GENIUS

GENIUS

STEVEN T. SEAGLE
&
TEDDY KRISTIANSEN

First Second
NEW YORK

It's always the little things...

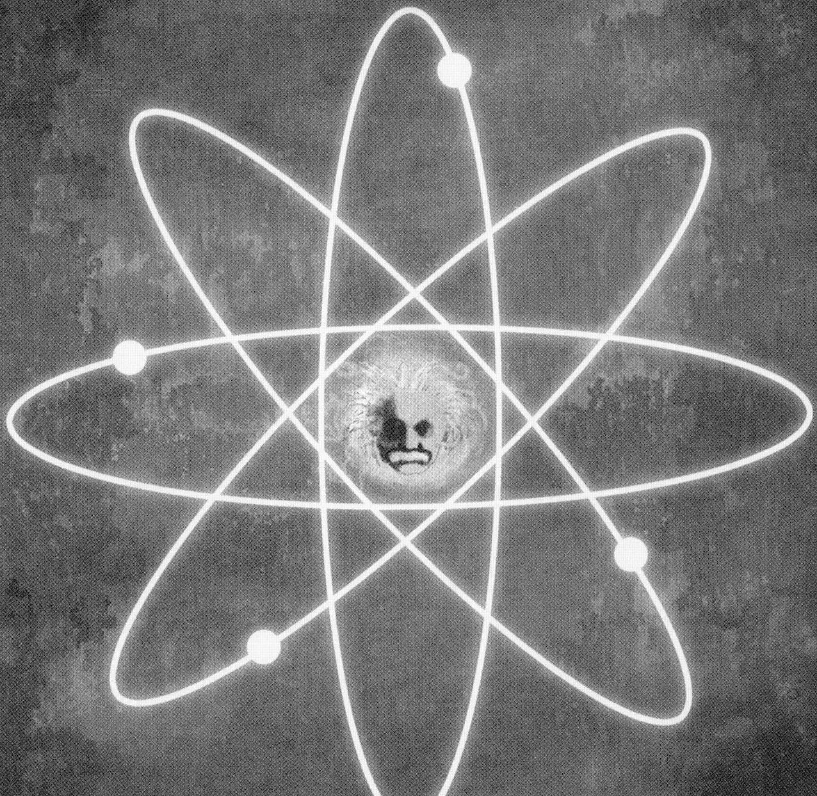

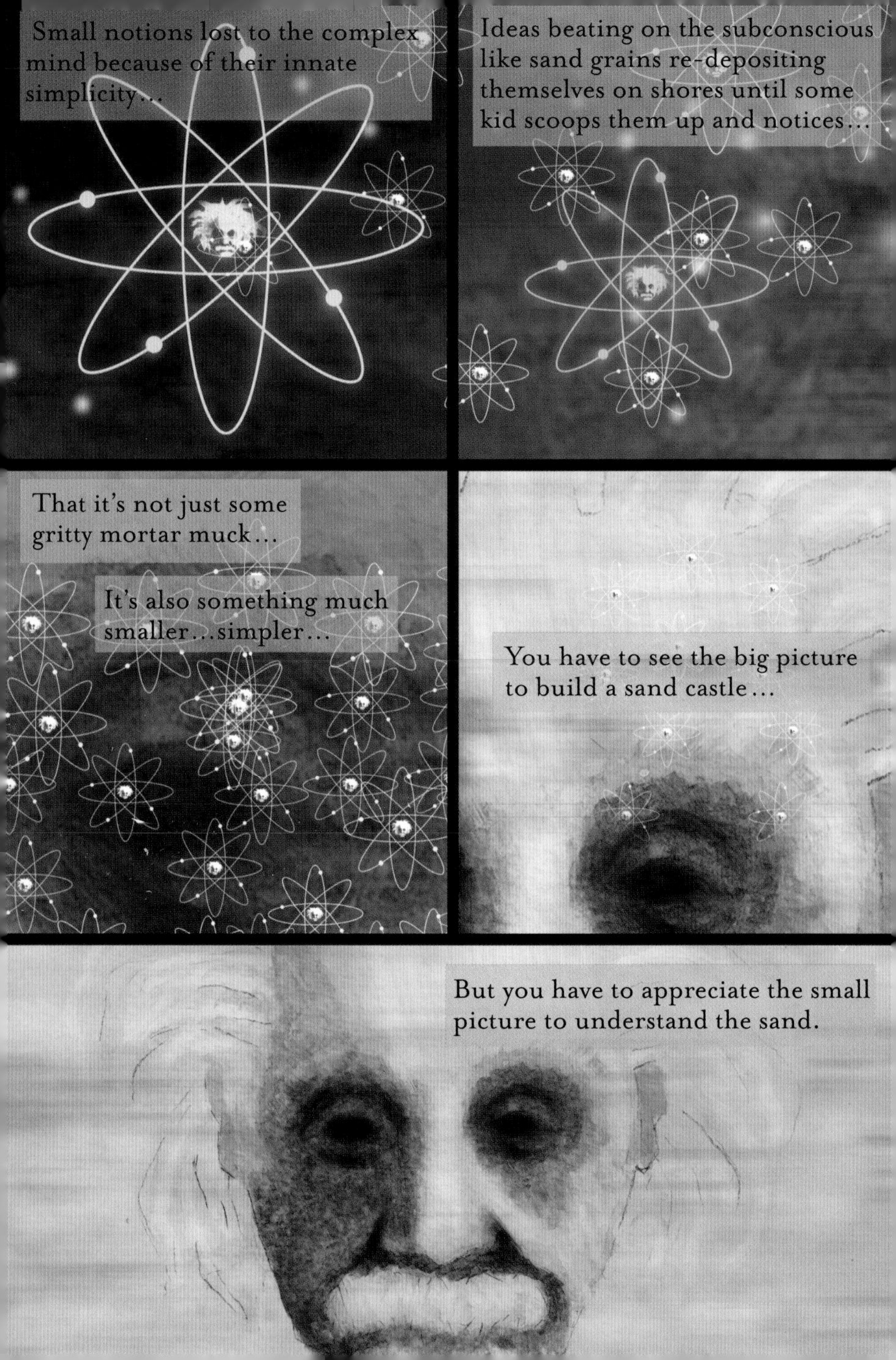
Small notions lost to the complex mind because of their innate simplicity...
Ideas beating on the subconscious like sand grains re-depositing themselves on shores until some kid scoops them up and notices...
That it's not just some gritty mortar muck...
It's also something much smaller...simpler...
You have to see the big picture to build a sand castle...
But you have to appreciate the small picture to understand the sand.

I was always pretty smart.

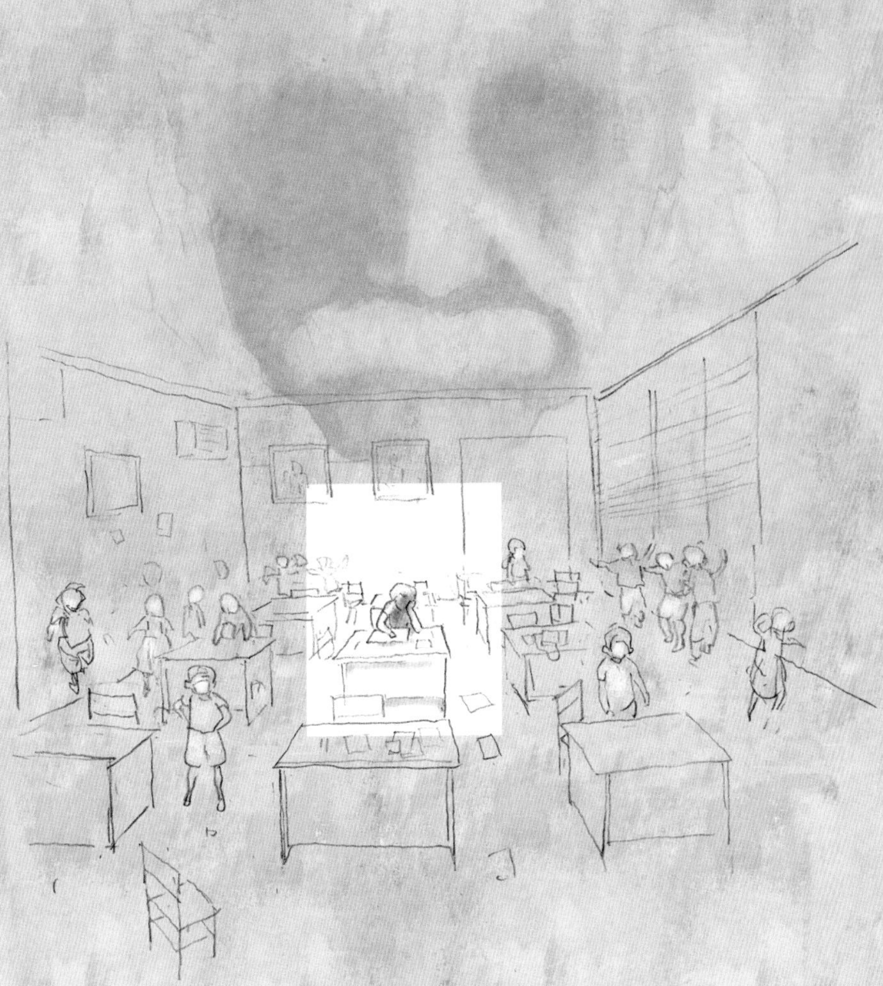

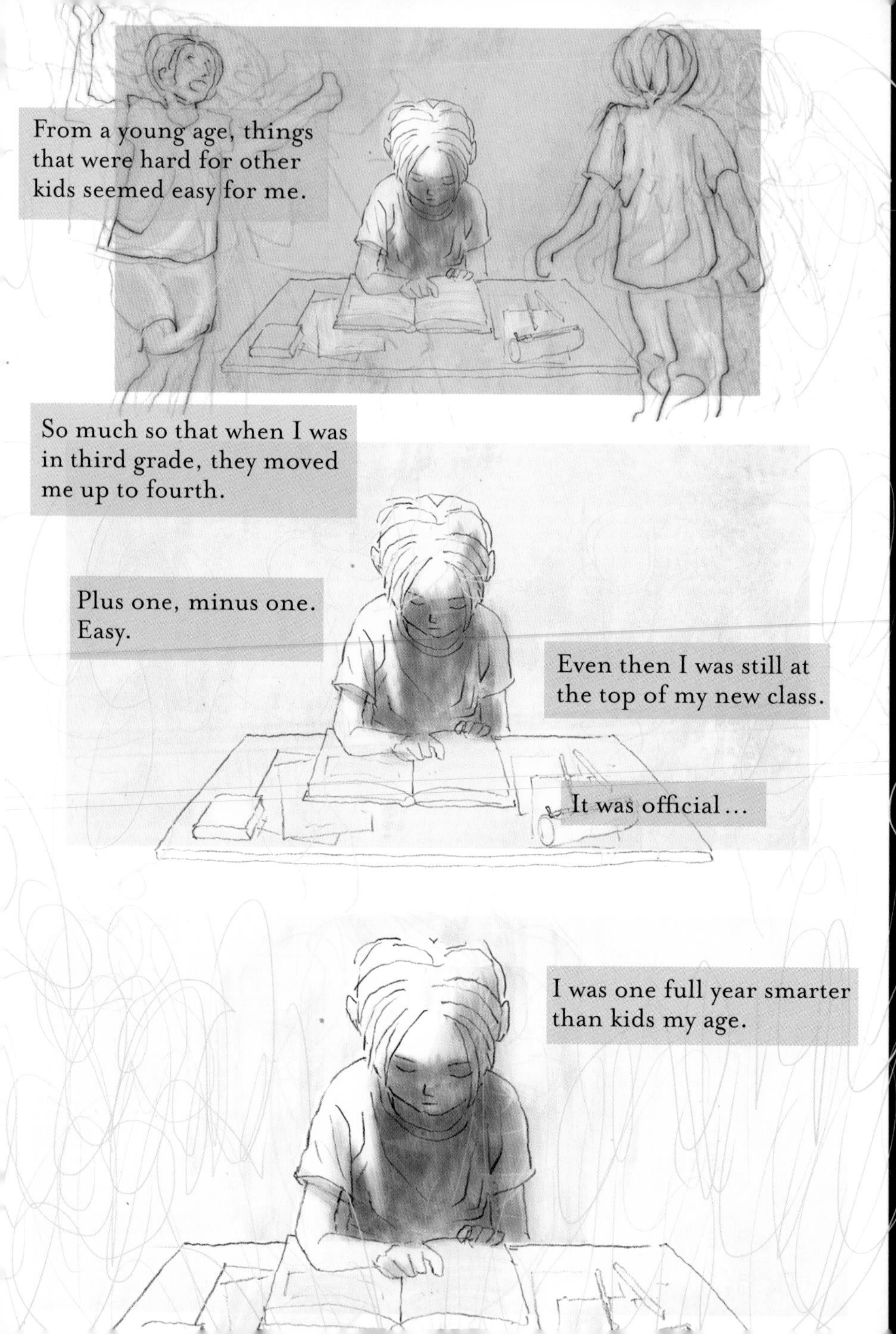
From a young age, things that were hard for other kids seemed easy for me.
So much so that when I was in third grade, they moved me up to fourth.
Plus one, minus one. Easy.
Even then I was still at the top of my new class.
It was official...
I was one full year smarter than kids my age.

I was reading about light.

The book first described light as rays, then particles.

But even as I read, I imagined light my own way...

Like pudding.

Not literally pudding, not like light was half milk, half sugar, and hawked by a Bill Cosby kind of guy.

I just thought light made more... sense...

As a semi-solid.

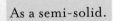

What kind of ten-year-old thinks up something like that?

Answer: a brilliant ten-year-old.

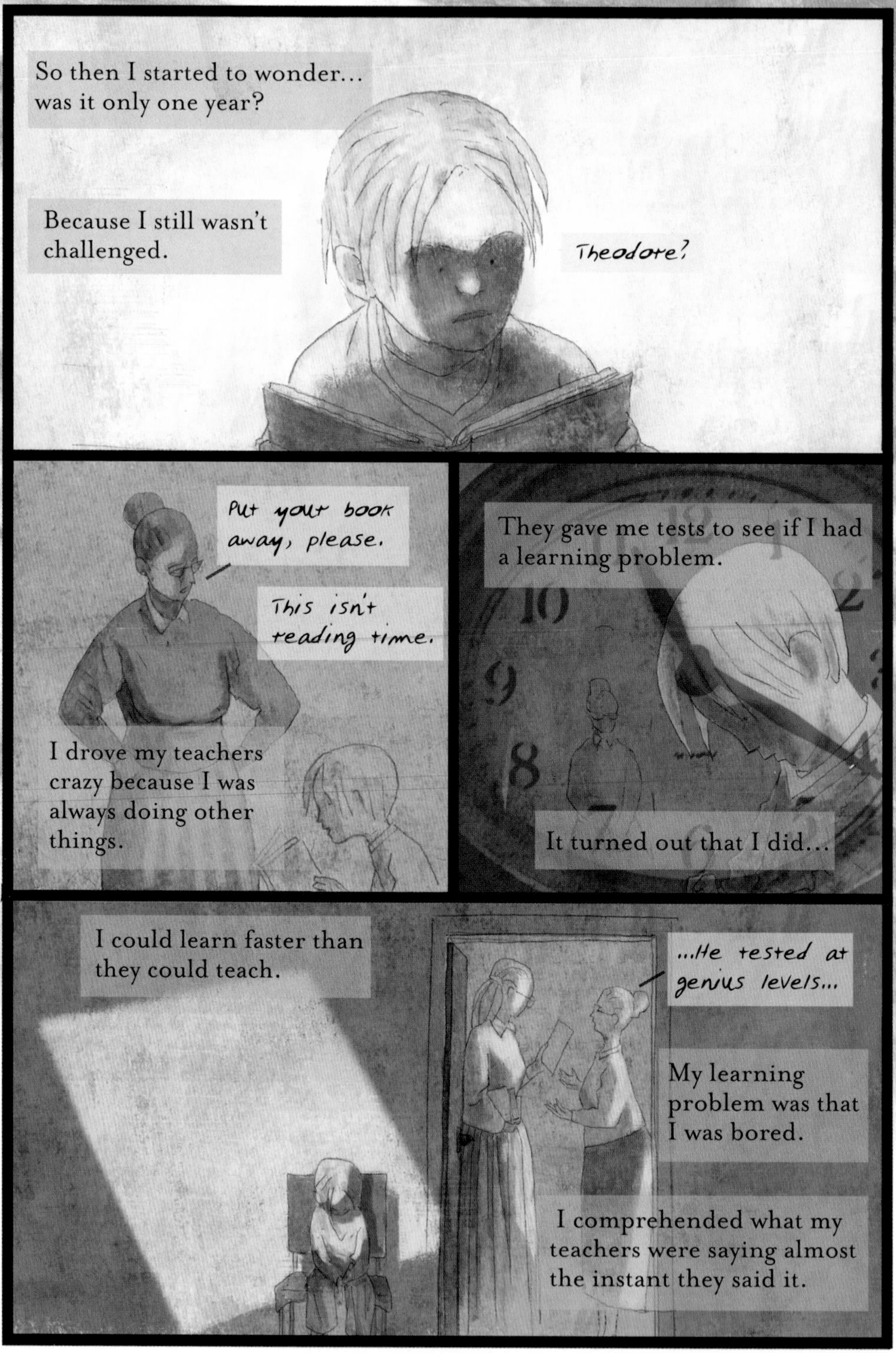
So then I started to wonder... was it only one year?
Because I still wasn't challenged.
Theodore?
Put your book away, please.
This isn't reading time.
I drove my teachers crazy because I was always doing other things.
They gave me tests to see if I had a learning problem.
It turned out that I did...
I could learn faster than they could teach.
...He tested at genius levels...
My learning problem was that I was bored.
I comprehended what my teachers were saying almost the instant they said it.

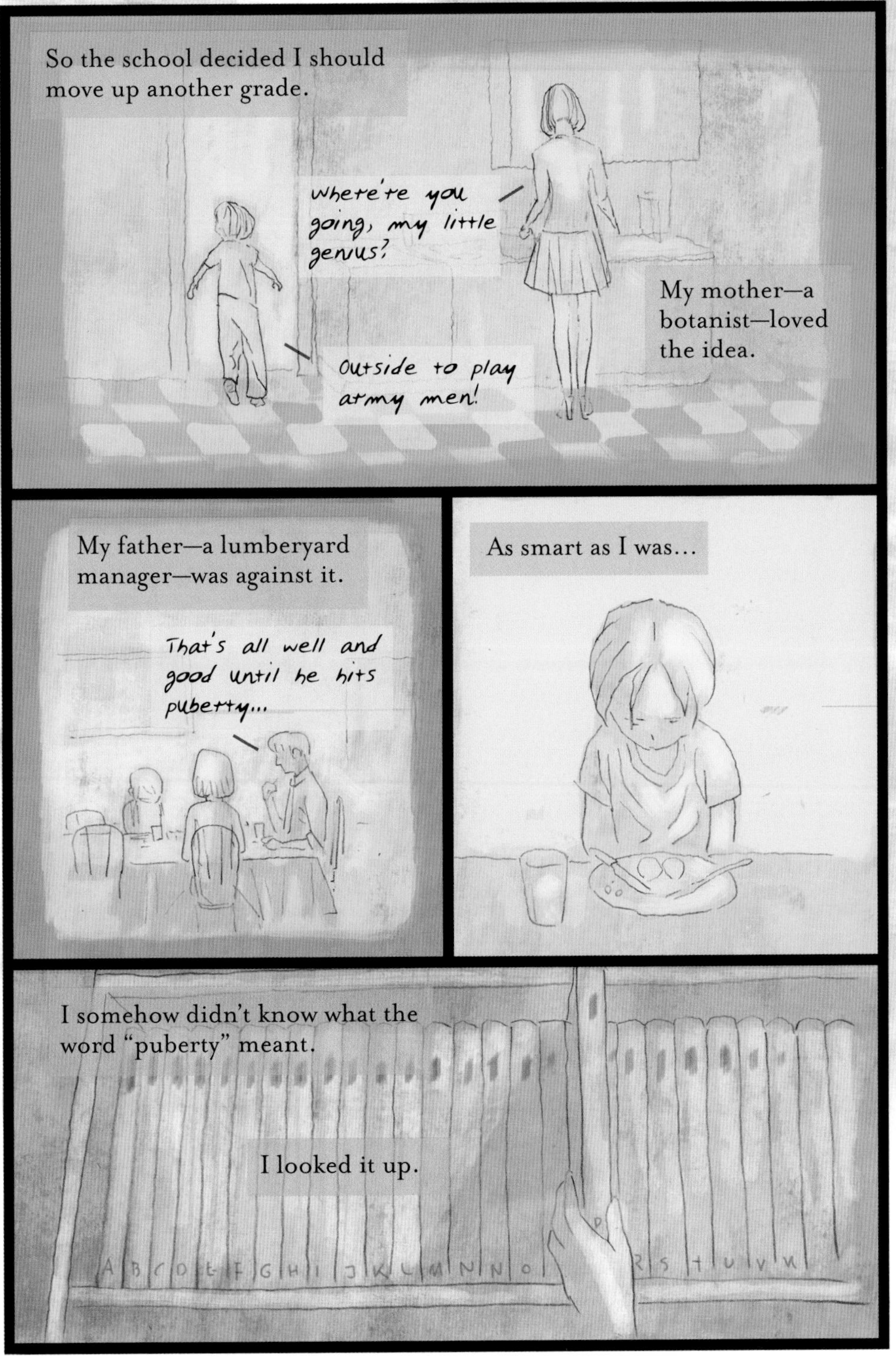
So the school decided I should move up another grade.
Where're you going, my little genius?
Outside to play army men!
My mother—a botanist—loved the idea.
My father—a lumberyard manager—was against it.
That's all well and good until he hits puberty...
As smart as I was...
I somehow didn't know what the word "puberty" meant.
I looked it up.

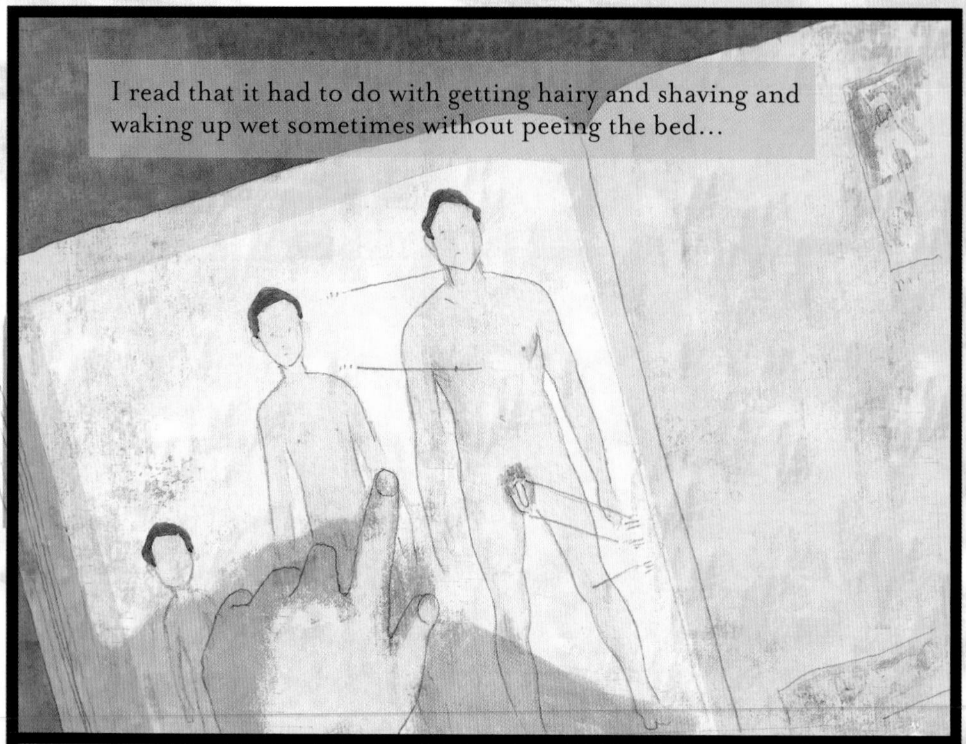
I read that it had to do with getting hairy and shaving and waking up wet sometimes without peeing the bed...

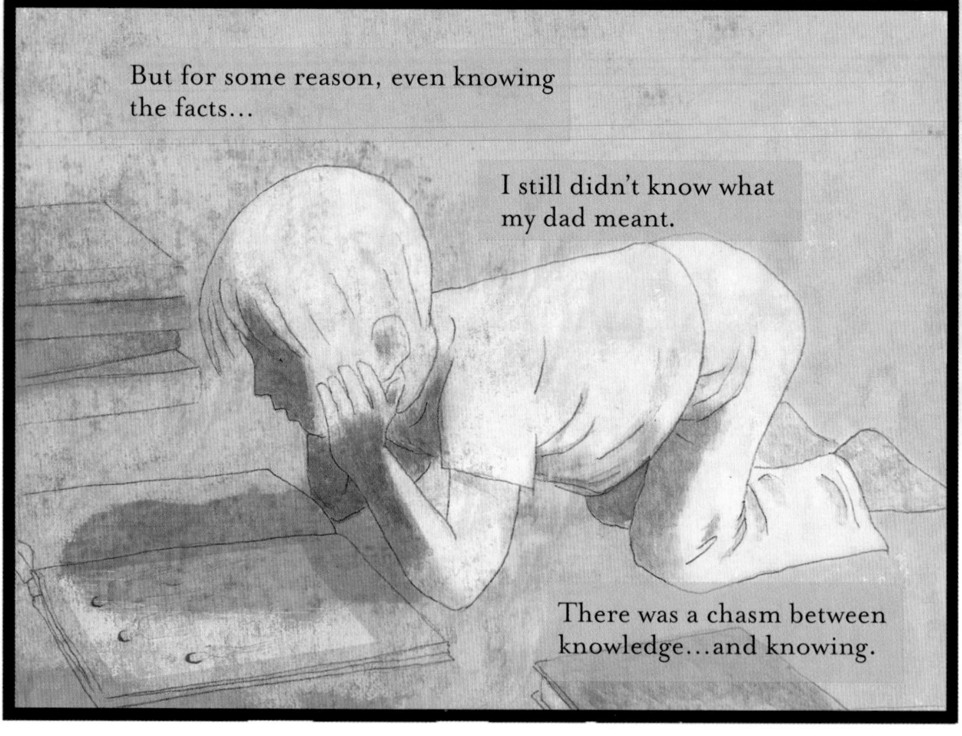
But for some reason, even knowing the facts...
I still didn't know what my dad meant.
There was a chasm between knowledge...and knowing.

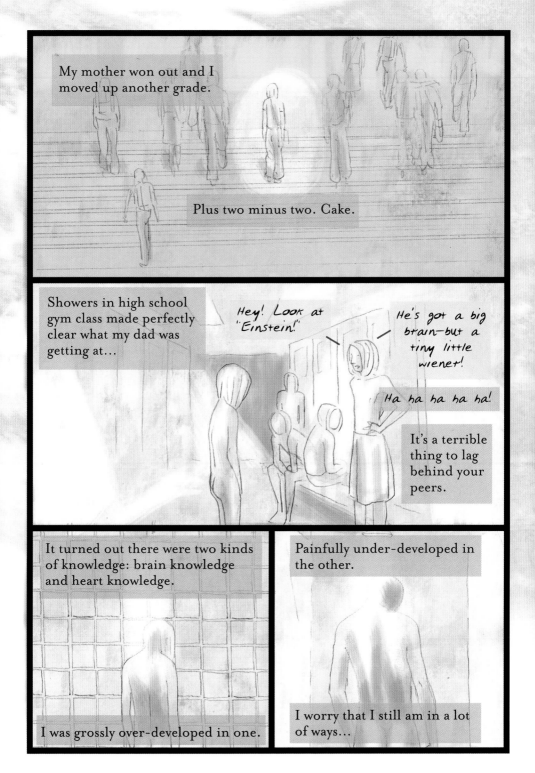

My mother won out and I moved up another grade.

Plus two minus two. Cake.

Showers in high school gym class made perfectly clear what my dad was getting at…

Hey! Look at "Einstein!"

He's got a big brain—but a tiny little wiener!

Ha ha ha ha ha!

It's a terrible thing to lag behind your peers.

It turned out there were two kinds of knowledge: brain knowledge and heart knowledge.

I was grossly over-developed in one.

Painfully under-developed in the other.

I worry that I still am in a lot of ways…

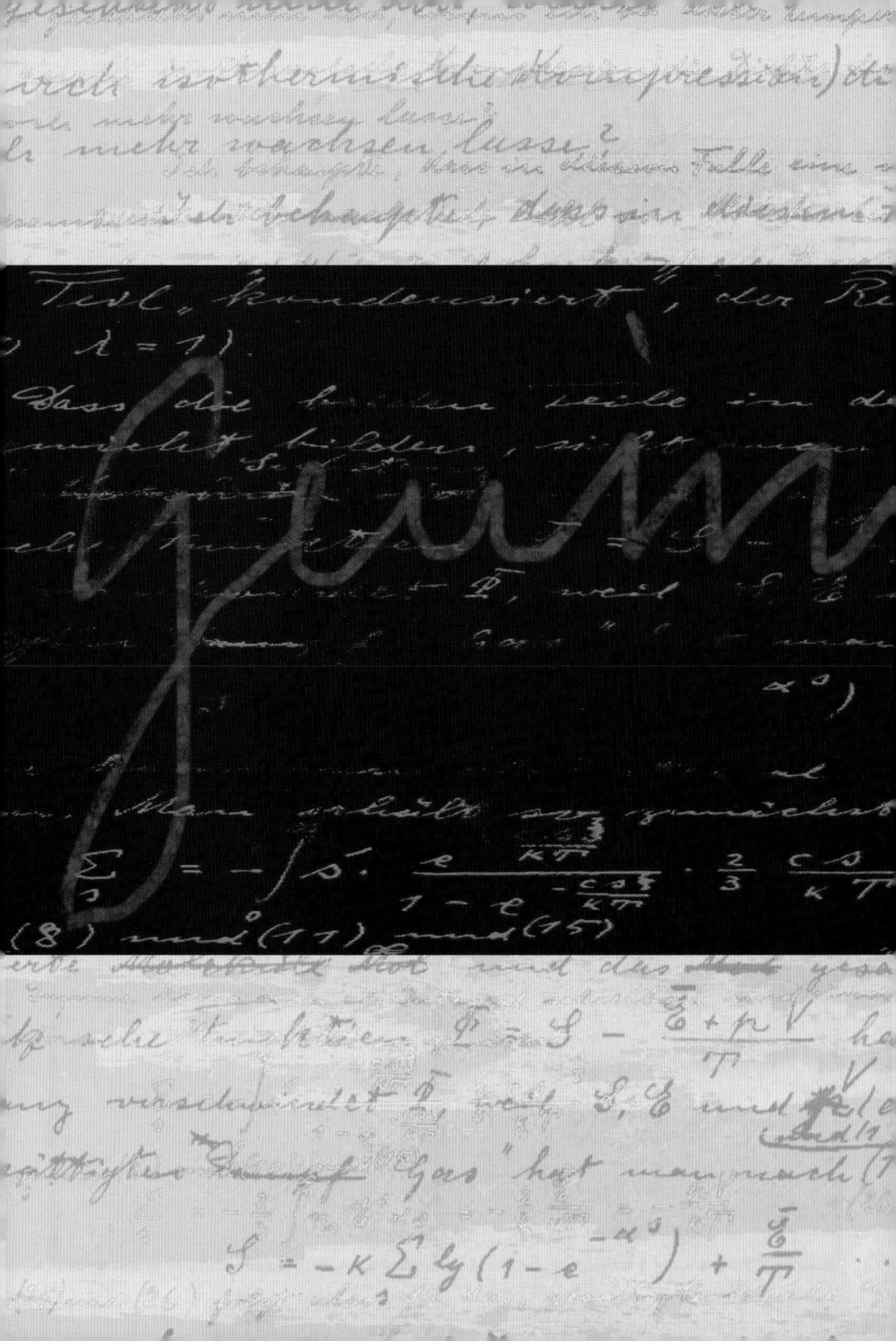

isotherm (die Kompression) ...

... mehr wachsen lasse?

... Ich behaupte, dass in diesem Falle eine ...

Teil kondensiert, der Re...

$\lambda = 1$).

dass die beiden Teile im ...

... $\overline{\Phi}_1$, weil ...

$x^0)$

$\sum_0 = -\int \dot{p} \cdot \dfrac{e^{\frac{c_5}{kT}}}{1 - e^{-\frac{c_5}{kT}}} \cdot \dfrac{2}{3} \cdot \dfrac{c_5}{kT}$

(8) und (11) und (15)

... Funktion $\overline{\Phi} = S - \dfrac{\overline{E} + p\overline{V}}{T}$ ...

... "Gas" hat man nach ...

$$S = -\kappa \sum_s \ell y \left(1 - e^{-x^0}\right) + \dfrac{\overline{E}}{T}$$

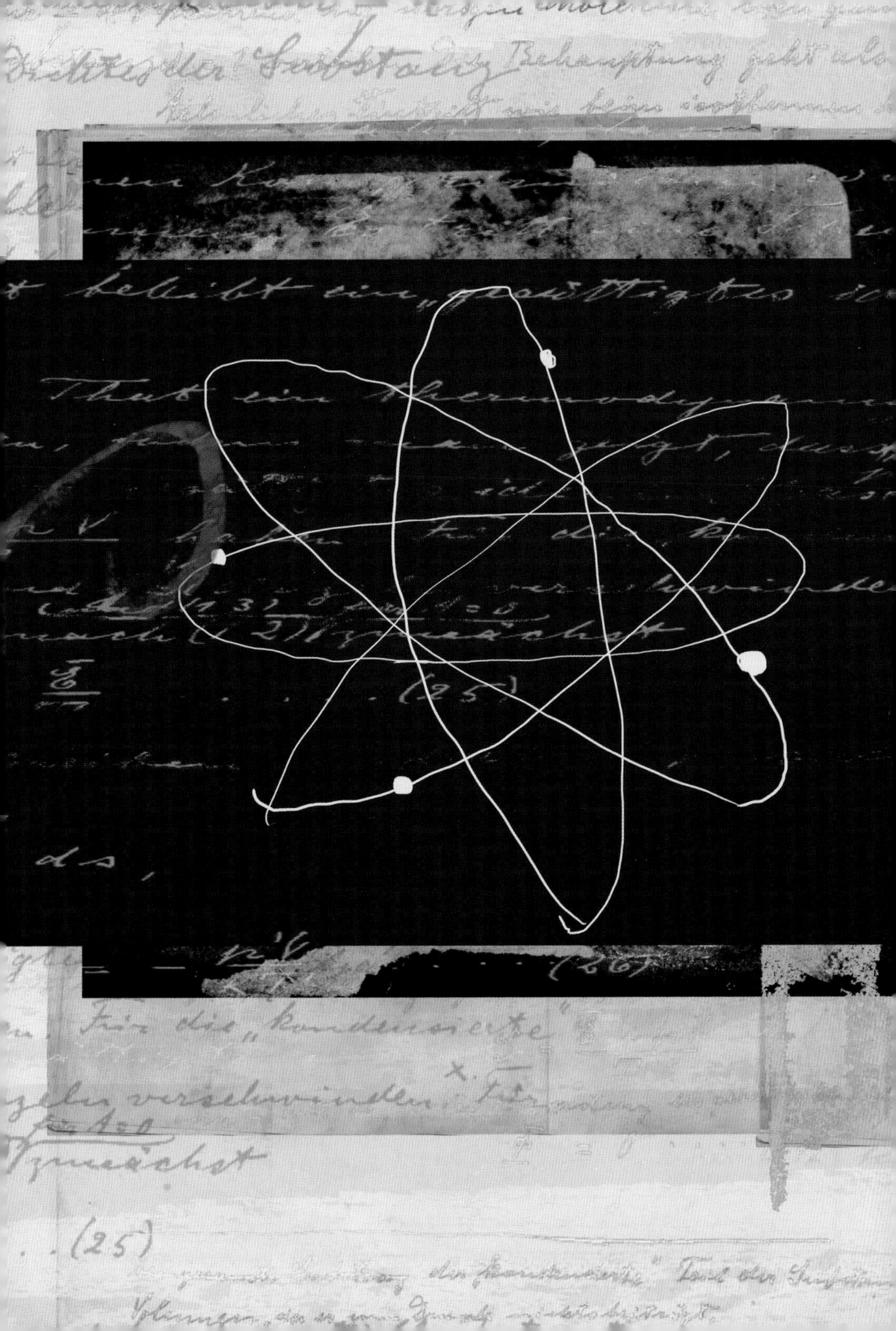

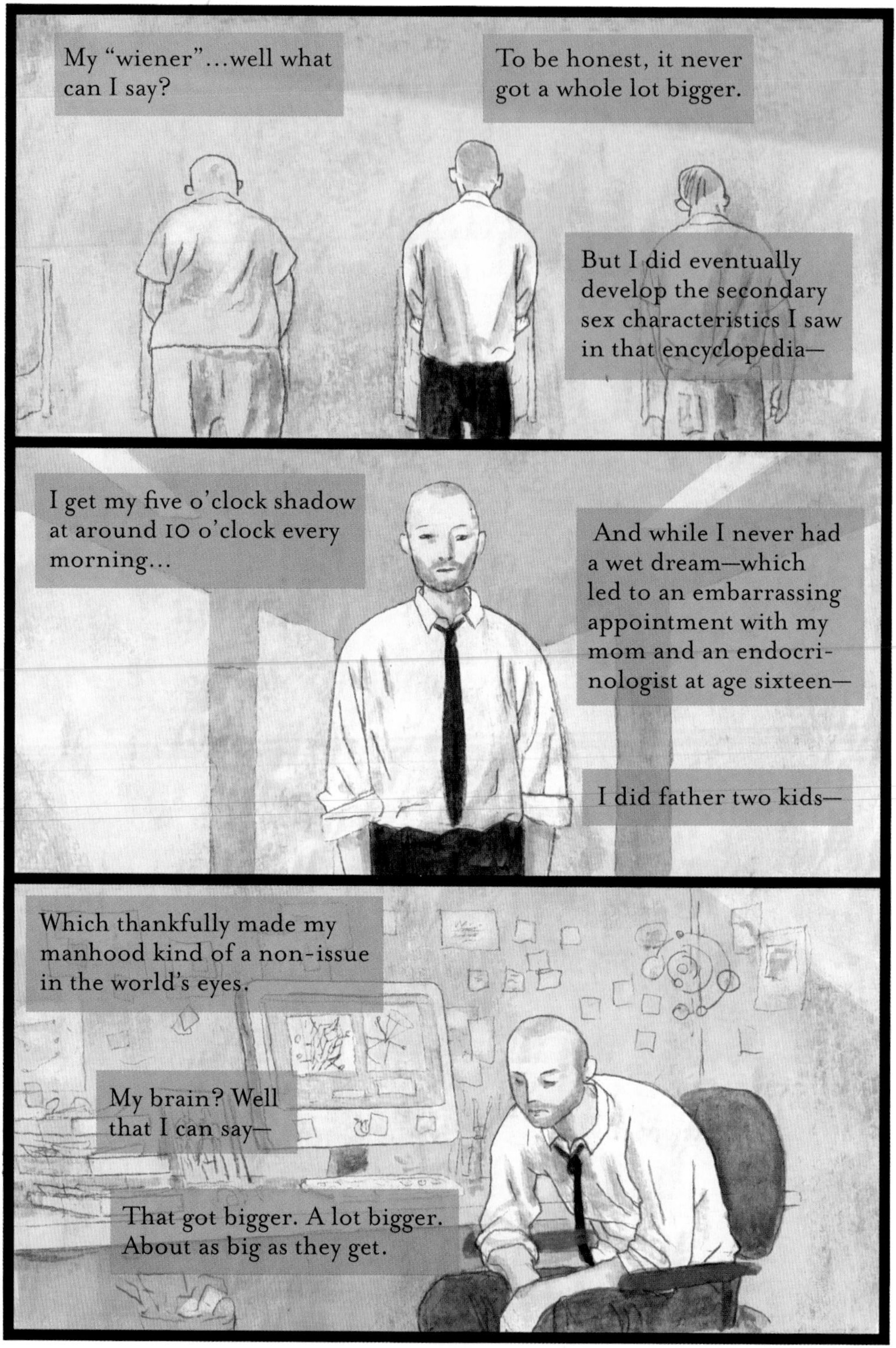
My "wiener"...well what can I say?
To be honest, it never got a whole lot bigger.
But I did eventually develop the secondary sex characteristics I saw in that encyclopedia—
I get my five o'clock shadow at around 10 o'clock every morning...
And while I never had a wet dream—which led to an embarrassing appointment with my mom and an endocrinologist at age sixteen—
I did father two kids—
Which thankfully made my manhood kind of a non-issue in the world's eyes.
My brain? Well that I can say—
That got bigger. A lot bigger. About as big as they get.

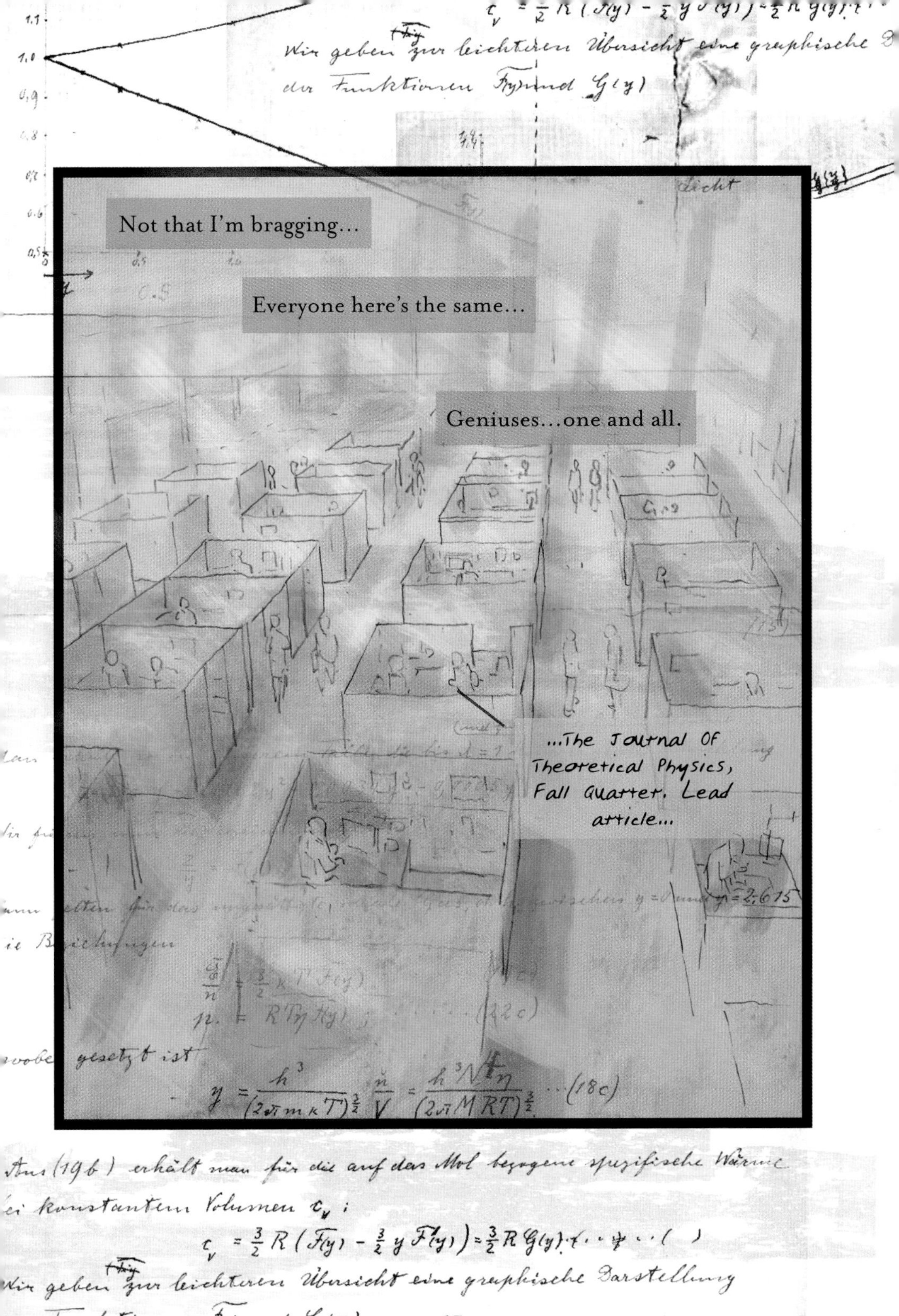

Not that I'm bragging…
Everyone here's the same…
Geniuses…one and all.
...The Journal Of Theoretical Physics, Fall Quarter. Lead article...

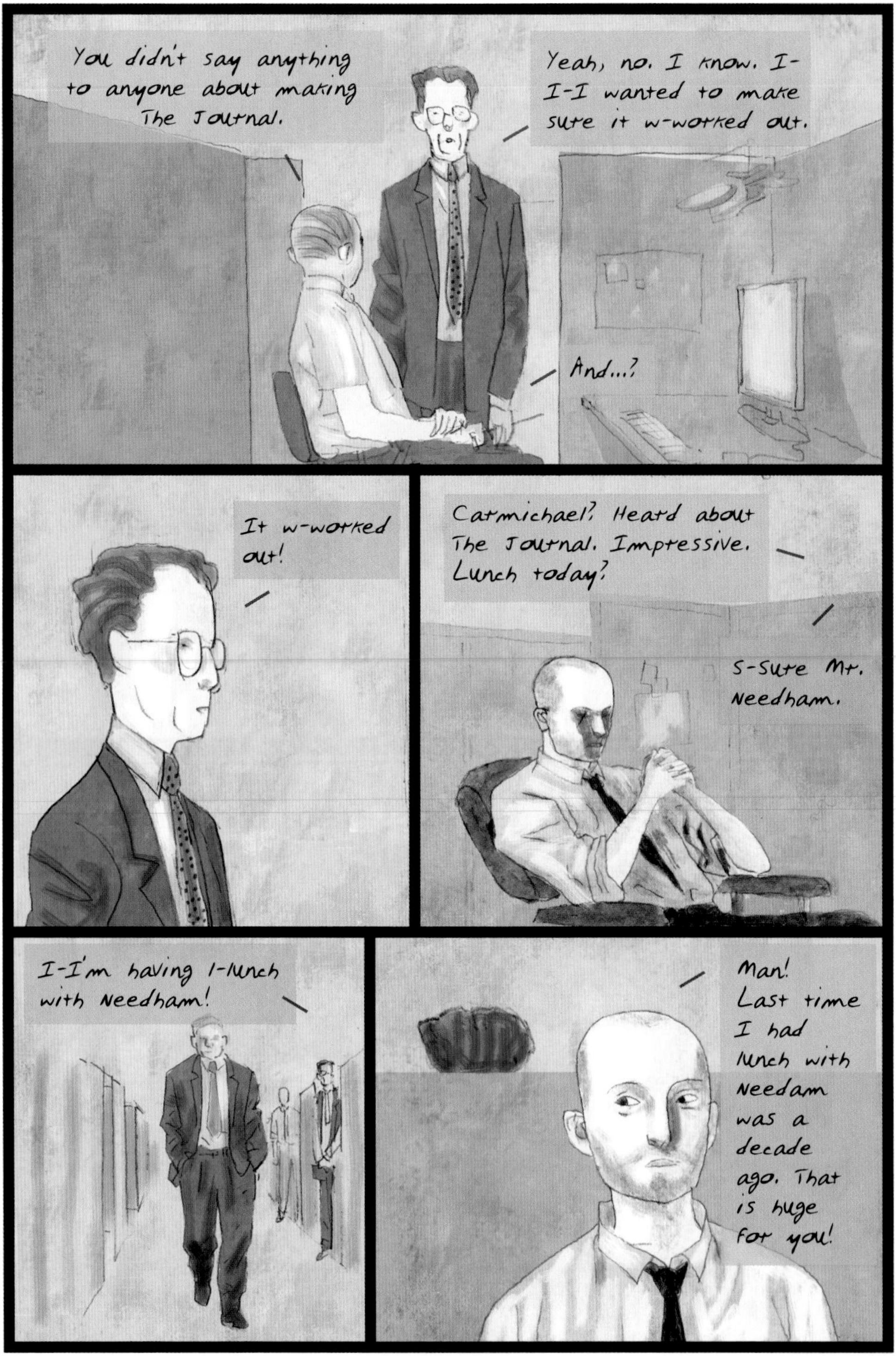
You didn't say anything to anyone about making The Journal.
Yeah, no. I know. I- I-I wanted to make sure it w-worked out.
And...?
It w-worked out!
Carmichael? Heard about The Journal. Impressive. Lunch today?
S-Sure Mr. Needham.
I-I'm having l-lunch with Needham!
Man! Last time I had lunch with Needam was a decade ago. That is huge for you!

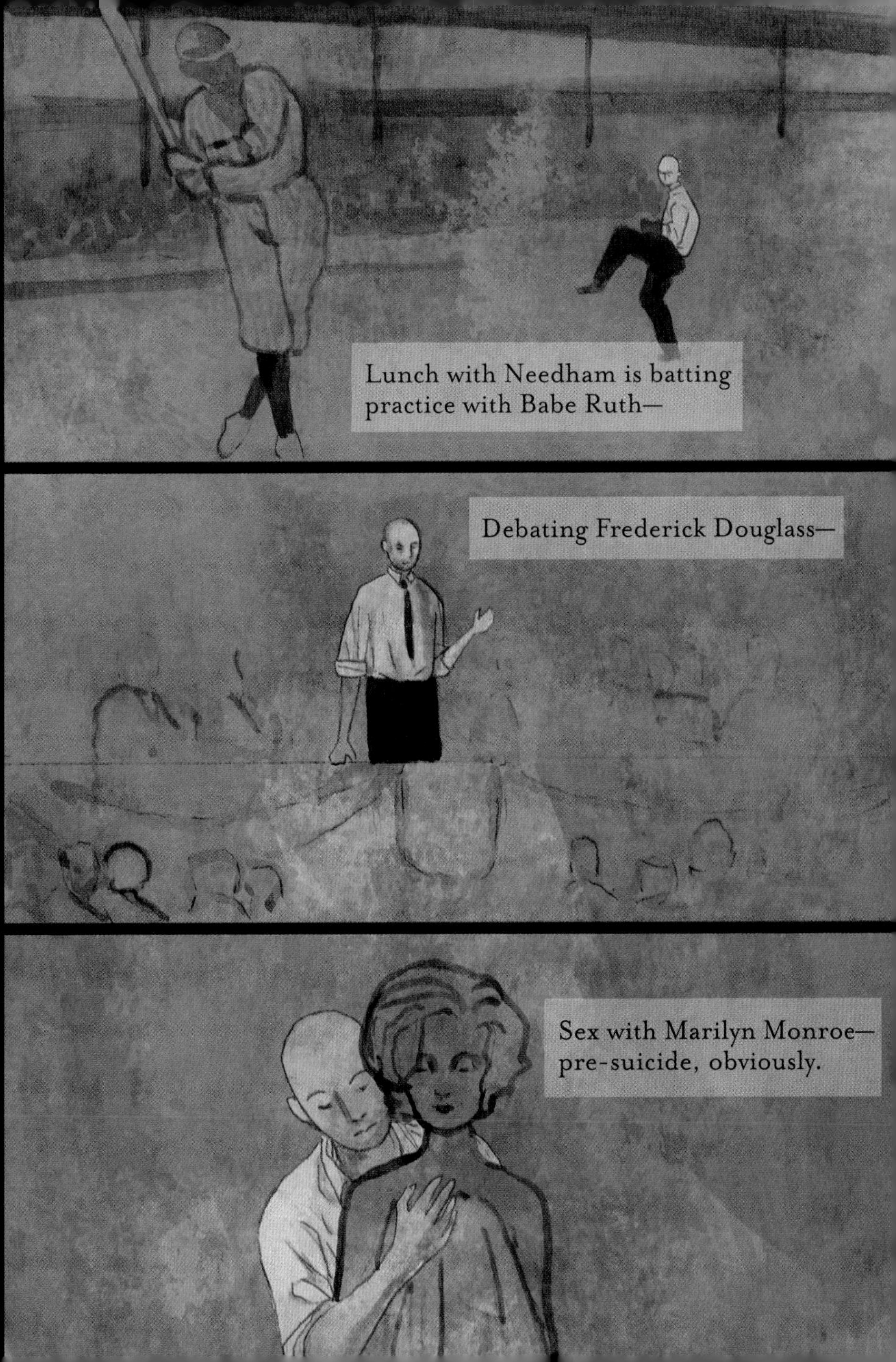
Lunch with Needham is batting practice with Babe Ruth—
Debating Frederick Douglass—
Sex with Marilyn Monroe—pre-suicide, obviously.

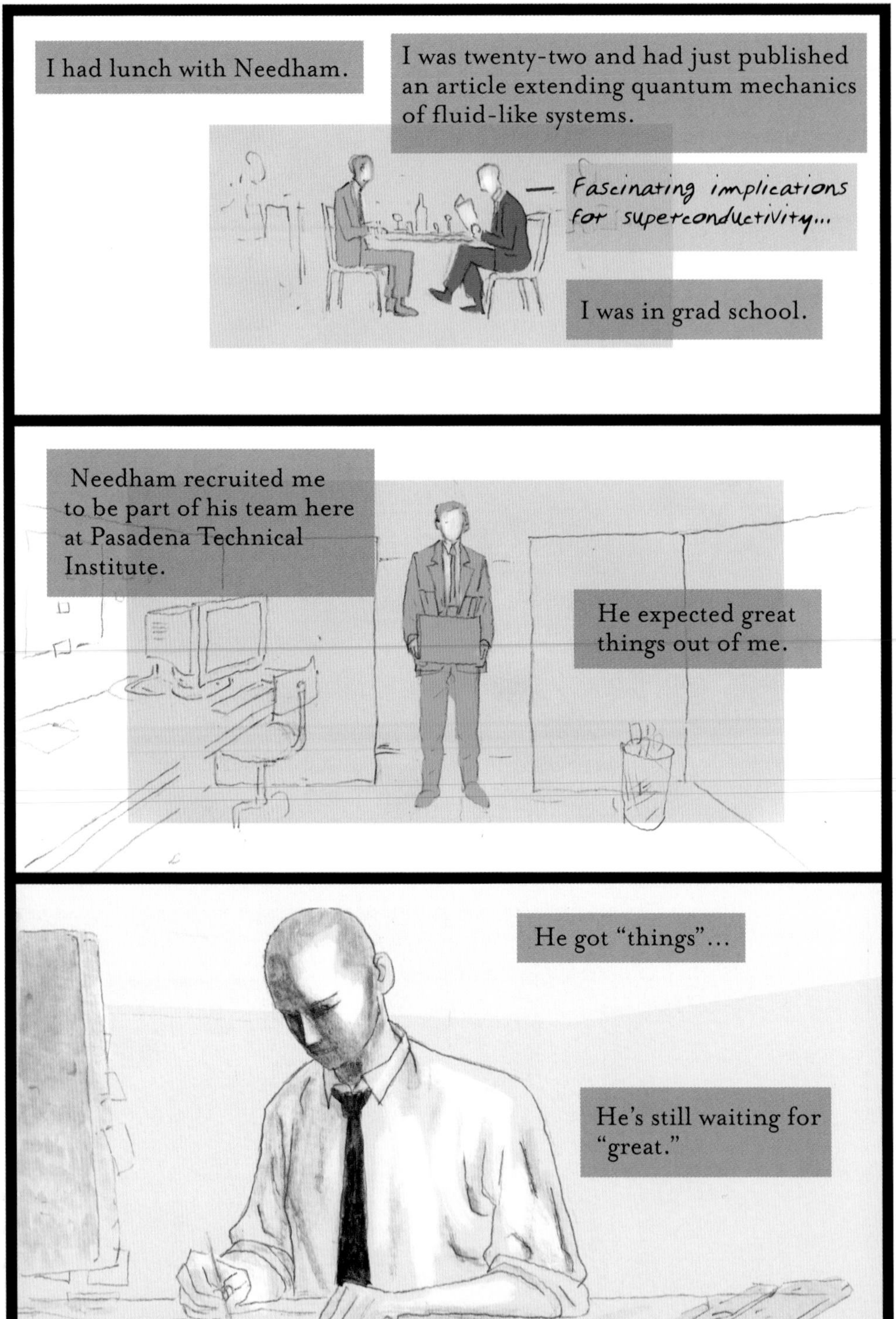
I had lunch with Needham.
I was twenty-two and had just published an article extending quantum mechanics of fluid-like systems.
— Fascinating implications for superconductivity...
I was in grad school.
Needham recruited me to be part of his team here at Pasadena Technical Institute.
He expected great things out of me.
He got "things"...
He's still waiting for "great."

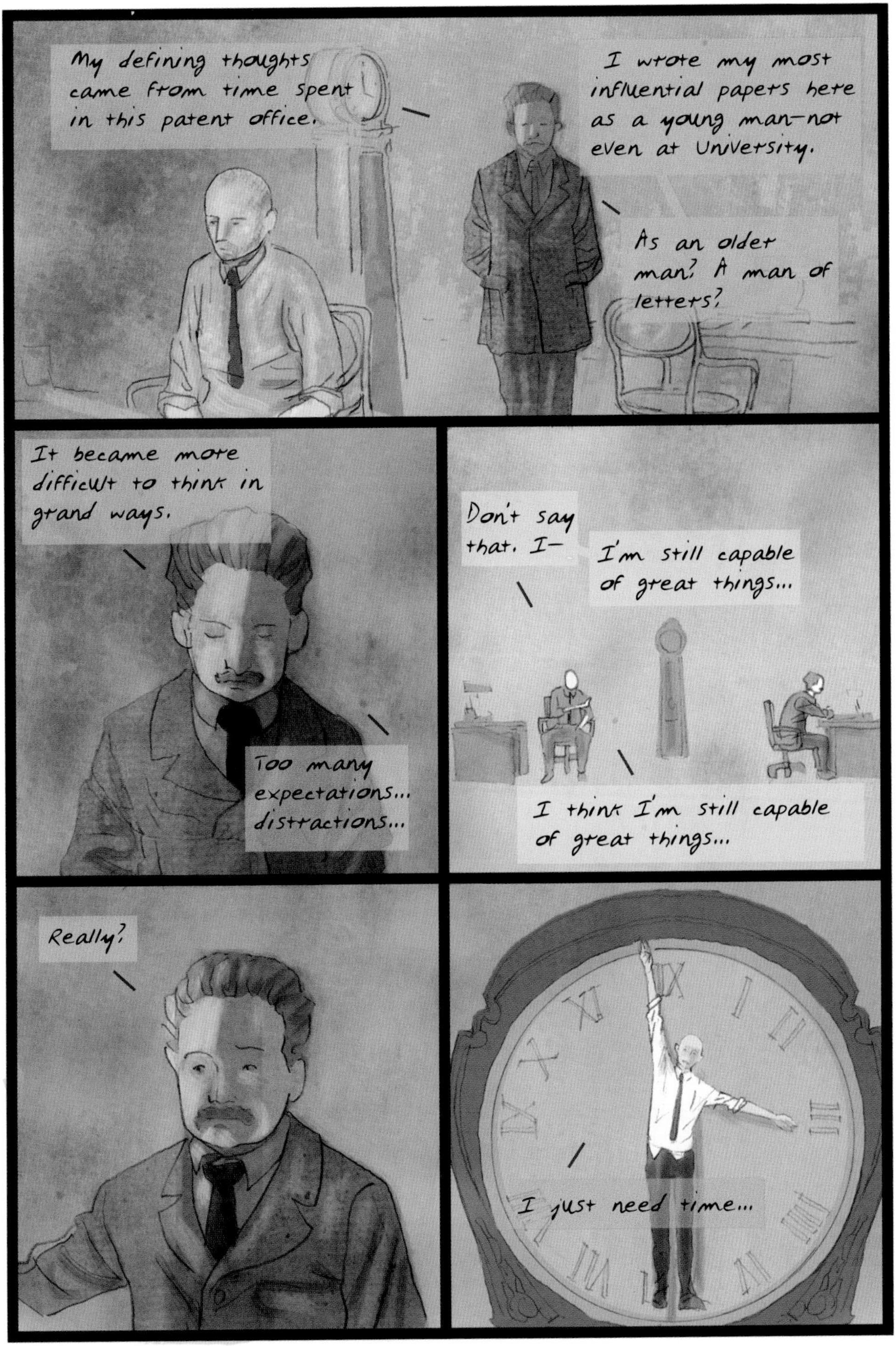
My defining thoughts came from time spent in this patent office.
I wrote my most influential papers here as a young man—not even at University.
As an older man? A man of letters?
It became more difficult to think in grand ways.
Too many expectations... distractions...
Don't say that. I—
I'm still capable of great things...
I think I'm still capable of great things...
Really?
I just need time...

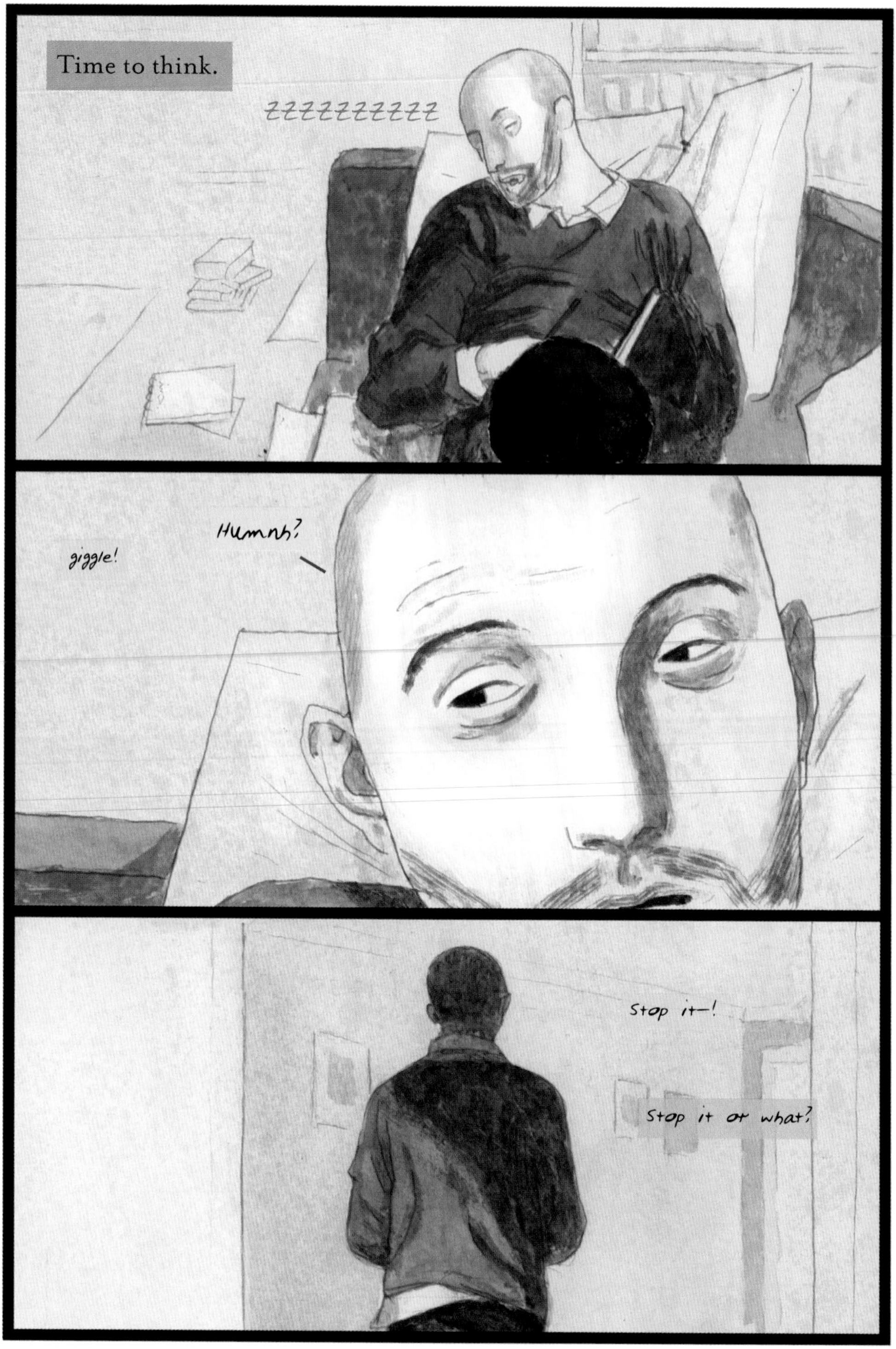
Time to think.
ZZZZZZZZZZ
giggle!
Humnh?
Stop it—!
Stop it or what?

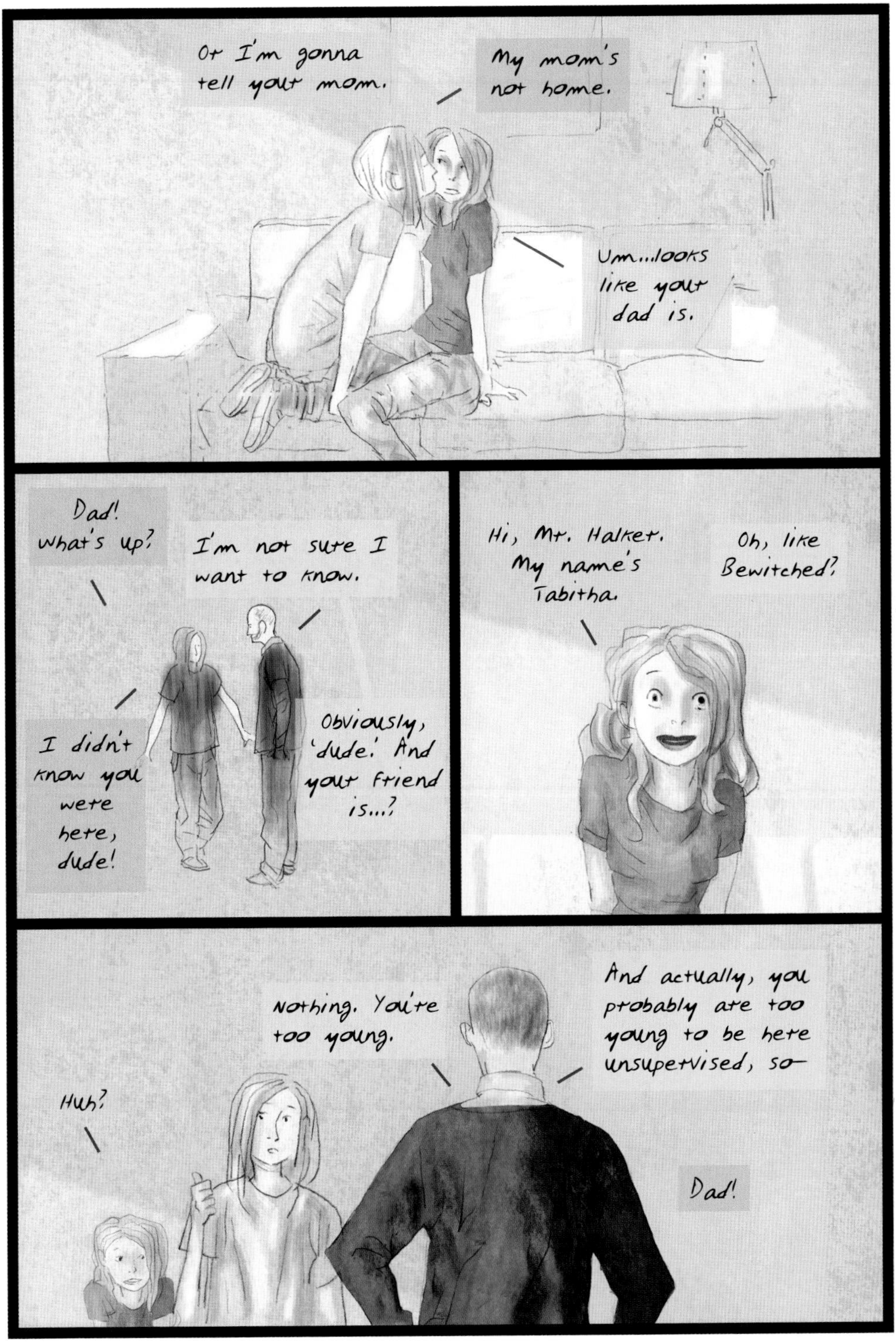
Or I'm gonna tell your mom.
My mom's not home.
Um...looks like your dad is.
Dad! What's up?
I'm not sure I want to know.
I didn't know you were here, dude!
Obviously, 'dude.' And your friend is...?
Hi, Mr. Halker. My name's Tabitha.
Oh, like Bewitched?
Huh?
Nothing. You're too young.
And actually, you probably are too young to be here unsupervised, so—
Dad!

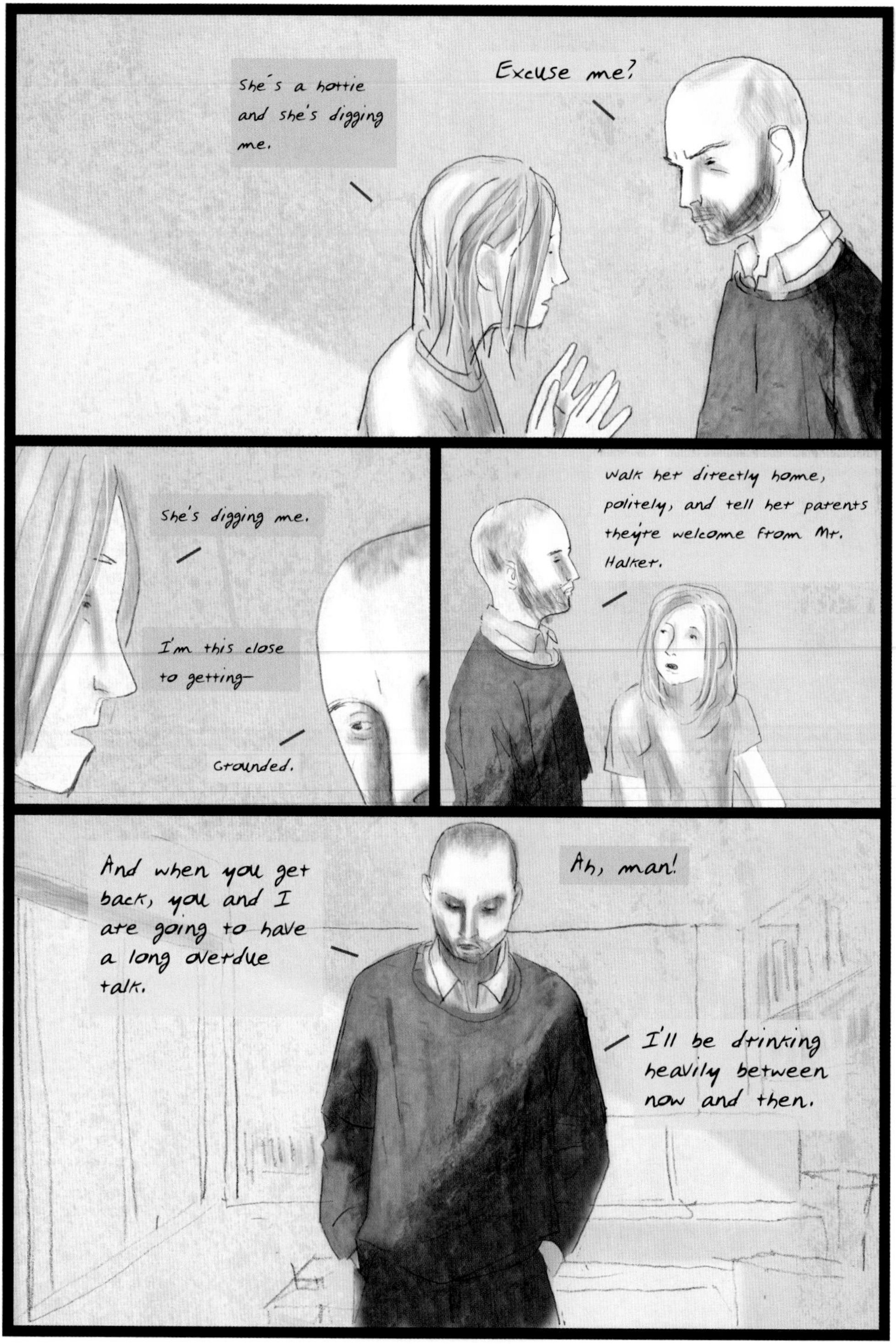
She's a hottie and she's digging me.
Excuse me?
She's digging me.
I'm this close to getting—
Grounded.
Walk her directly home, politely, and tell her parents they're welcome from Mr. Halker.
And when you get back, you and I are going to have a long overdue talk.
Ah, man!
I'll be drinking heavily between now and then.

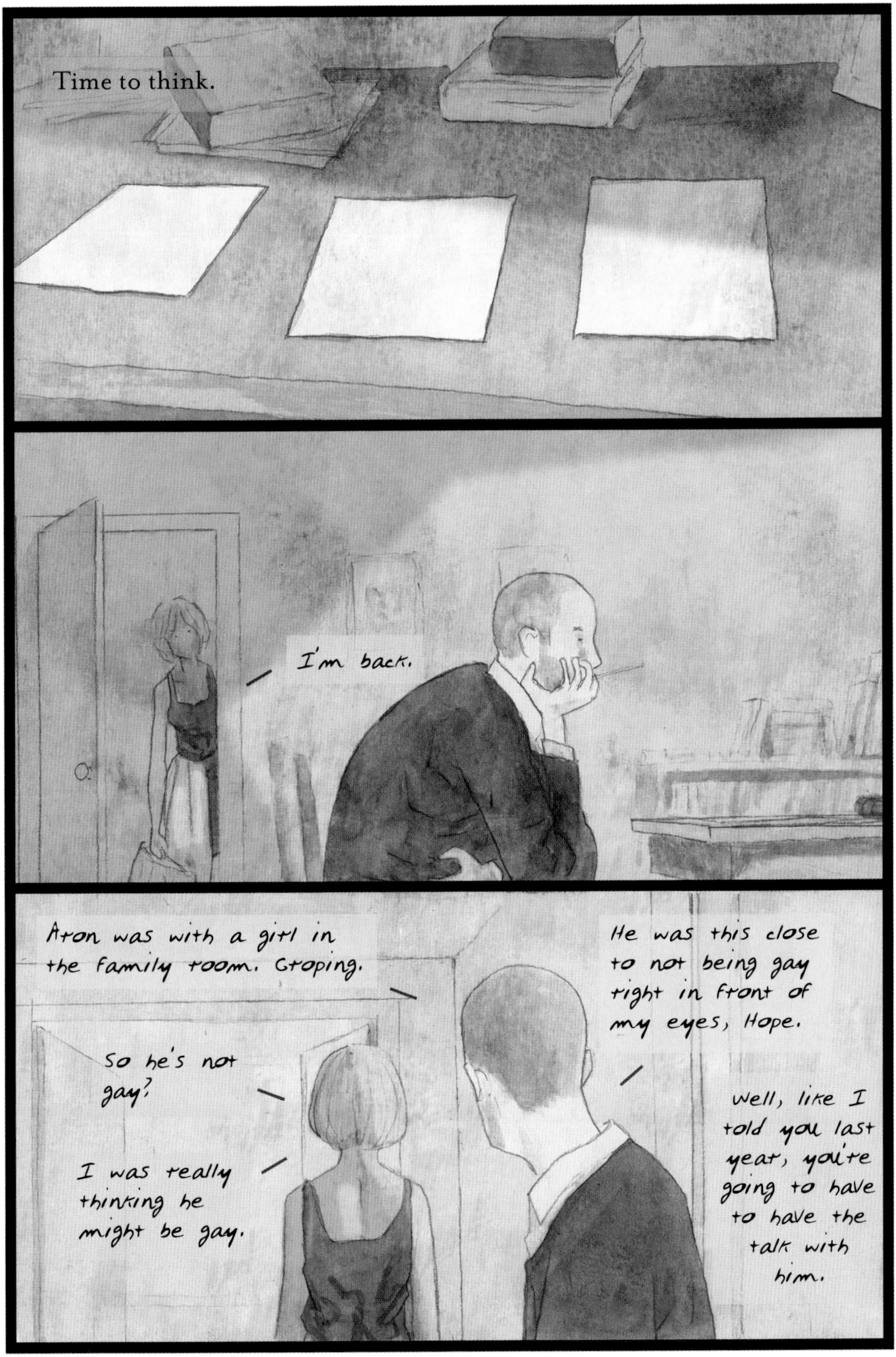
Time to think.
I'm back.
Aron was with a girl in the family room. Groping.
He was this close to not being gay right in front of my eyes, Hope.
So he's not gay?
I was really thinking he might be gay.
Well, like I told you last year, you're going to have to have the talk with him.

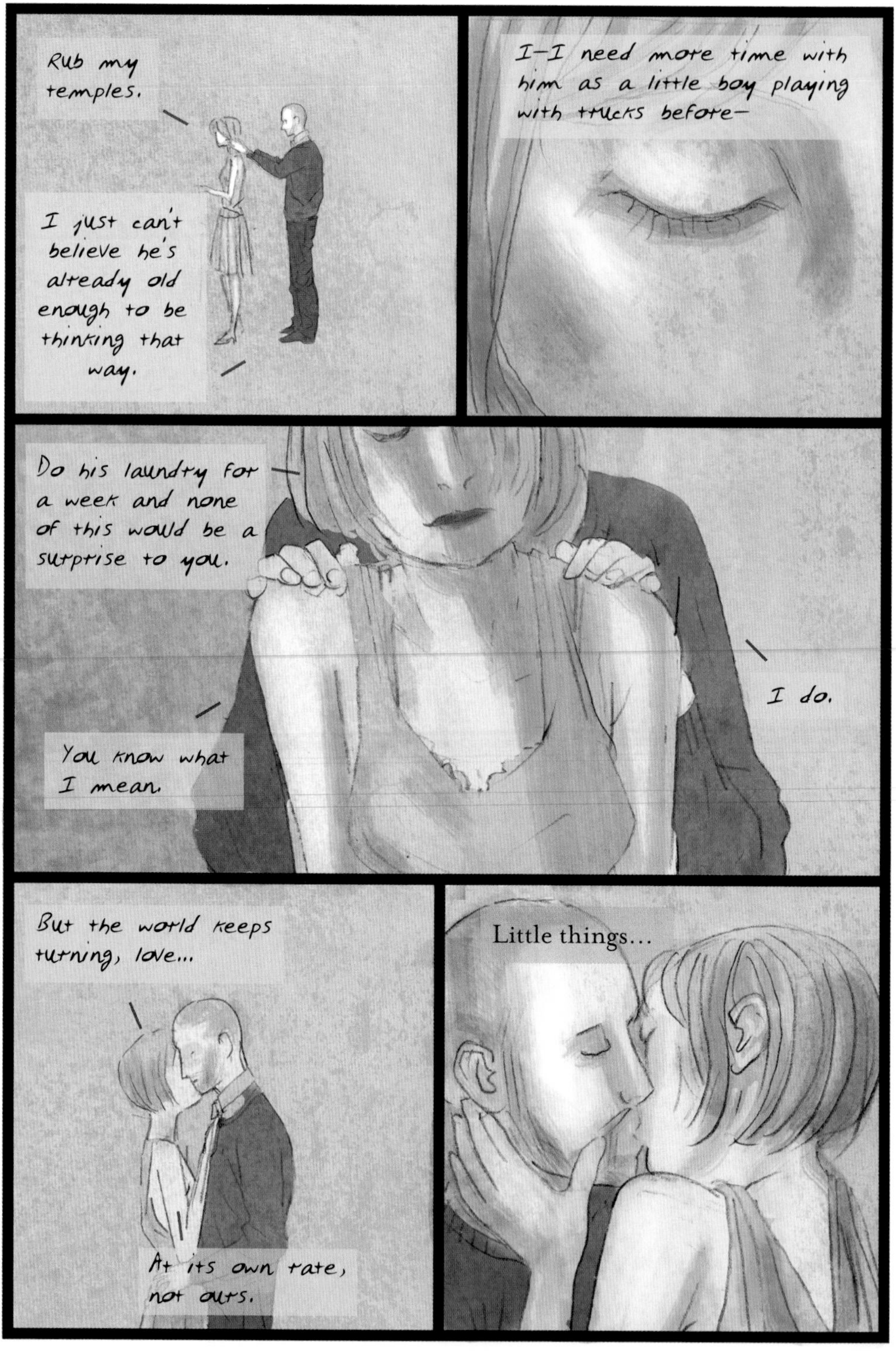
Rub my temples.
I just can't believe he's already old enough to be thinking that way.
I—I need more time with him as a little boy playing with trucks before—
Do his laundry for a week and none of this would be a surprise to you.
I do.
You know what I mean.
But the world keeps turning, love...
At its own rate, not ours.
Little things...

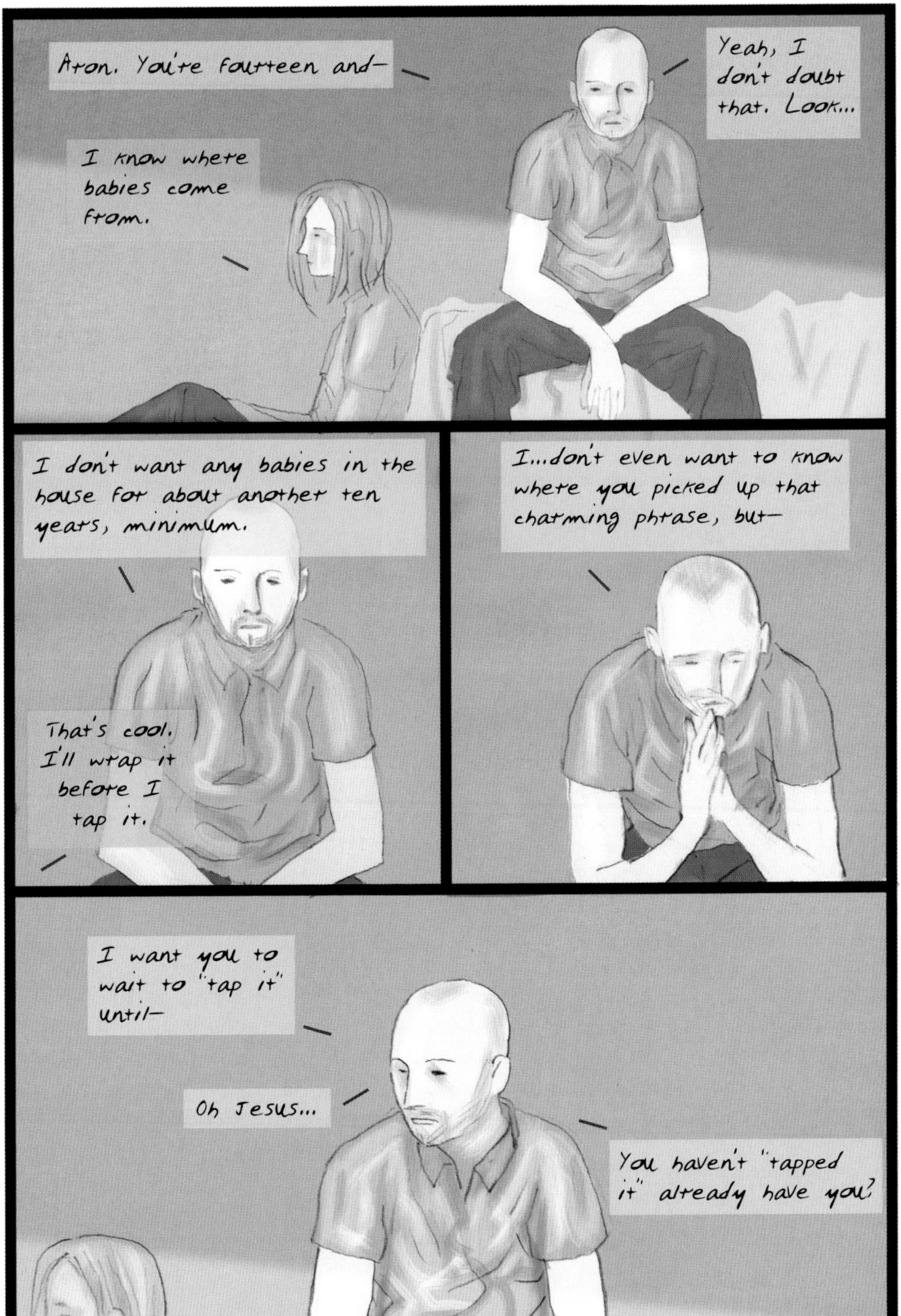
Aron. You're fourteen and—
Yeah, I don't doubt that. Look...
I know where babies come from.
I don't want any babies in the house for about another ten years, minimum.
That's cool. I'll wrap it before I tap it.
I...don't even want to know where you picked up that charming phrase, but—
I want you to wait to "tap it" until—
Oh Jesus...
You haven't "tapped it" already have you?

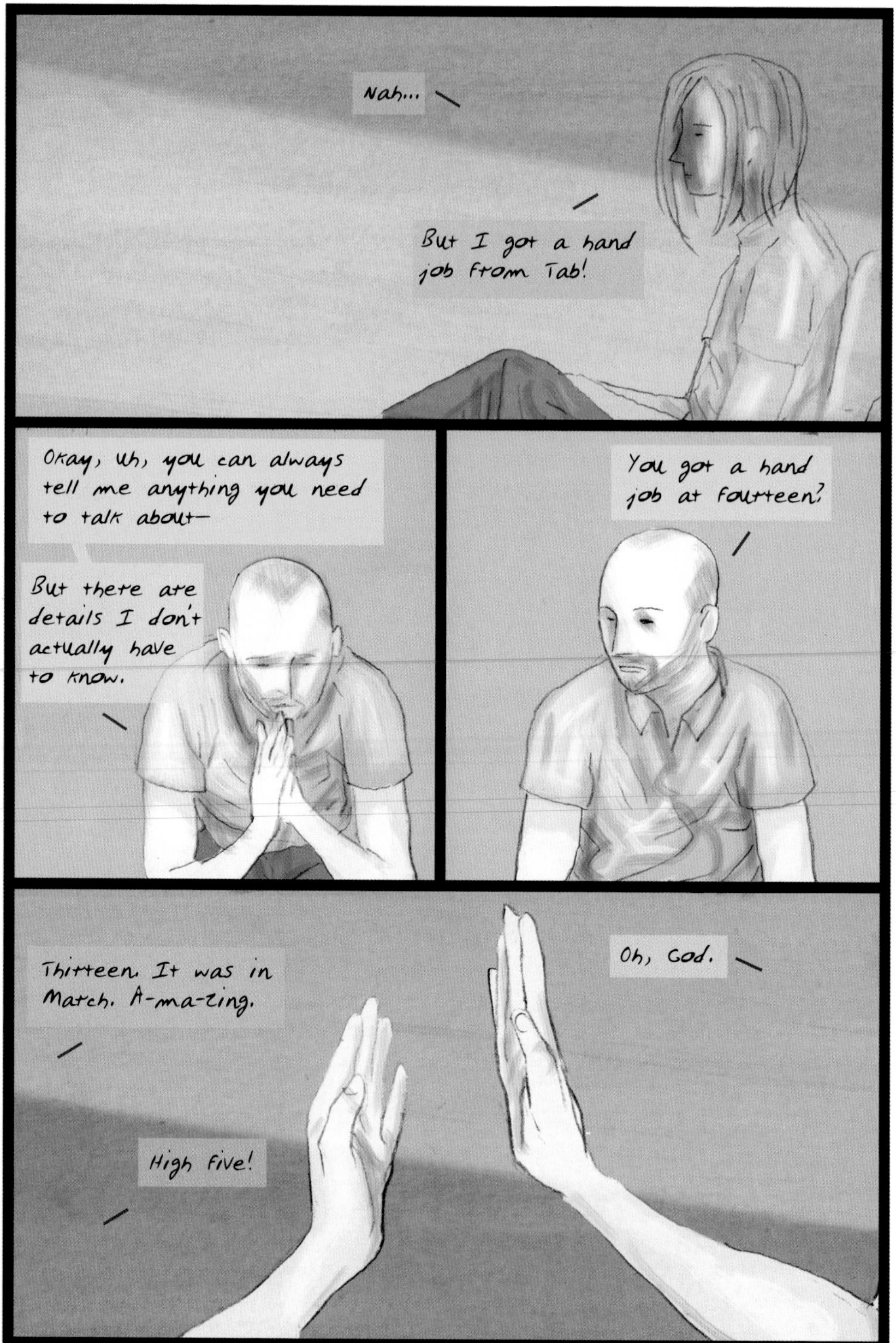
Nah...
But I got a hand job from Tab!
Okay, uh, you can always tell me anything you need to talk about—
But there are details I don't actually have to know.
You got a hand job at fourteen?
Thirteen. It was in March. A-ma-zing.
Oh, God.
High five!

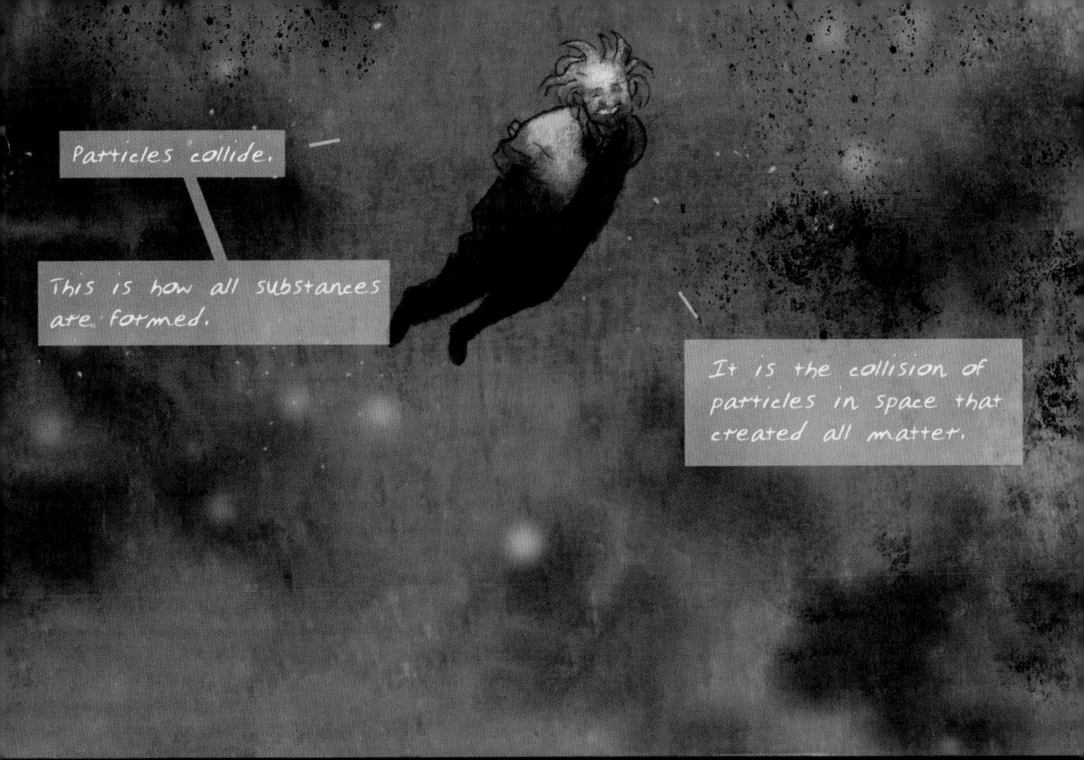
Particles collide.
This is how all substances are formed.
It is the collision of particles in space that created all matter.

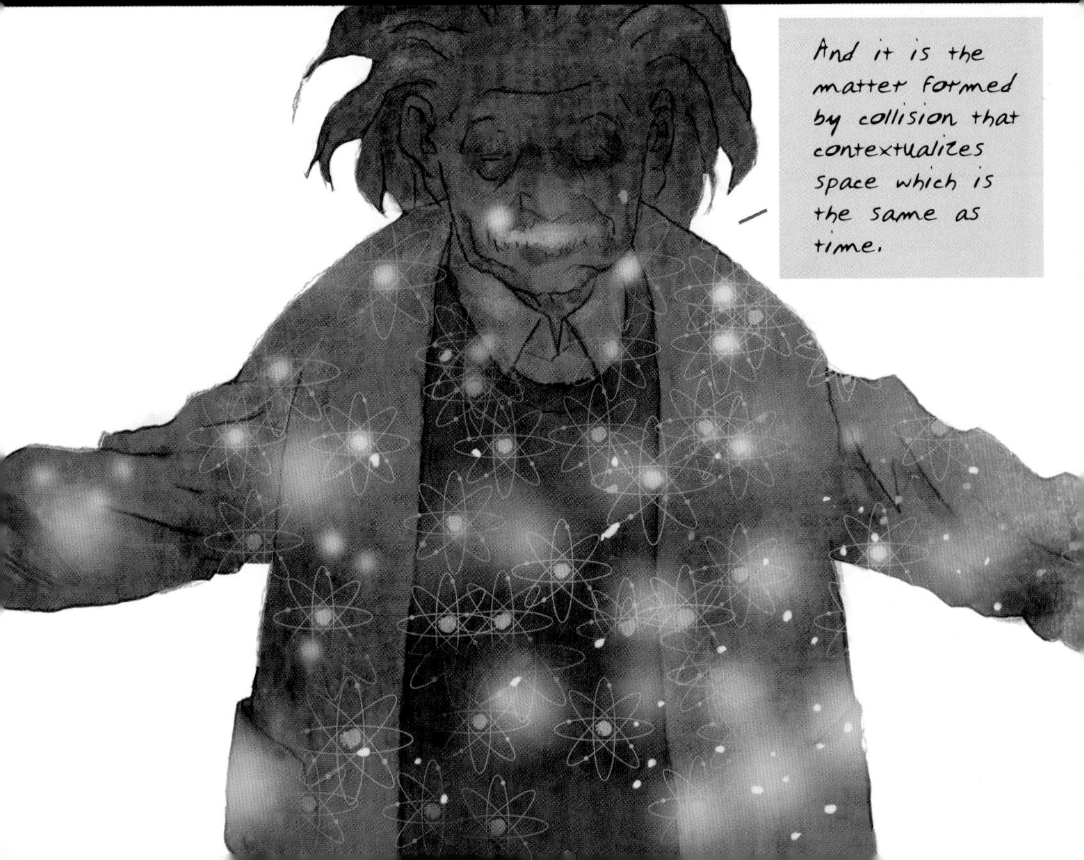
And it is the matter formed by collision that contextualizes space which is the same as time.

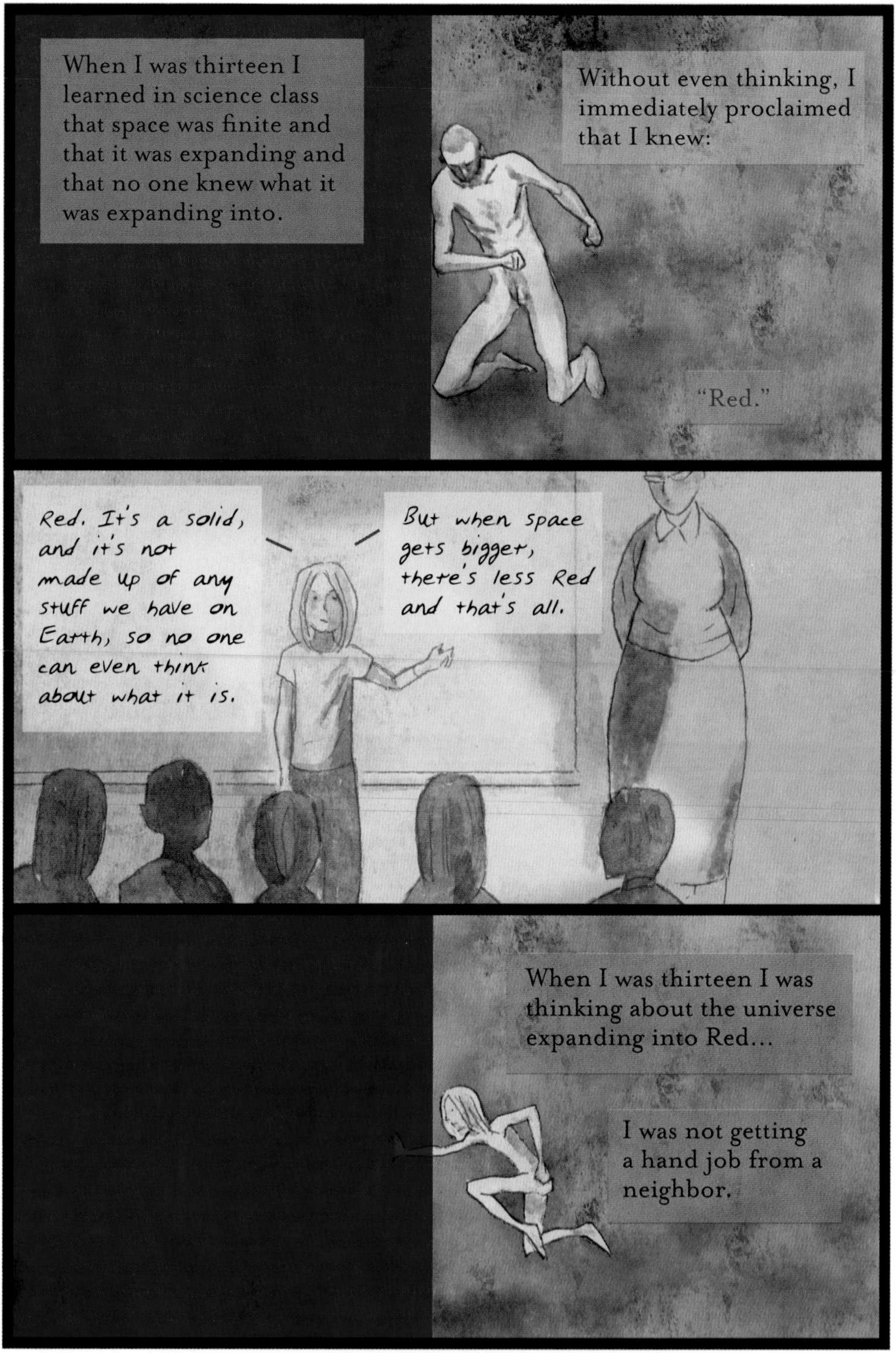
When I was thirteen I learned in science class that space was finite and that it was expanding and that no one knew what it was expanding into.
Without even thinking, I immediately proclaimed that I knew:
"Red."
Red. It's a solid, and it's not made up of any stuff we have on Earth, so no one can even think about what it is.
But when space gets bigger, there's less Red and that's all.
When I was thirteen I was thinking about the universe expanding into Red...
I was not getting a hand job from a neighbor.

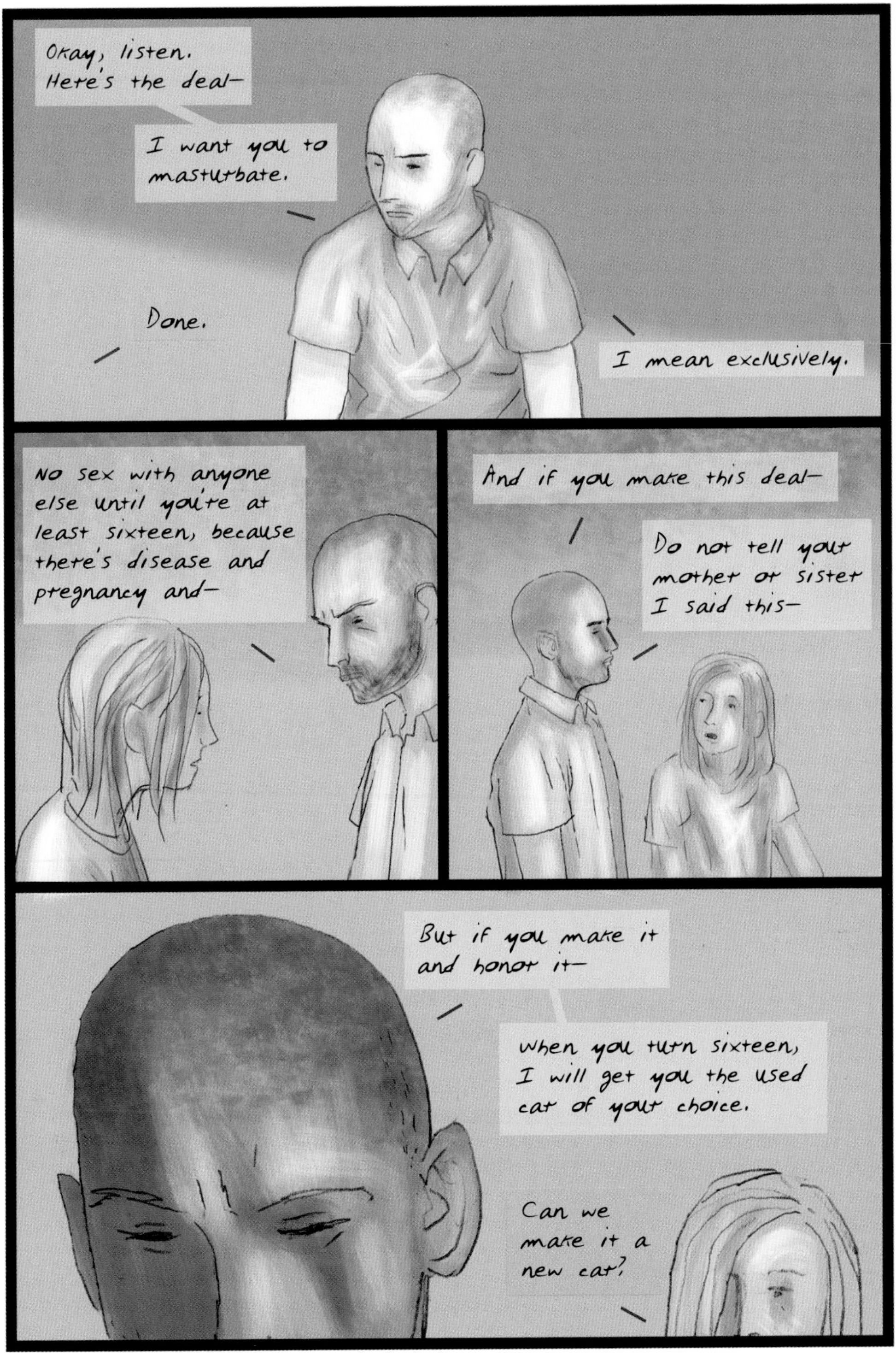
Okay, listen. Here's the deal—
I want you to masturbate.
Done.
I mean exclusively.
No sex with anyone else until you're at least sixteen, because there's disease and pregnancy and—
And if you make this deal—
Do not tell your mother or sister I said this—
But if you make it and honor it—
When you turn sixteen, I will get you the used car of your choice.
Can we make it a new car?

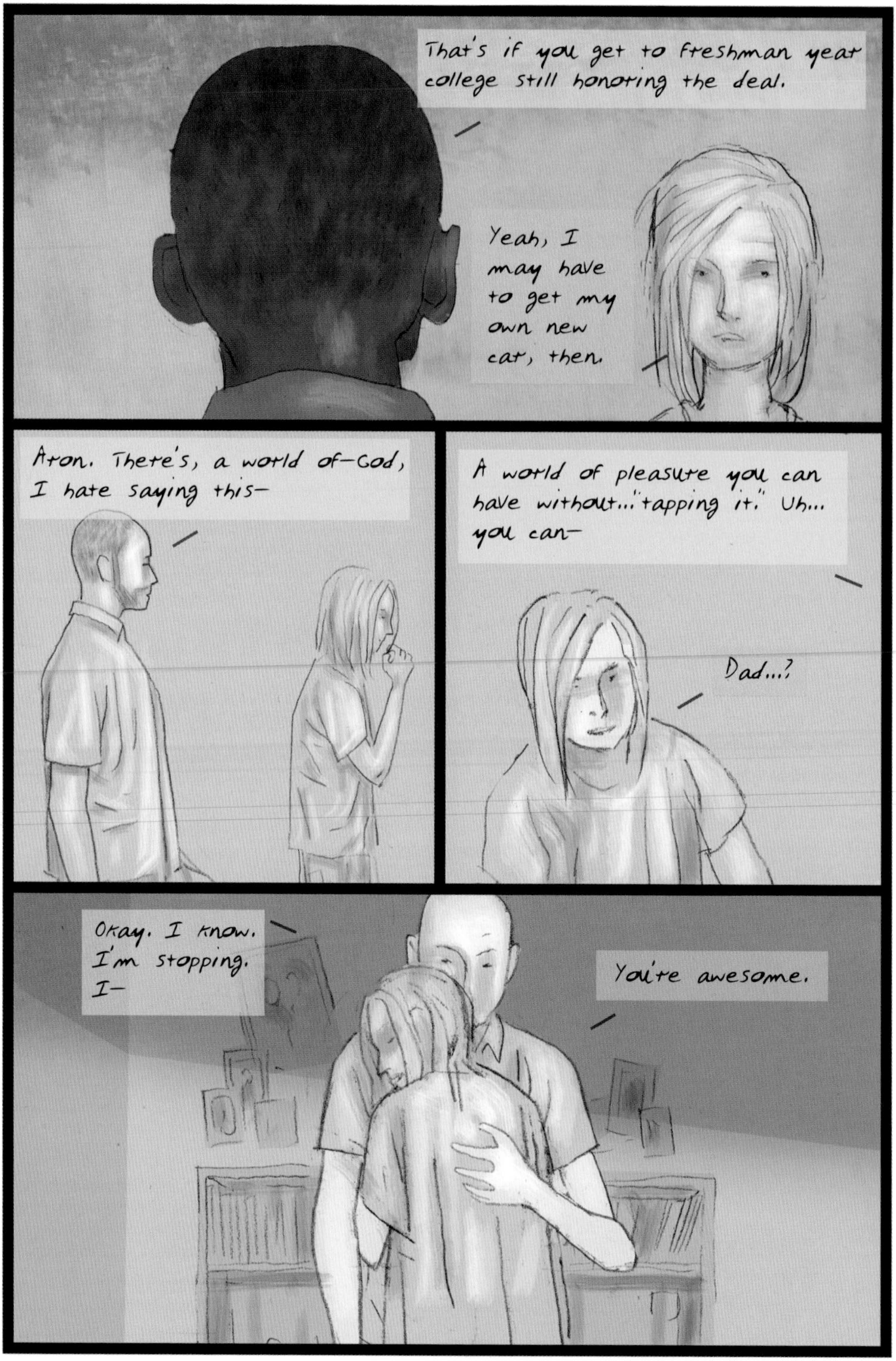
That's if you get to freshman year college still honoring the deal.
Yeah, I may have to get my own new car, then.
Aron. There's, a world of—God, I hate saying this—
A world of pleasure you can have without..."tapping it." Uh... you can—
Dad...?
Okay. I know. I'm stopping. I—
You're awesome.

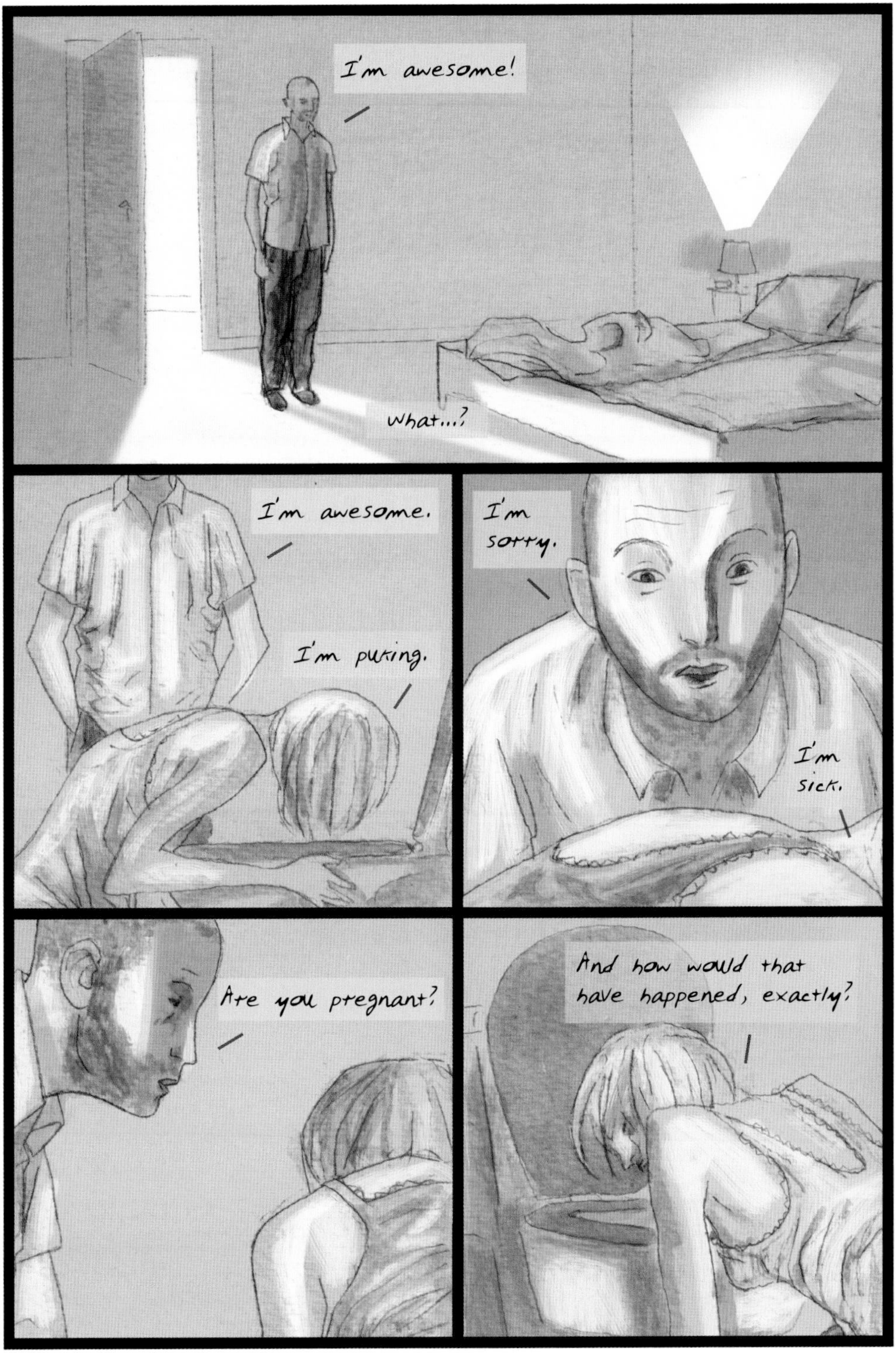
I'm awesome!
what...?
I'm awesome.
I'm puking.
I'm sorry.
I'm sick.
Are you pregnant?
And how would that have happened, exactly?

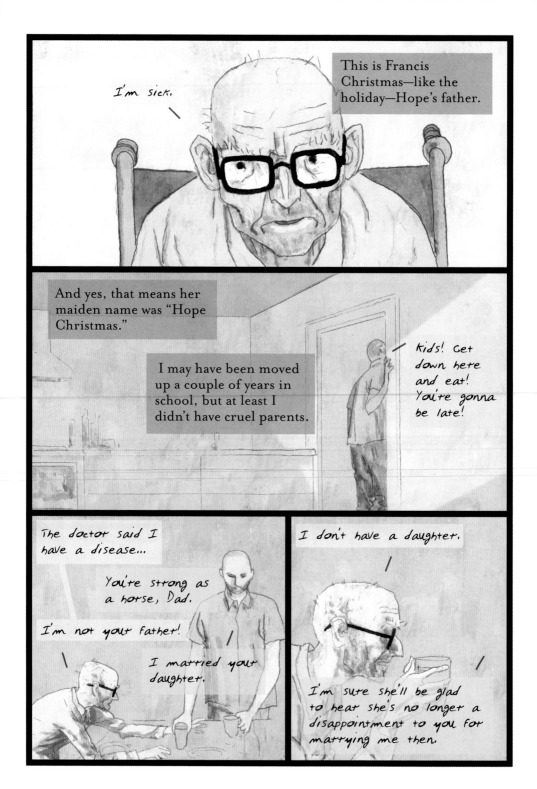

I'm sick.

This is Francis Christmas—like the holiday—Hope's father.

And yes, that means her maiden name was "Hope Christmas."

I may have been moved up a couple of years in school, but at least I didn't have cruel parents.

Kids! Get down here and eat! You're gonna be late!

The doctor said I have a disease...

You're strong as a horse, Dad.

I'm not your father!

I married your daughter.

I don't have a daughter.

I'm sure she'll be glad to hear she's no longer a disappointment to you for marrying me then.

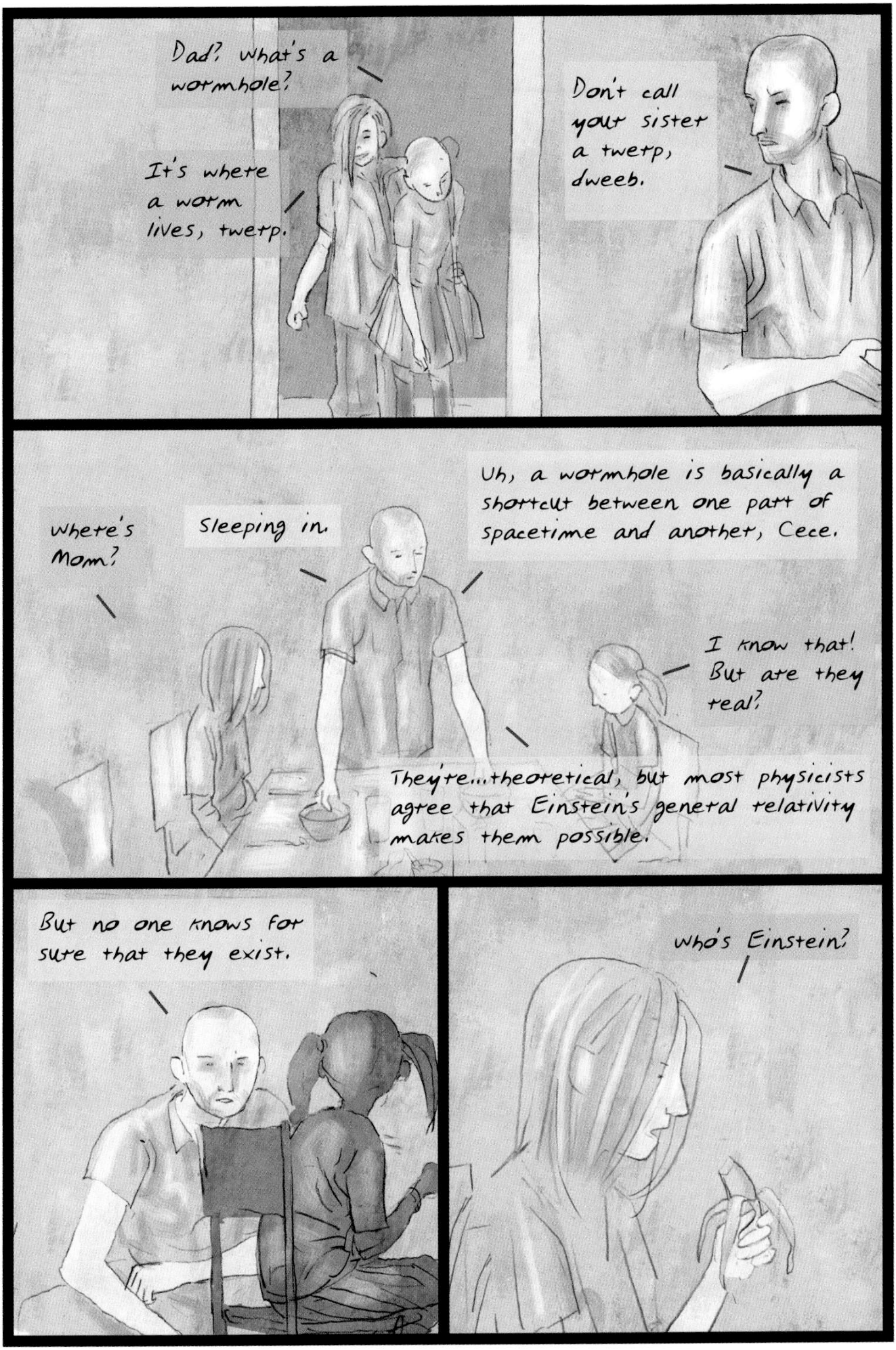
Dad? What's a wormhole?
It's where a worm lives, twerp.
Don't call your sister a twerp, dweeb.
Where's Mom?
Sleeping in.
Uh, a wormhole is basically a shortcut between one part of spacetime and another, Cece.
I know that! But are they real?
They're...theoretical, but most physicists agree that Einstein's general relativity makes them possible.
But no one knows for sure that they exist.
Who's Einstein?

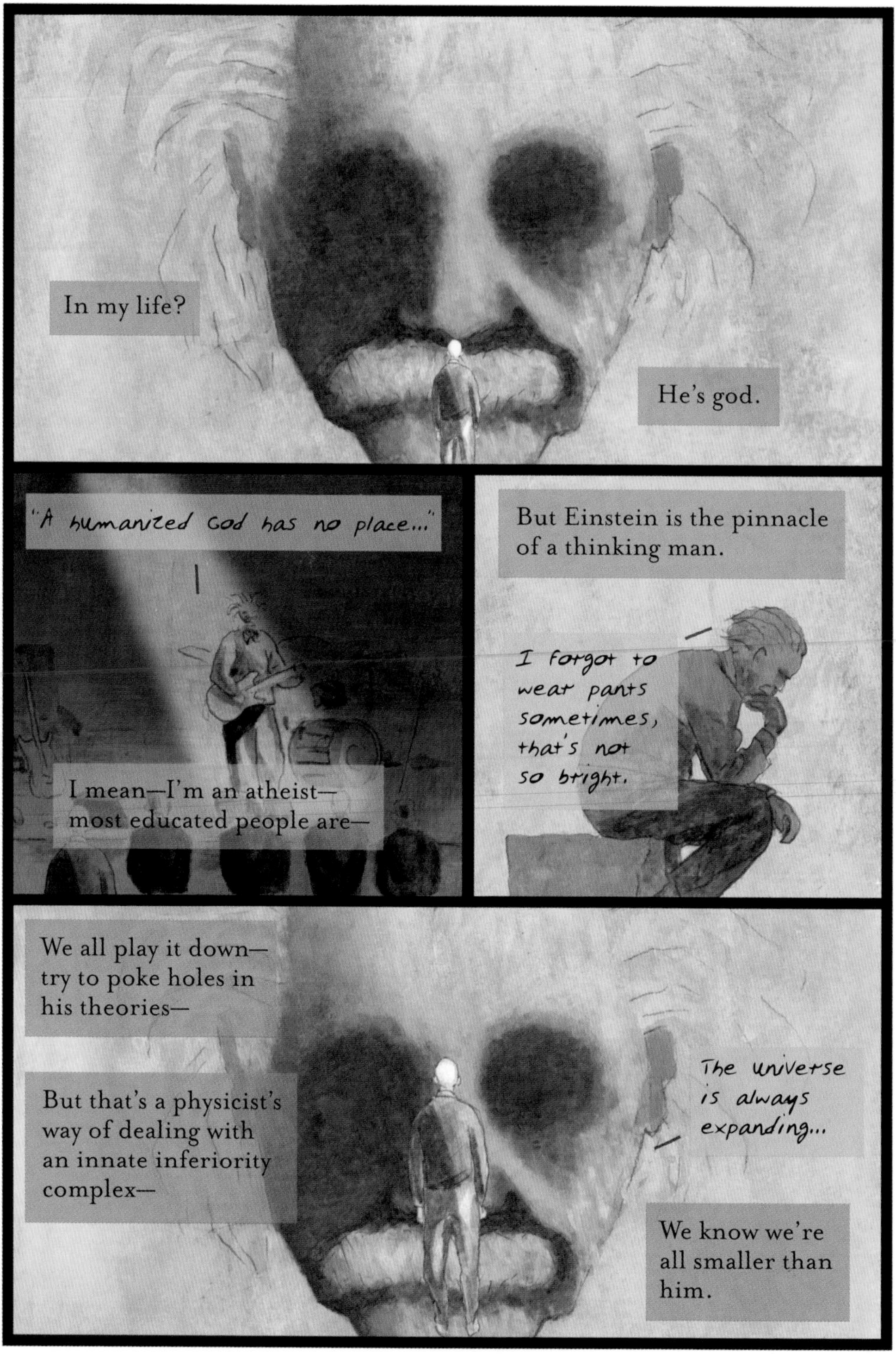
In my life?
He's god.
"A humanized God has no place..."
I mean—I'm an atheist—most educated people are—
But Einstein is the pinnacle of a thinking man.
I forgot to wear pants sometimes, that's not so bright.
We all play it down—try to poke holes in his theories—
But that's a physicist's way of dealing with an innate inferiority complex—
The universe is always expanding...
We know we're all smaller than him.

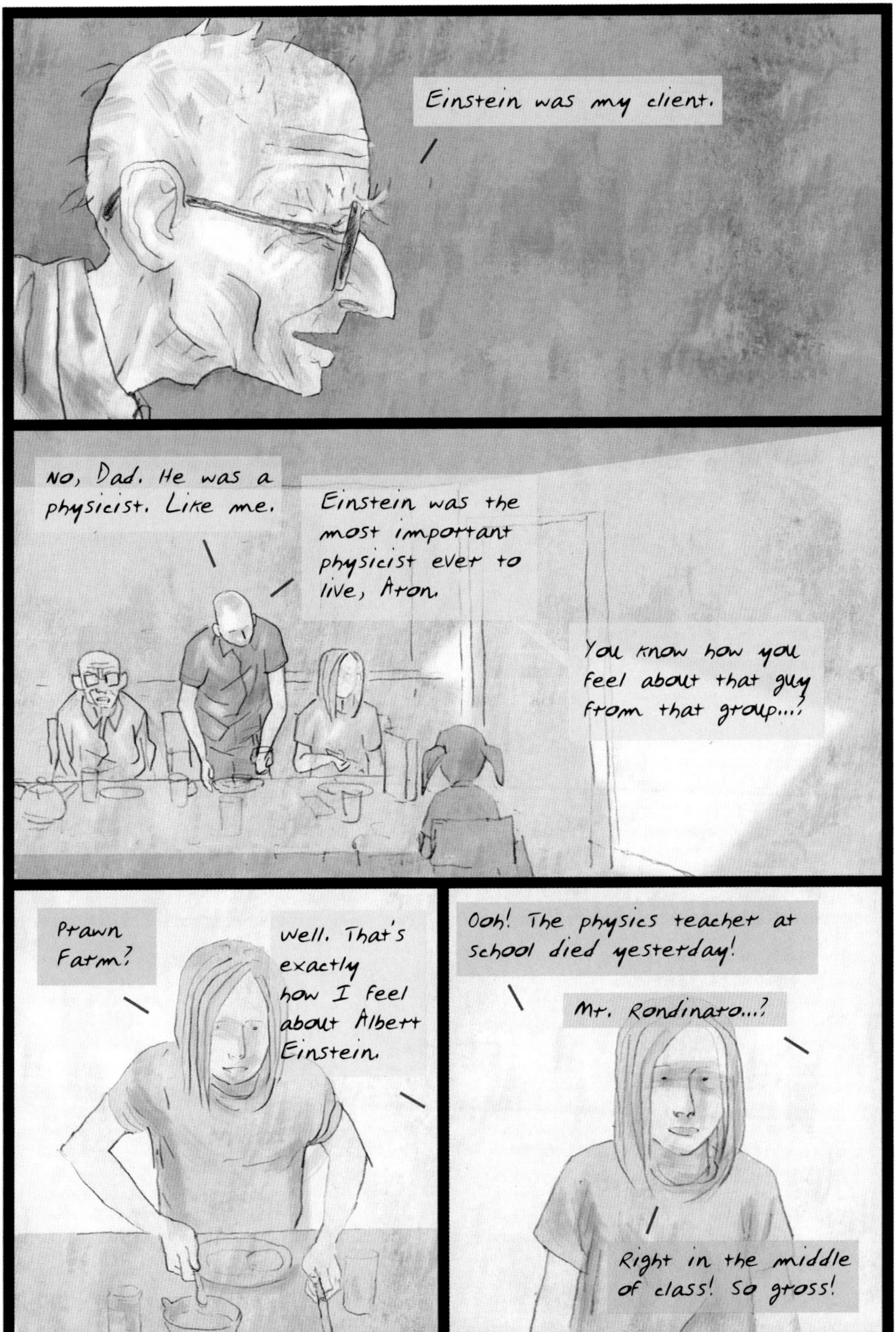
Einstein was my client.
No, Dad. He was a physicist. Like me.
Einstein was the most important physicist ever to live, Aron.
You know how you feel about that guy from that group...?
Prawn Farm?
Well. That's exactly how I feel about Albert Einstein.
Ooh! The physics teacher at school died yesterday!
Mr. Rondinaro...?
Right in the middle of class! So gross!

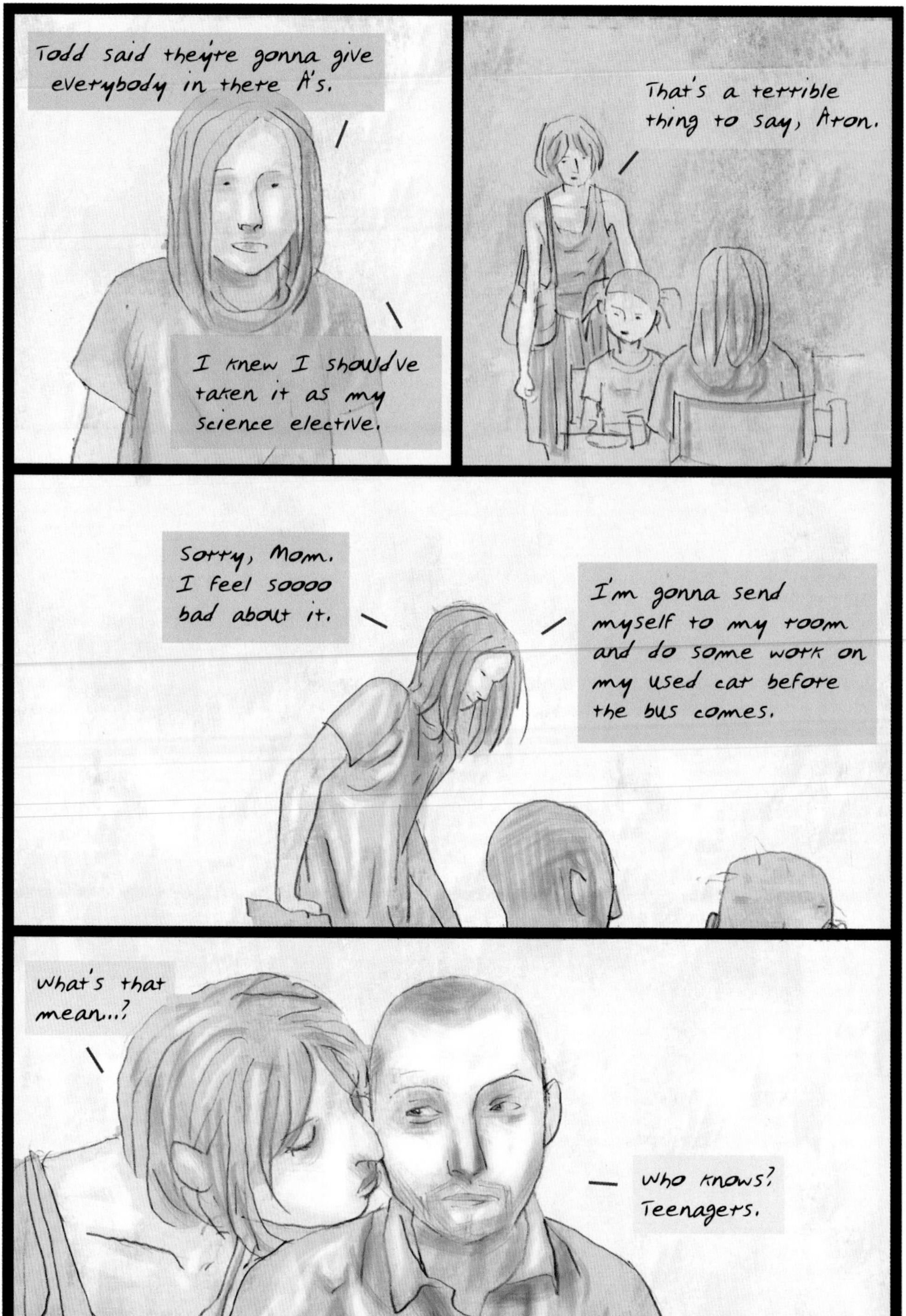

Todd said they're gonna give everybody in there A's.
I knew I should've taken it as my science elective.
That's a terrible thing to say, Aron.
Sorry, Mom. I feel soooo bad about it.
I'm gonna send myself to my room and do some work on my used car before the bus comes.
What's that mean...?
Who knows? Teenagers.

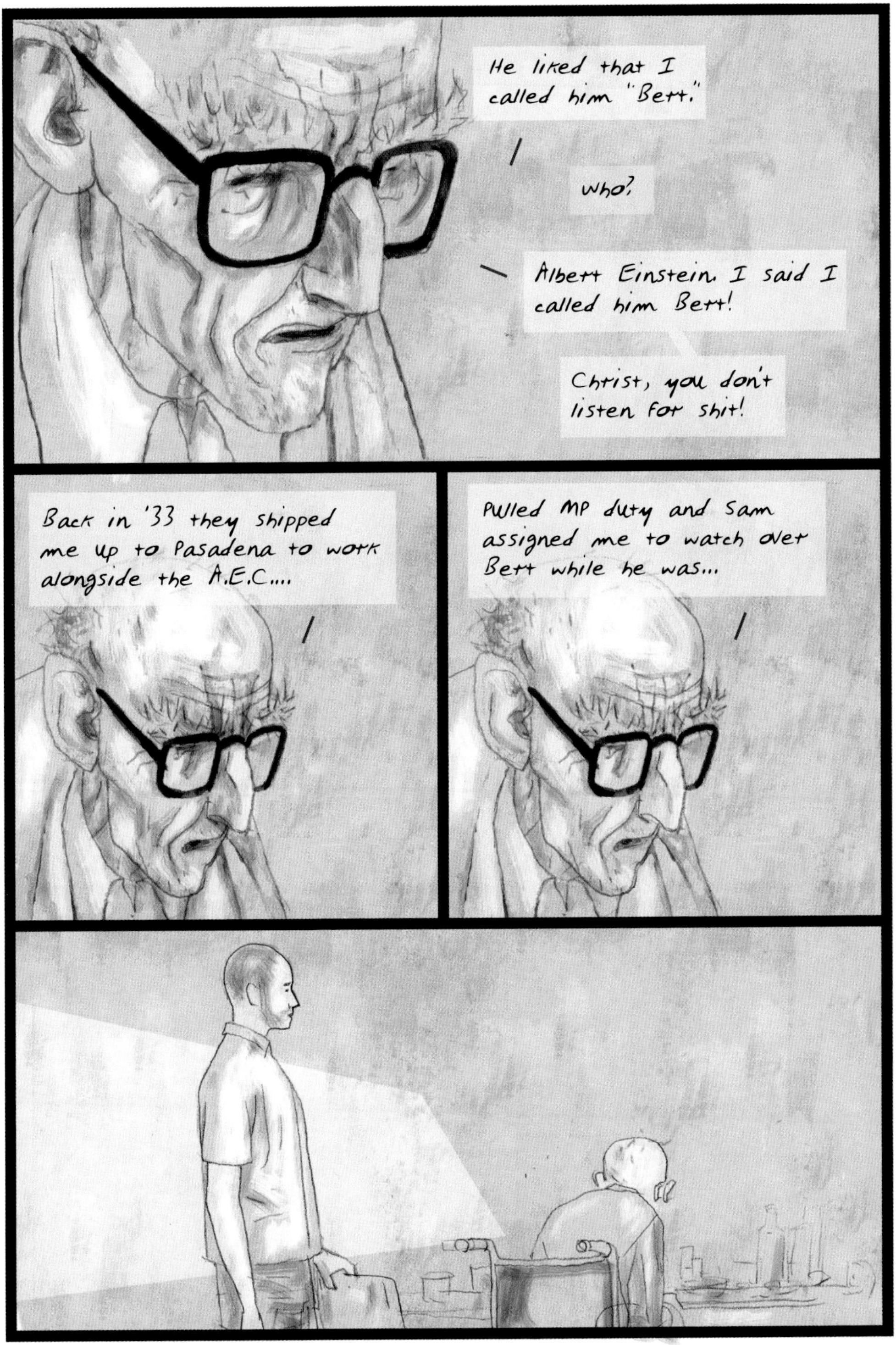
He liked that I called him "Bert."
who?
Albert Einstein. I said I called him Bert!
Christ, you don't listen for shit!
Back in '33 they shipped me up to Pasadena to work alongside the A.E.C....
Pulled MP duty and Sam assigned me to watch over Bert while he was...

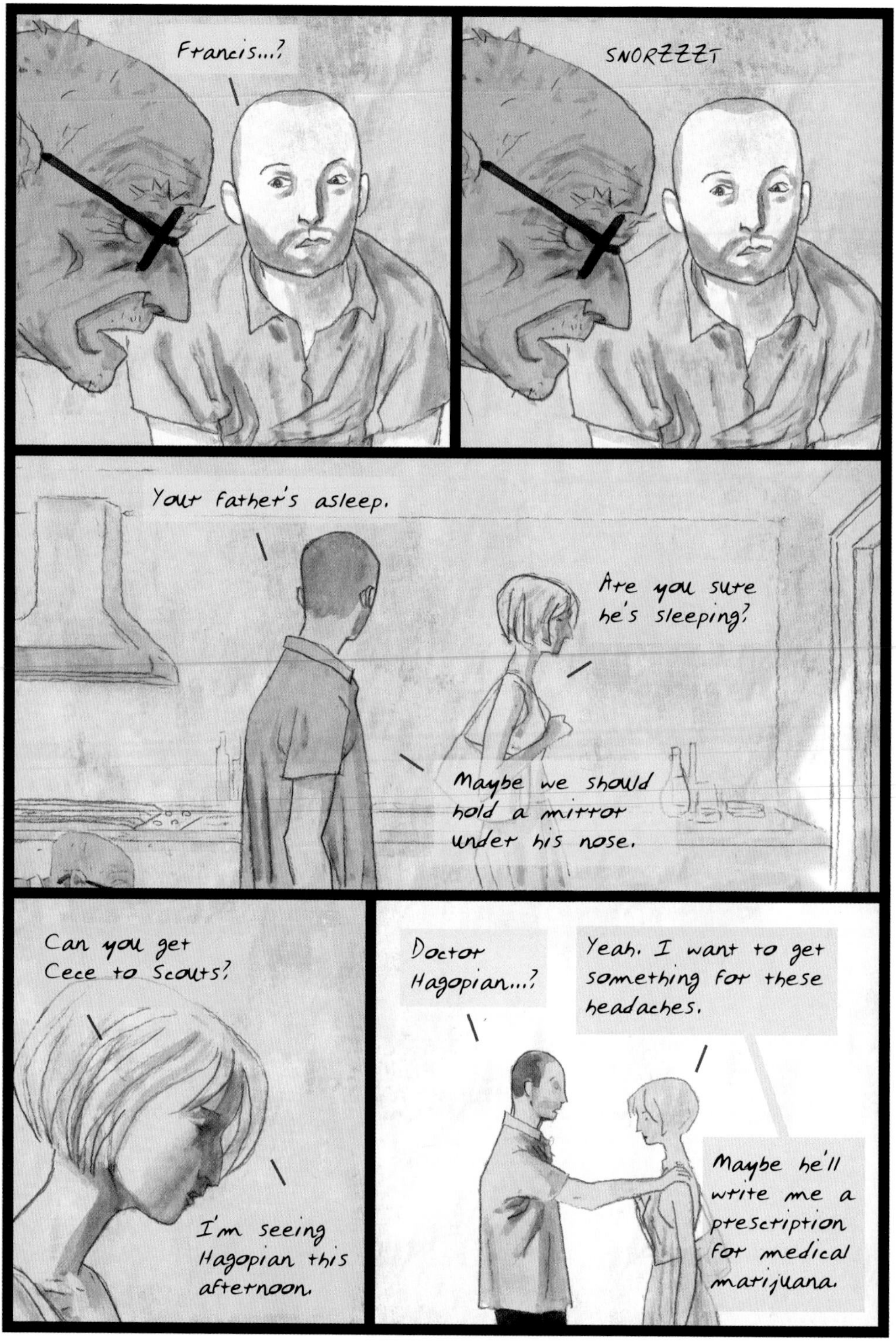
Francis...?
SNORZZZT
Your father's asleep.
Are you sure he's sleeping?
Maybe we should hold a mirror under his nose.
Can you get Cece to Scouts?
I'm seeing Hagopian this afternoon.
Doctor Hagopian...?
Yeah. I want to get something for these headaches.
Maybe he'll write me a prescription for medical marijuana.

I've never smoked.

I've never had more than a sip of liquor at any one time.

I've never cheated on Hope.

I kissed Maryann Nichols in a moment of weakness at an office party one year when Hope and I were having troubles.

I confessed, but Hope said it didn't count because there was mistletoe...

And because Maryann Nichols was horse-faced so if I could stand to kiss that mug, more power to me.

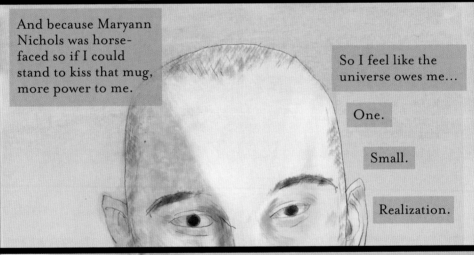

So I feel like the universe owes me...

One.

Small.

Realization.

Sooner than later.

Really great, Catmichael.

Thanks, M-Mr. Needham.

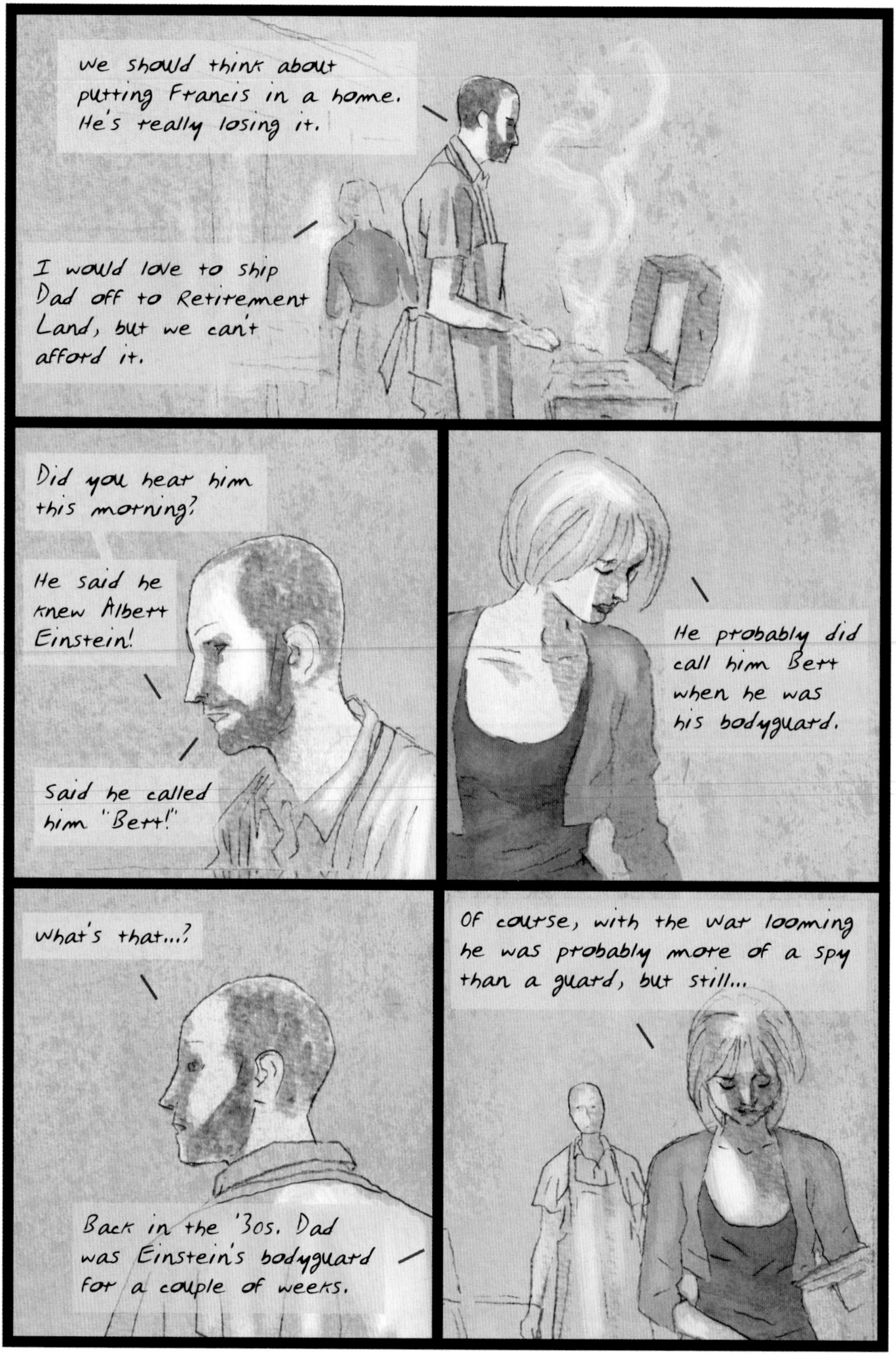
We should think about putting Francis in a home. He's really losing it.
I would love to ship Dad off to Retirement Land, but we can't afford it.
Did you hear him this morning?
He said he knew Albert Einstein!
Said he called him "Bert!"
He probably did call him Bert when he was his bodyguard.
What's that...?
Back in the '30s. Dad was Einstein's bodyguard for a couple of weeks.
Of course, with the war looming he was probably more of a spy than a guard, but still...

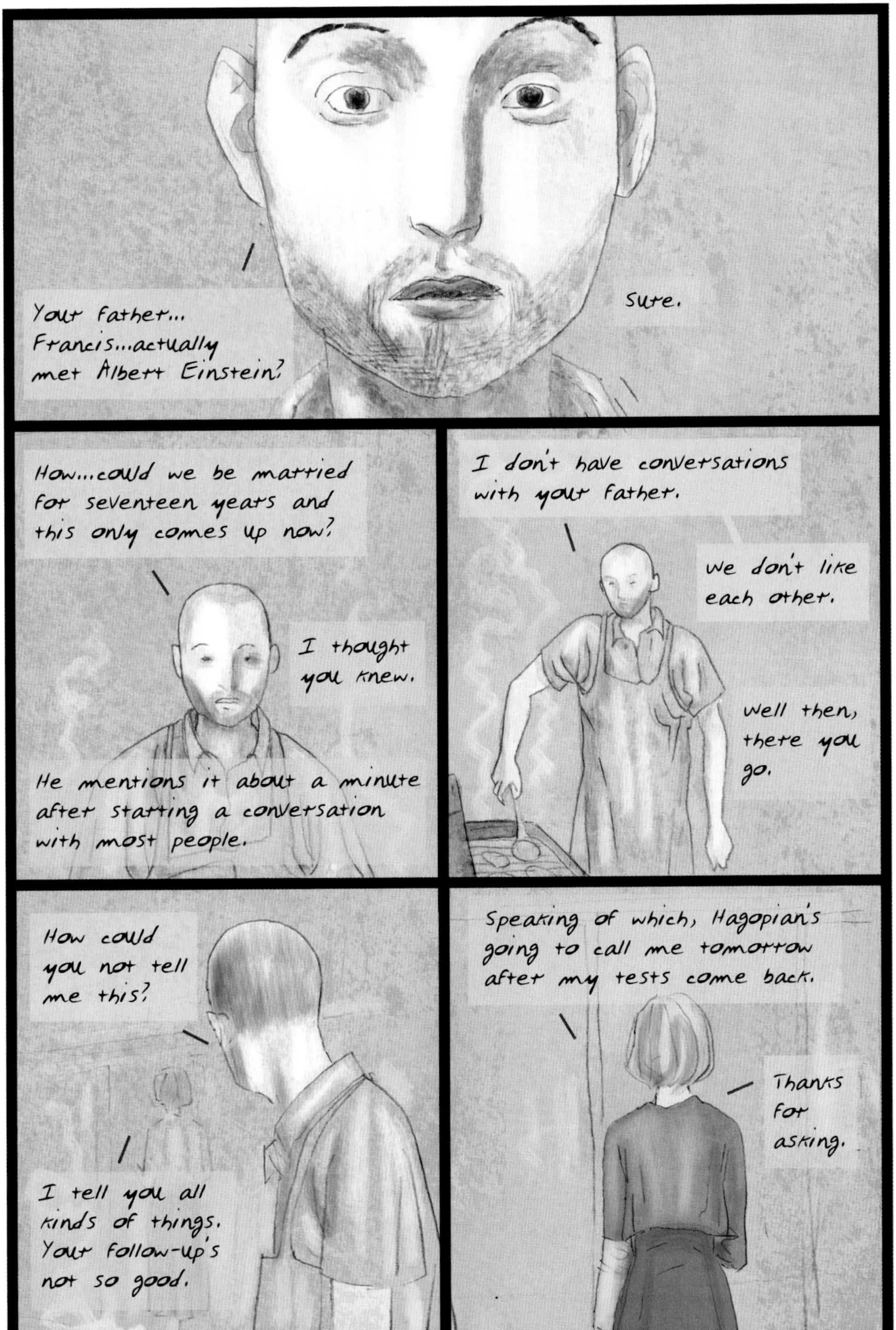
Your father...
Francis...actually
met Albert Einstein?
Sure.
How...could we be married for seventeen years and this only comes up now?
I thought you knew.
He mentions it about a minute after starting a conversation with most people.
I don't have conversations with your father.
We don't like each other.
Well then, there you go.
How could you not tell me this?
I tell you all kinds of things. Your follow-up's not so good.
Speaking of which, Hagopian's going to call me tomorrow after my tests come back.
Thanks for asking.

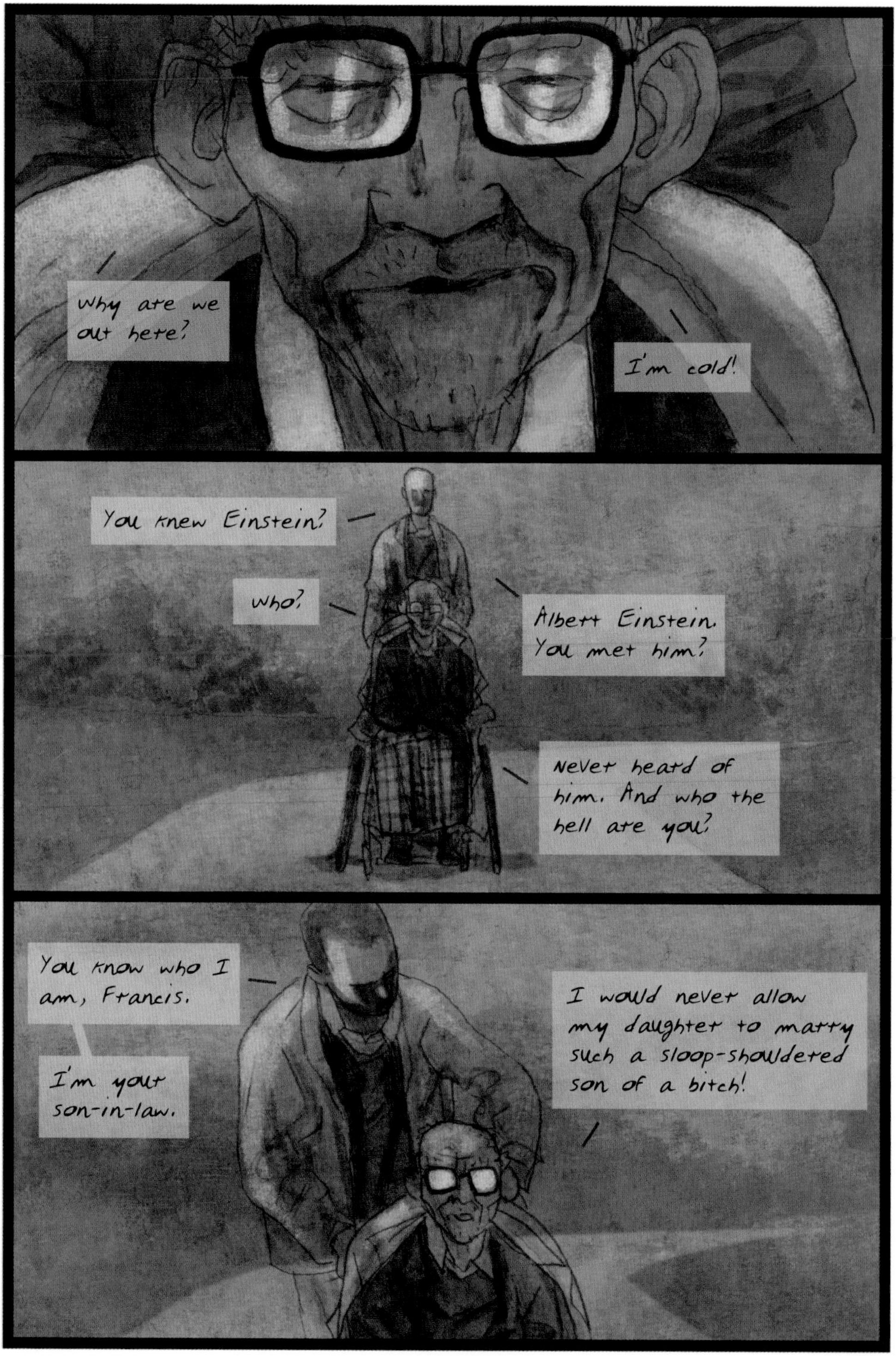
Why are we out here?
I'm cold!
You knew Einstein?
Who?
Albert Einstein. You met him?
Never heard of him. And who the hell are you?
You know who I am, Francis.
I'm your son-in-law.
I would never allow my daughter to marry such a sloop-shouldered son of a bitch!

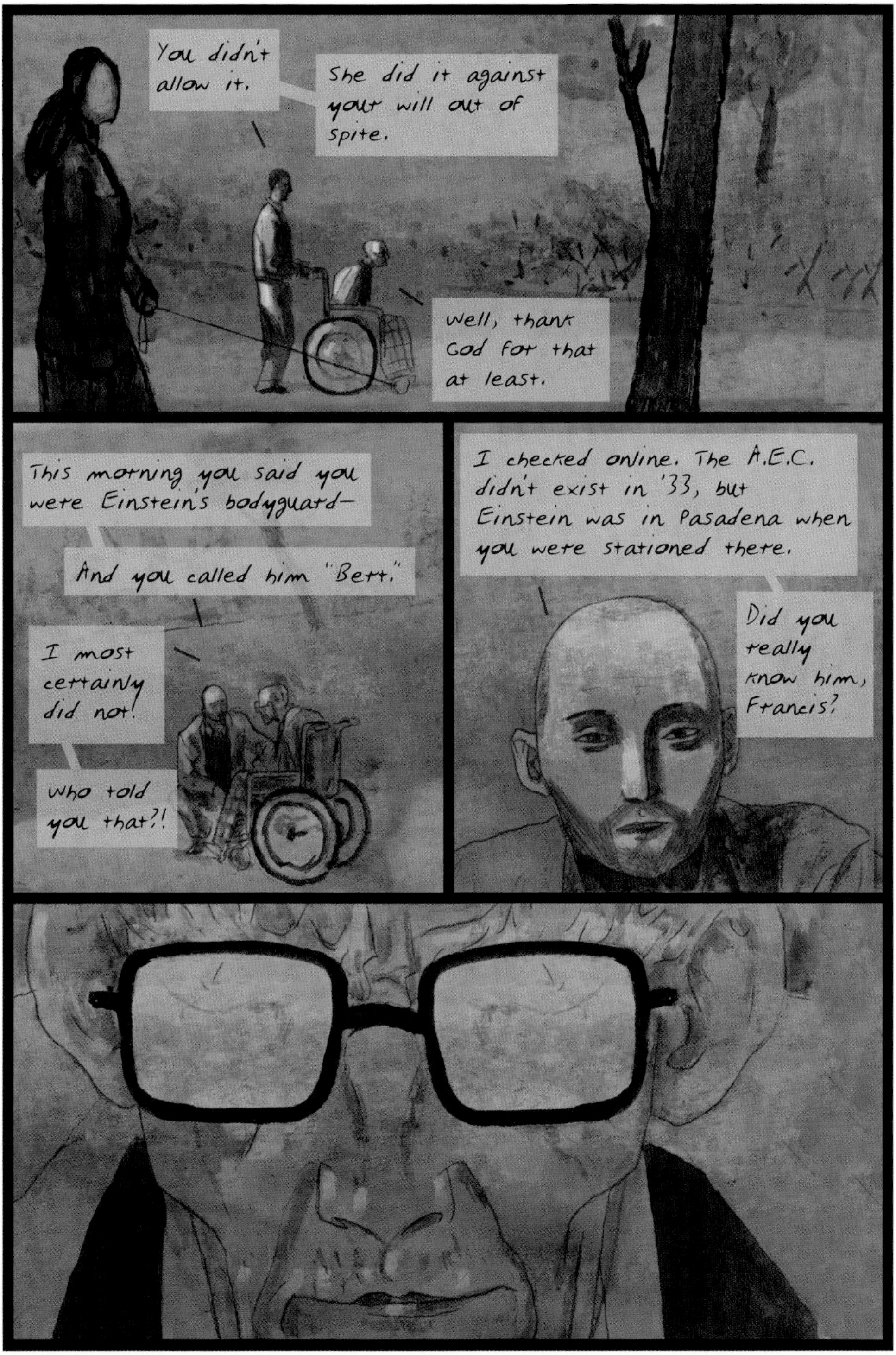
You didn't allow it.
She did it against your will out of spite.
Well, thank God for that at least.
This morning you said you were Einstein's bodyguard—
And you called him "Bert."
I most certainly did not!
Who told you that?!
I checked online. The A.E.C. didn't exist in '33, but Einstein was in Pasadena when you were stationed there.
Did you really know him, Francis?

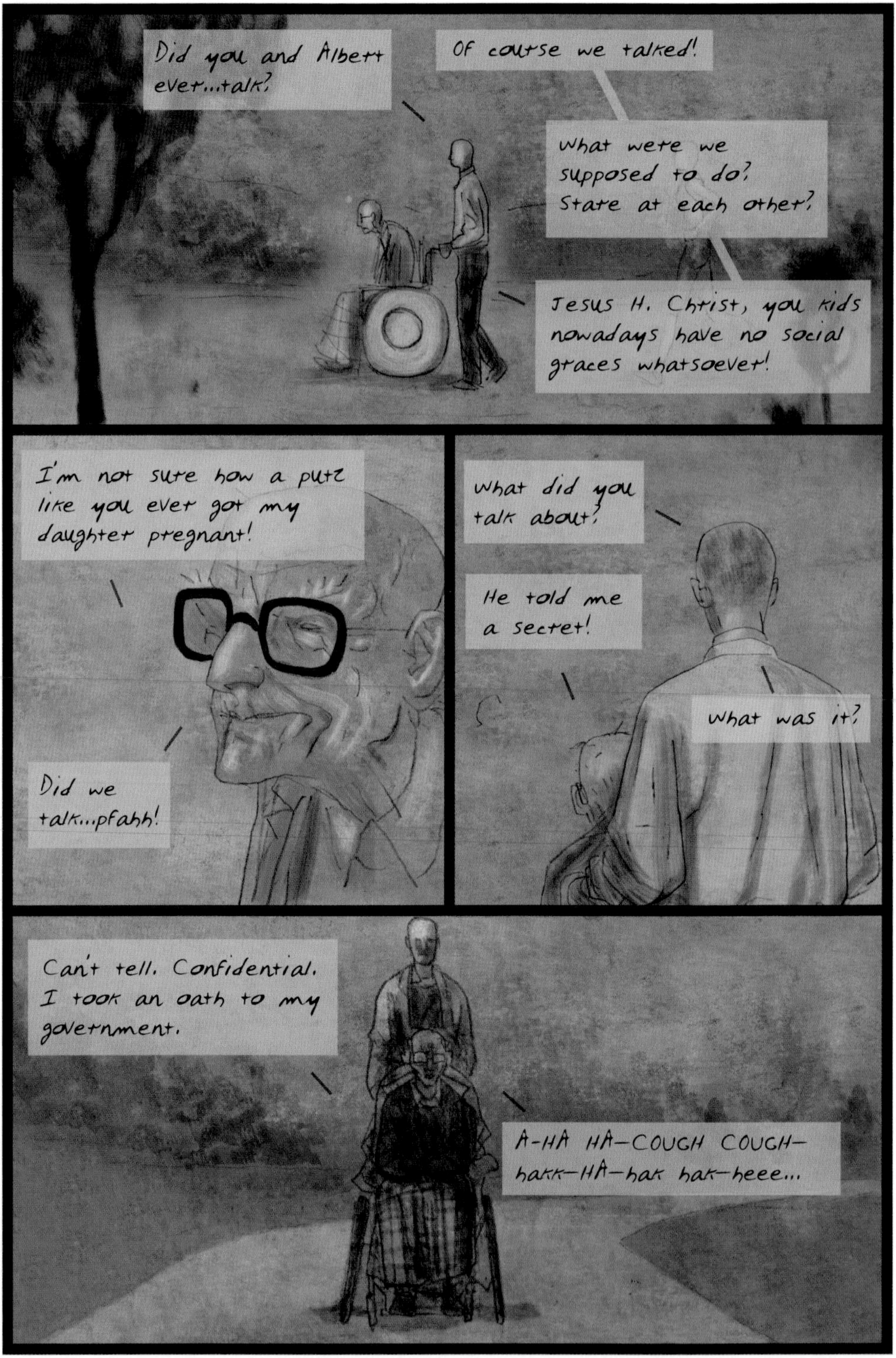
Did you and Albert ever...talk?
Of course we talked!
What were we supposed to do? Stare at each other?
Jesus H. Christ, you kids nowadays have no social graces whatsoever!
I'm not sure how a putz like you ever got my daughter pregnant!
Did we talk...pfahh!
What did you talk about?
He told me a secret!
What was it?
Can't tell. Confidential. I took an oath to my government.
A-HA HA—COUGH COUGH—hakk—HA—hak hak—heee...

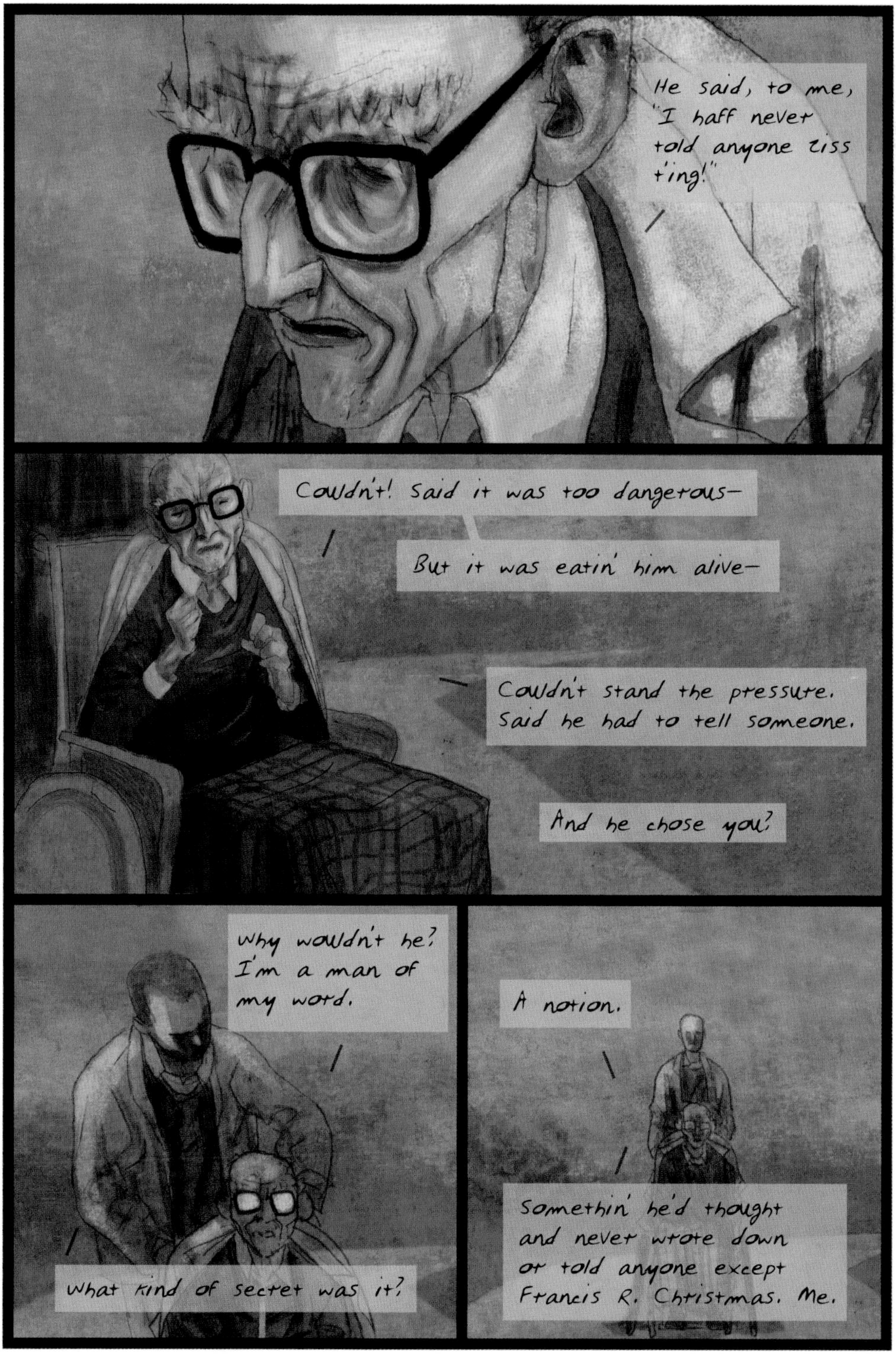
He said, to me, "I haff never told anyone ziss ting!"
Couldn't! Said it was too dangerous—
But it was eatin' him alive—
Couldn't stand the pressure. Said he had to tell someone.
And he chose you?
Why wouldn't he? I'm a man of my word.
What kind of secret was it?
A notion.
Somethin' he'd thought and never wrote down or told anyone except Francis R. Christmas. Me.

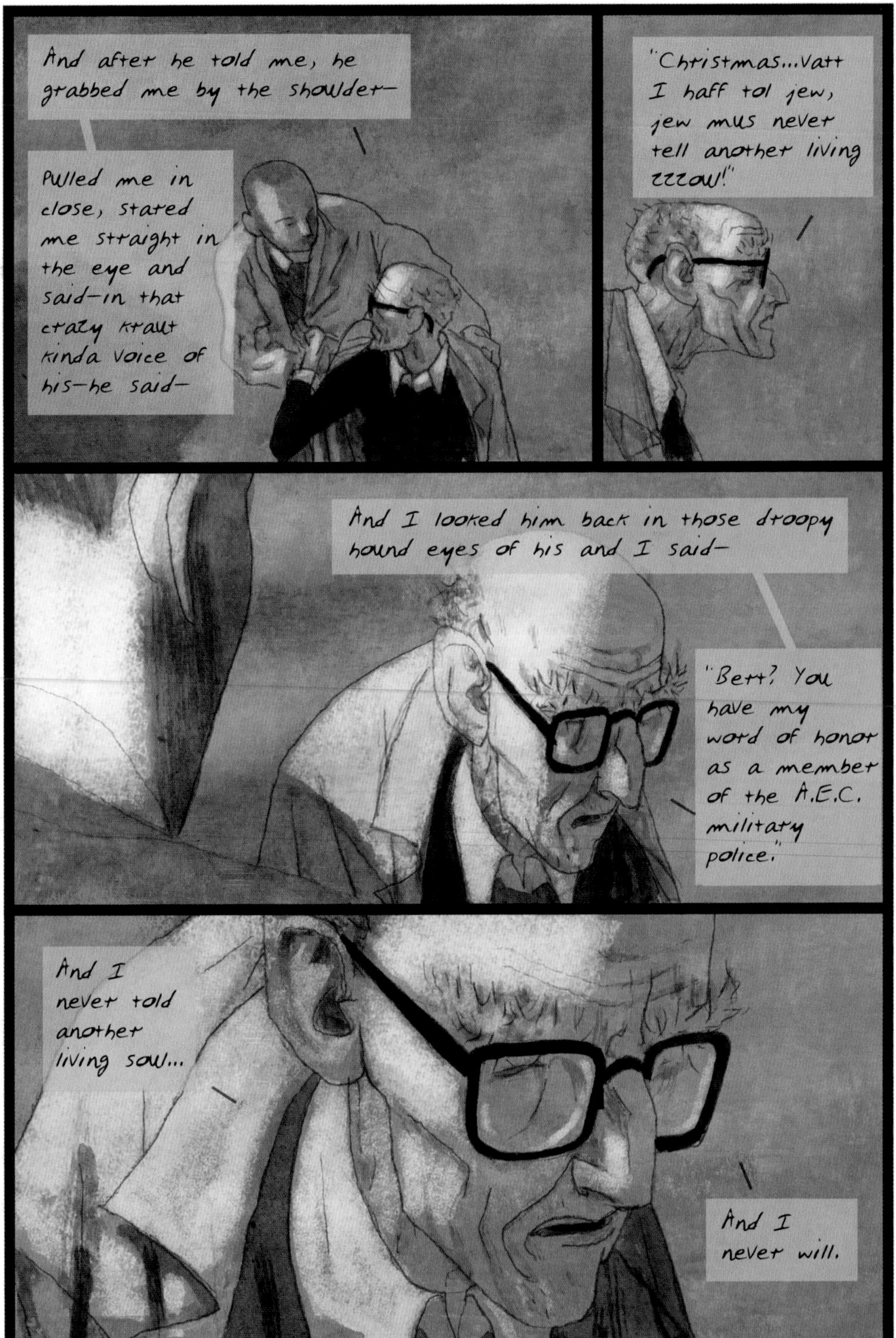
And after he told me, he grabbed me by the shoulder–
Pulled me in close, stared me straight in the eye and said–in that crazy kraut kinda voice of his–he said–
"Christmas...Vatt I haff tol jew, jew mus never tell another living zzzoul!"
And I looked him back in those droopy hound eyes of his and I said–
"Bert? You have my word of honor as a member of the A.E.C. military police."
And I never told another living soul...
And I never will.

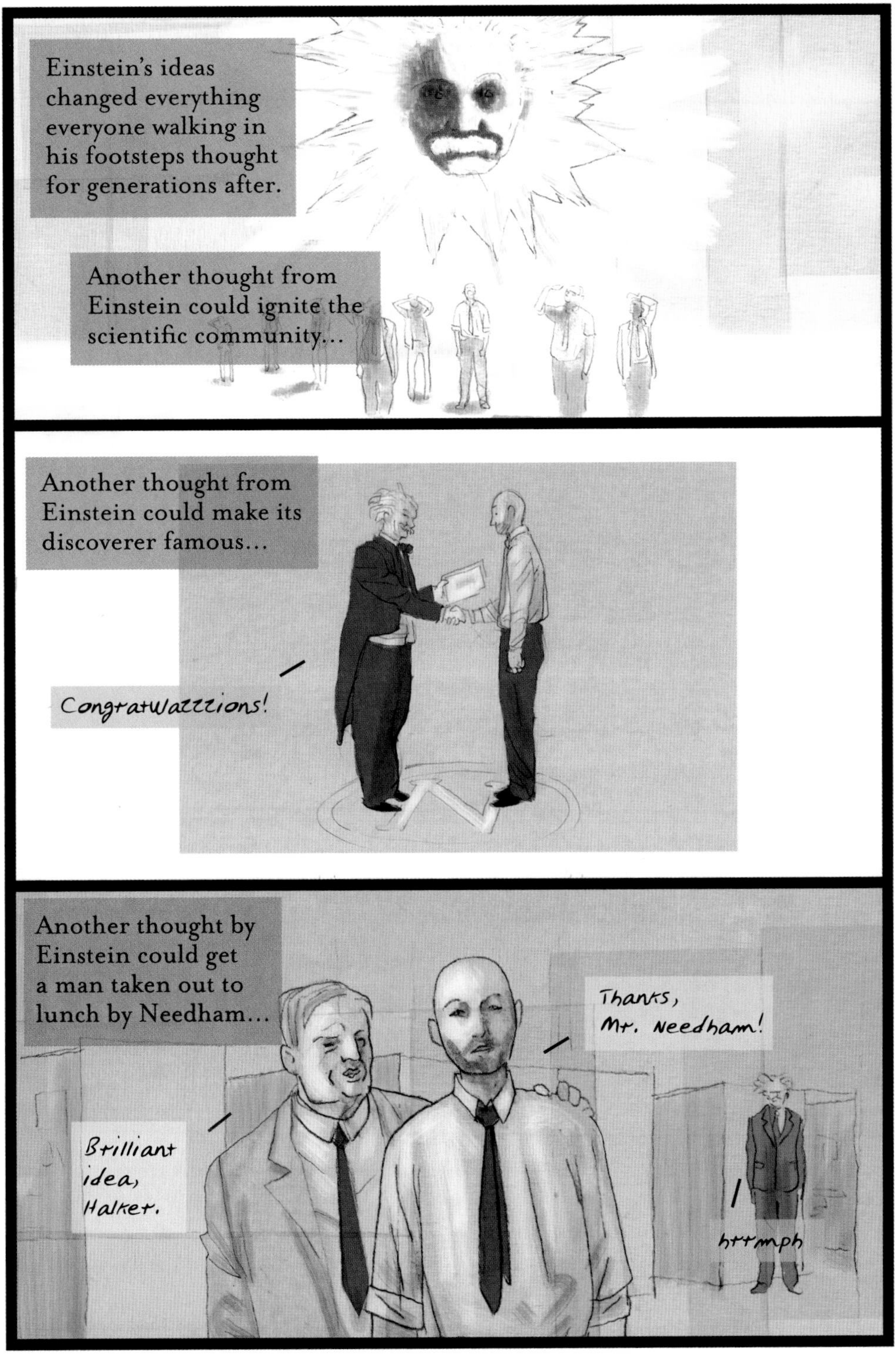
Einstein's ideas changed everything everyone walking in his footsteps thought for generations after.
Another thought from Einstein could ignite the scientific community...
Another thought from Einstein could make its discoverer famous...
CongratWazzzions!
Another thought by Einstein could get a man taken out to lunch by Needham...
Thanks, Mr. Needham!
Brilliant idea, Halker.
hrrmph

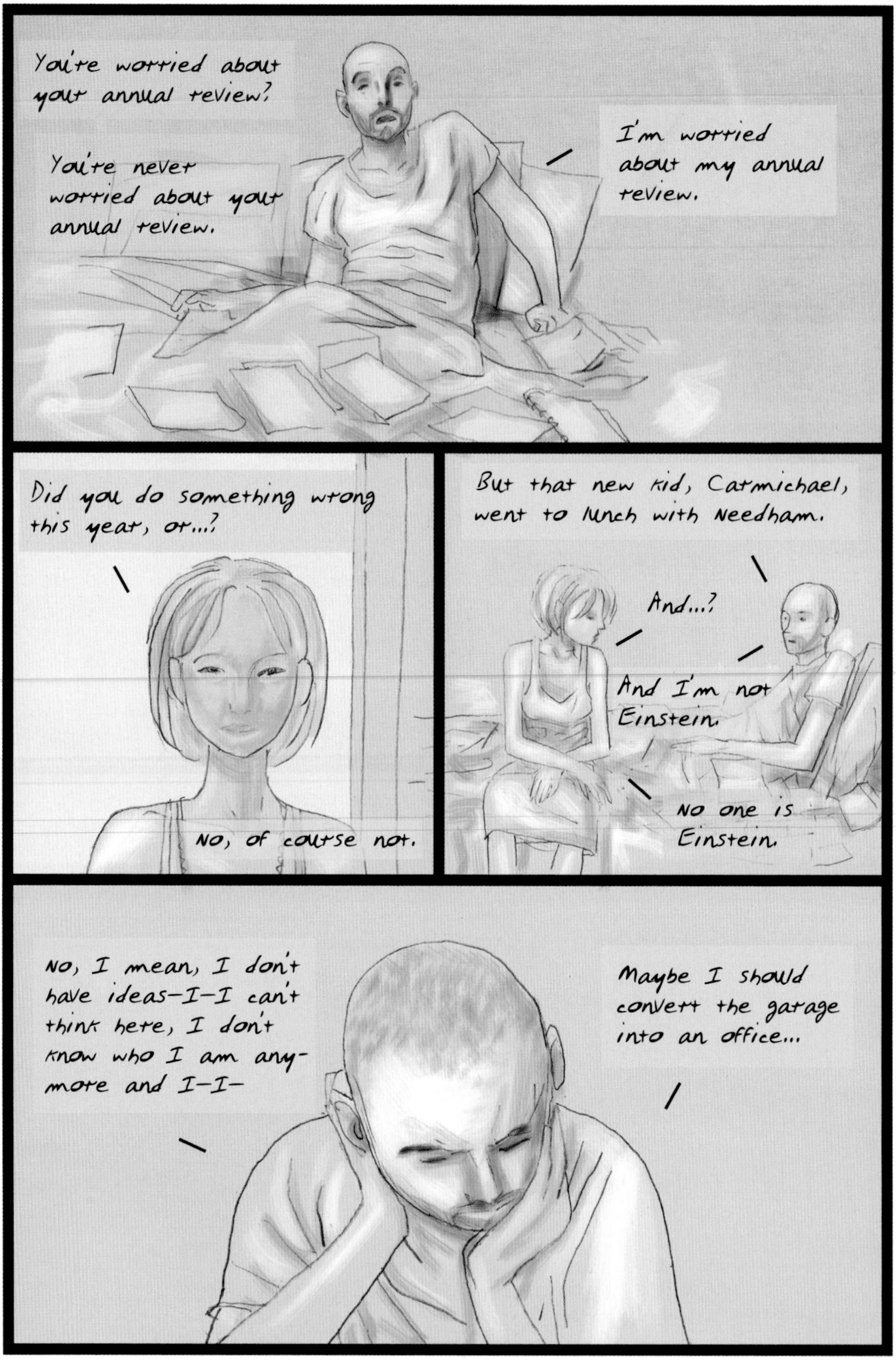
You're worried about your annual review?
You're never worried about your annual review.
I'm worried about my annual review.
Did you do something wrong this year, or...?
No, of course not.
But that new kid, Carmichael, went to lunch with Needham.
And...?
And I'm not Einstein.
No one is Einstein.
No, I mean, I don't have ideas—I—I can't think here, I don't know who I am anymore and I—I—
Maybe I should convert the garage into an office...

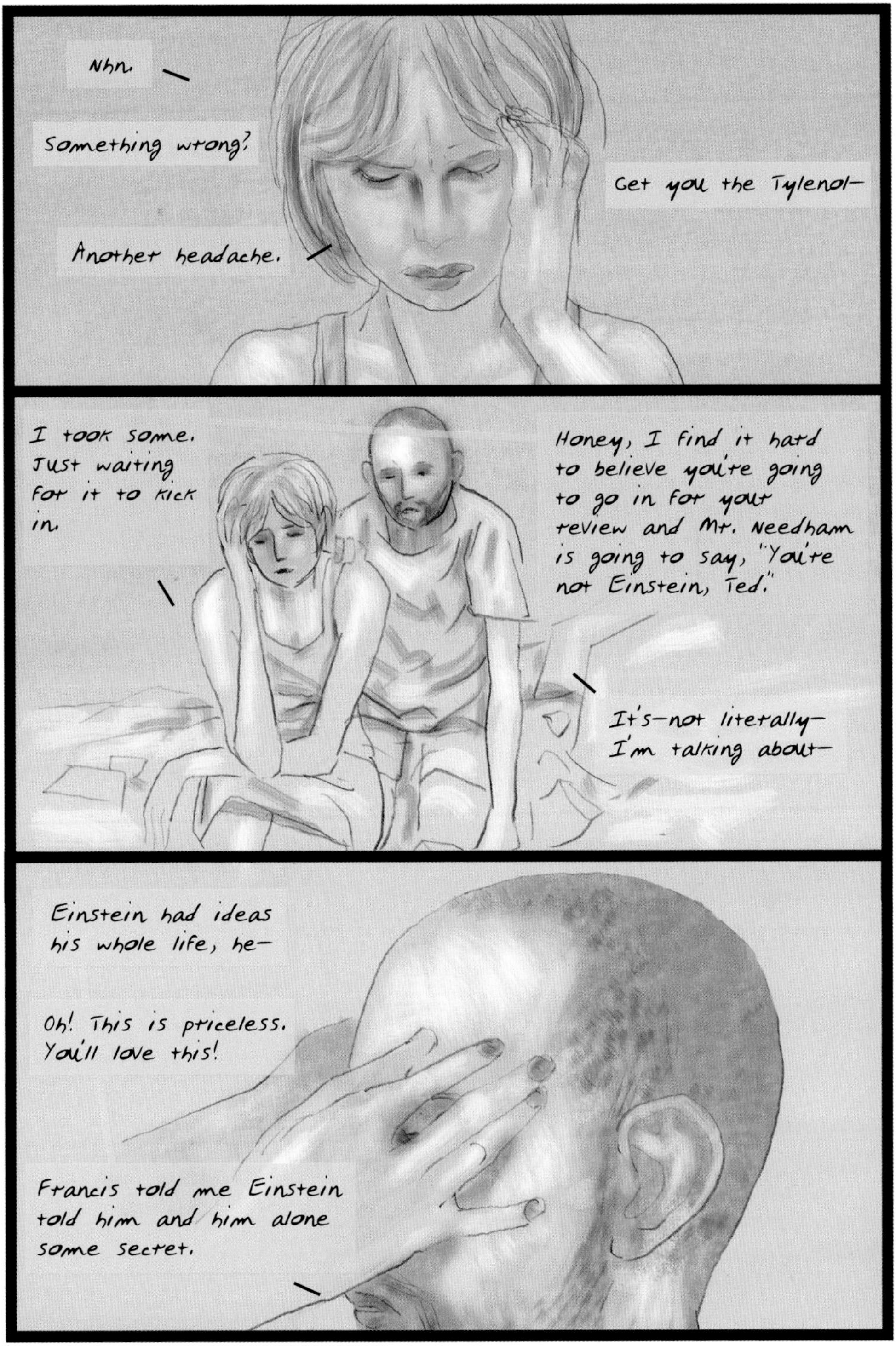
Nhn.
Something wrong?
Get you the Tylenol—
Another headache.
I took some. Just waiting for it to kick in.
Honey, I find it hard to believe you're going to go in for your review and Mr. Needham is going to say, "You're not Einstein, Ted."
It's—not literally—I'm talking about—
Einstein had ideas his whole life, he—
Oh! This is priceless. You'll love this!
Francis told me Einstein told him and him alone some secret.

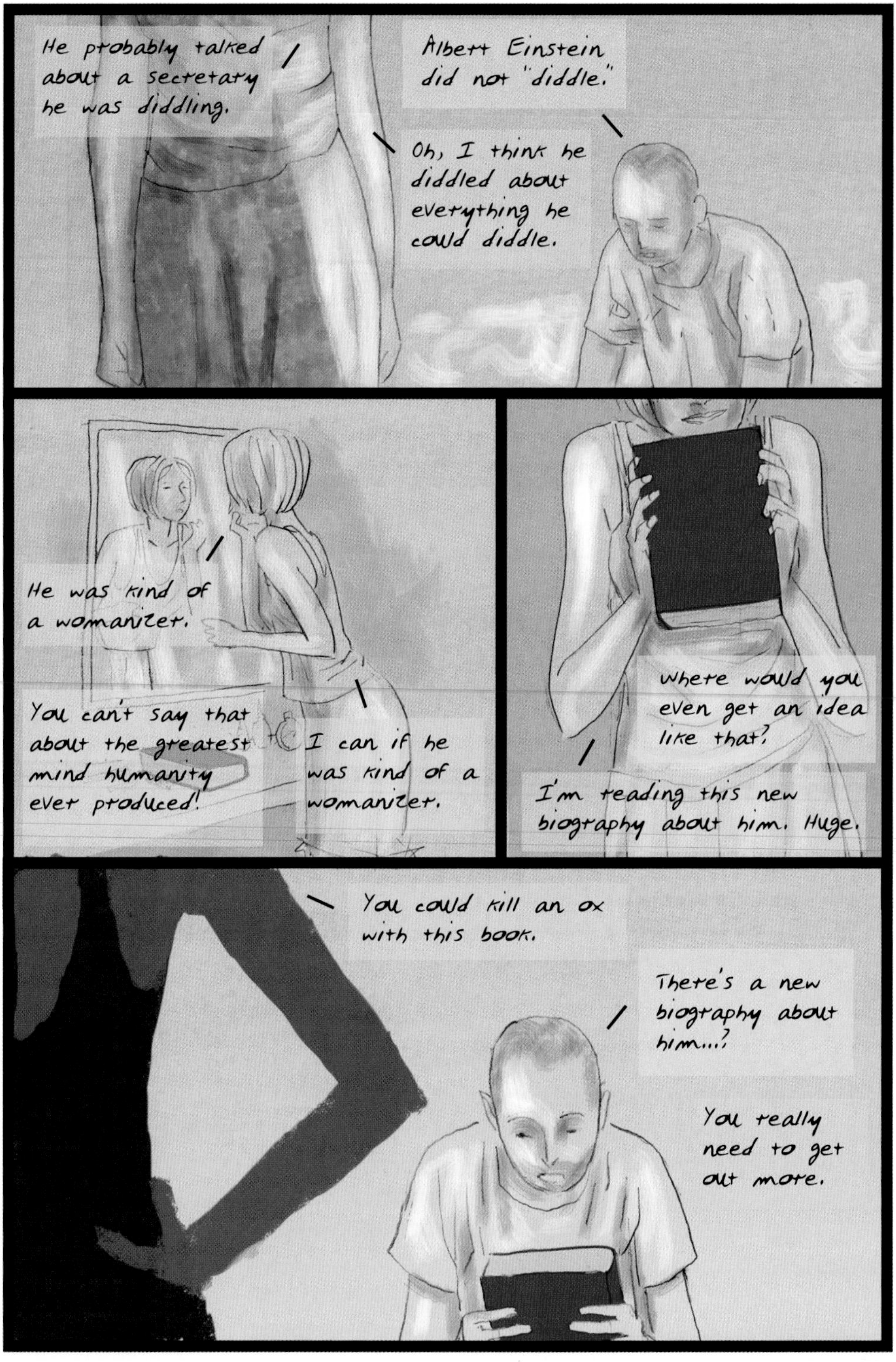
He probably talked about a secretary he was diddling.
Albert Einstein did not "diddle."
Oh, I think he diddled about everything he could diddle.
He was kind of a womanizer.
You can't say that about the greatest mind humanity ever produced!
I can if he was kind of a womanizer.
Where would you even get an idea like that?
I'm reading this new biography about him. Huge.
You could kill an ox with this book.
There's a new biography about him...?
You really need to get out more.

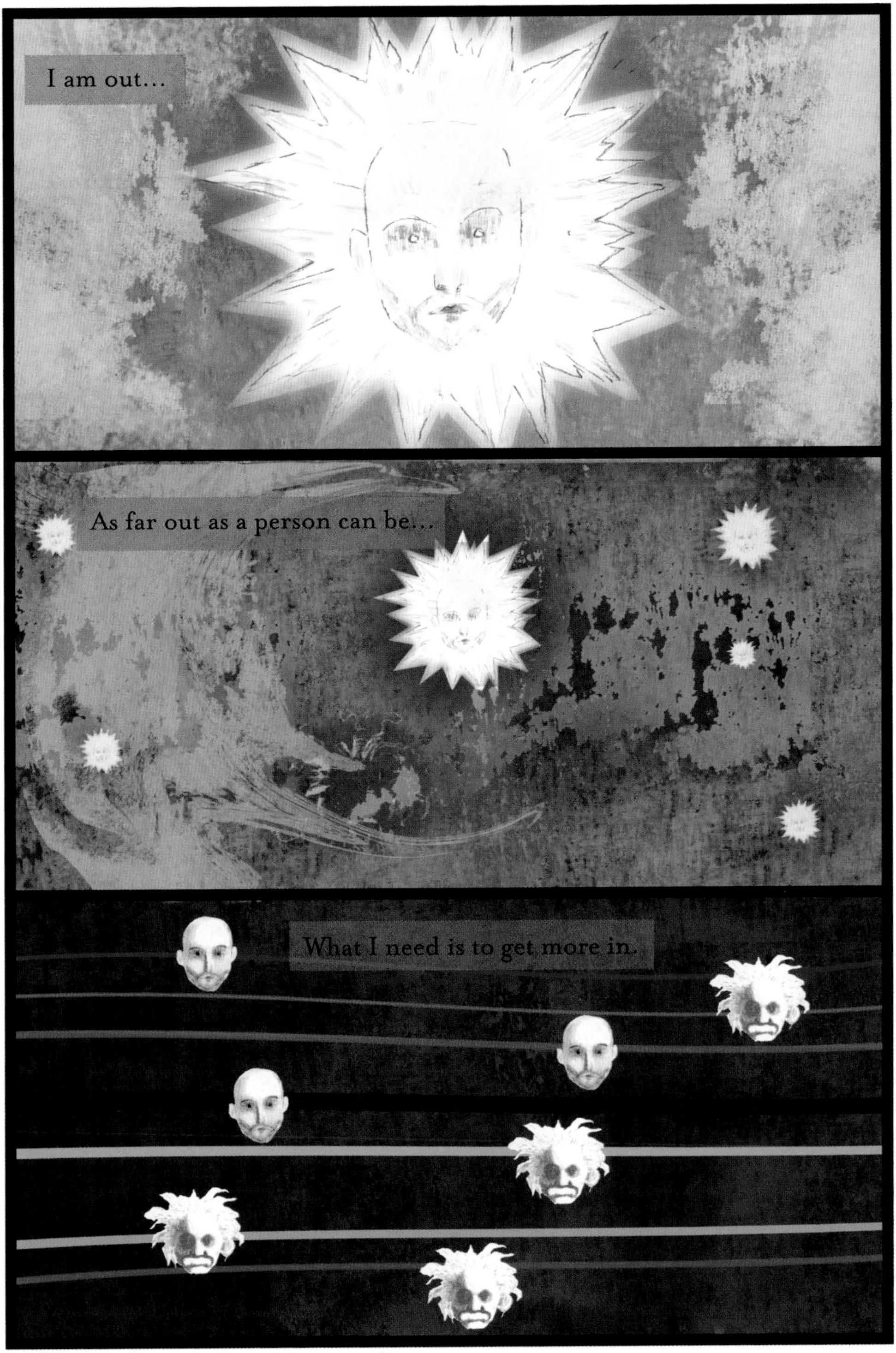
I am out...
As far out as a person can be...
What I need is to get more in.

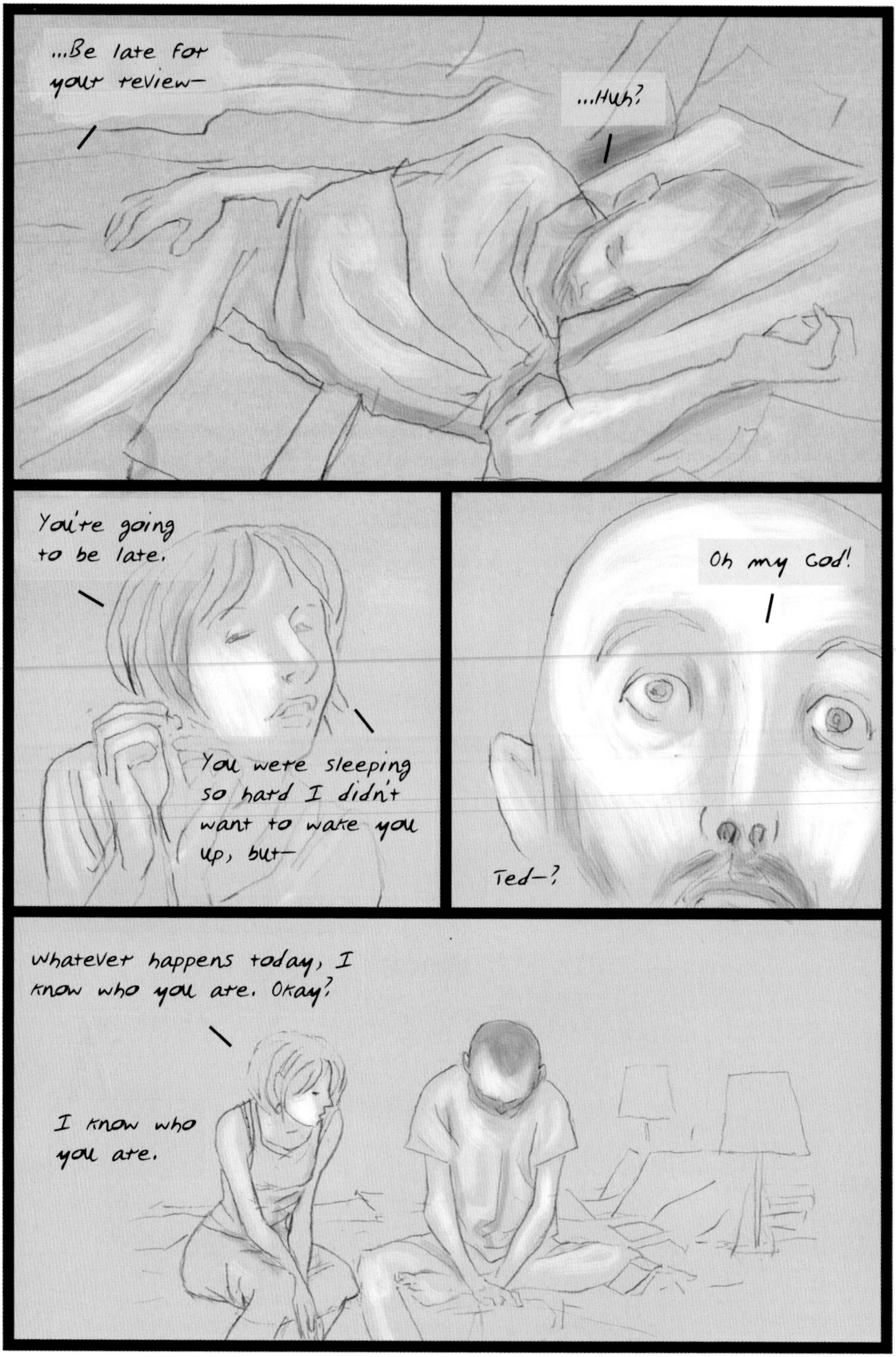
...Be late for your review—
...Huh?
You're going to be late.
You were sleeping so hard I didn't want to wake you up, but—
Oh my God!
Ted—?
Whatever happens today, I know who you are. Okay?
I know who you are.

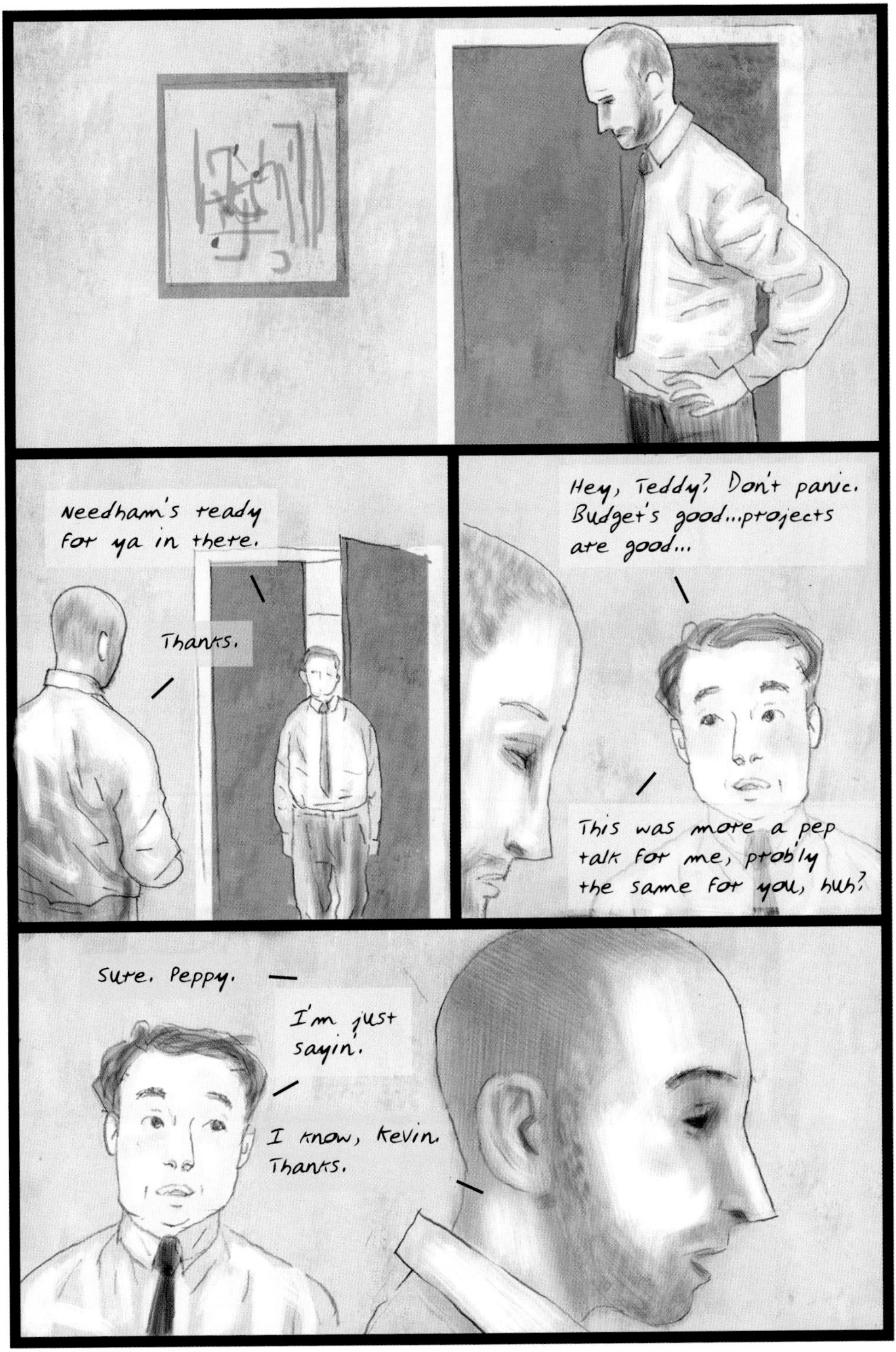
Needham's ready for ya in there.
Thanks.
Hey, Teddy? Don't panic. Budget's good...projects are good...
This was more a pep talk for me, prob'ly the same for you, huh?
Sure. Peppy.
I'm just sayin'.
I know, Kevin. Thanks.

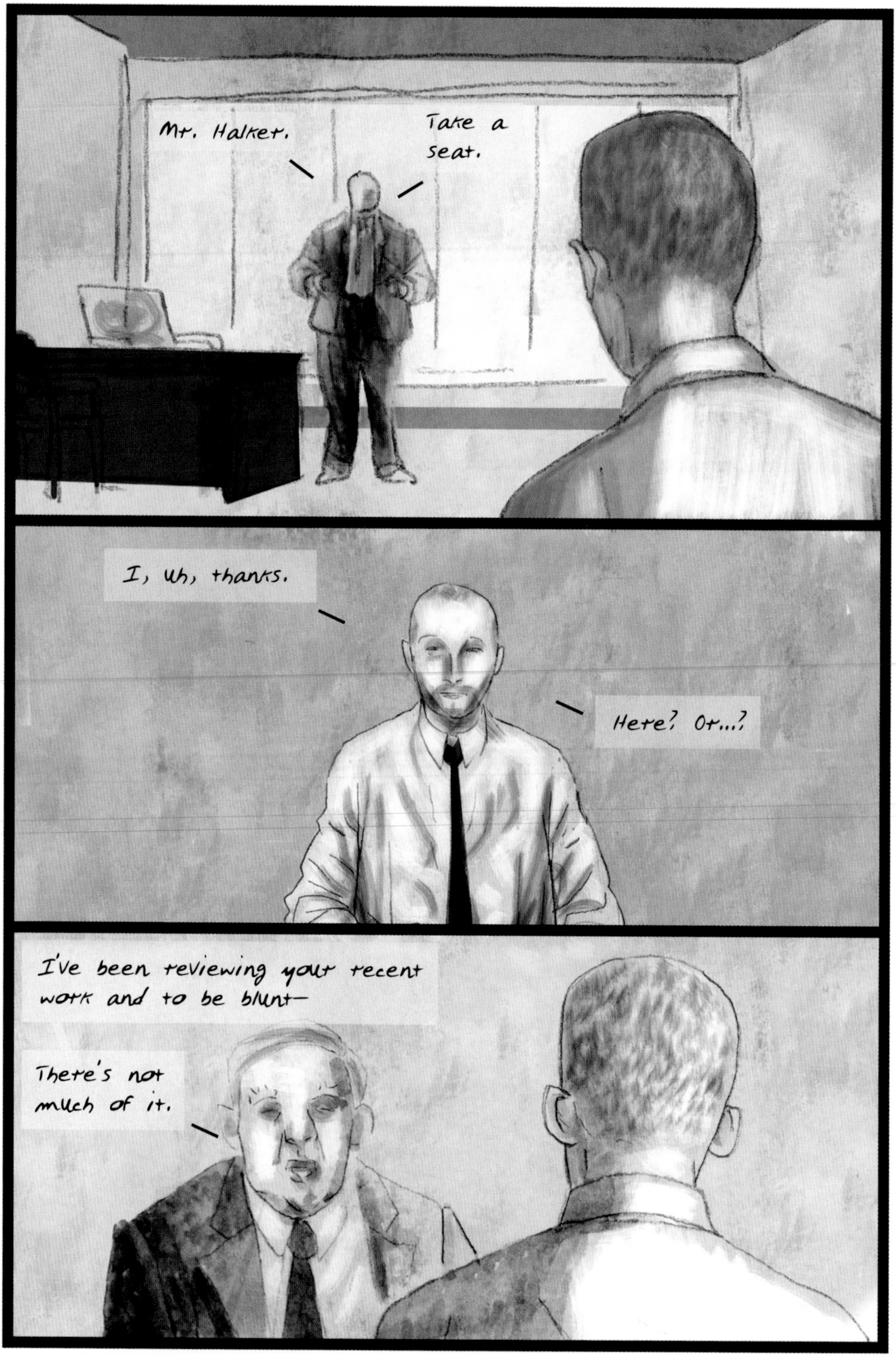
Mr. Halker.
Take a seat.
I, uh, thanks.
Here? Or...?
I've been reviewing your recent work and to be blunt—
There's not much of it.

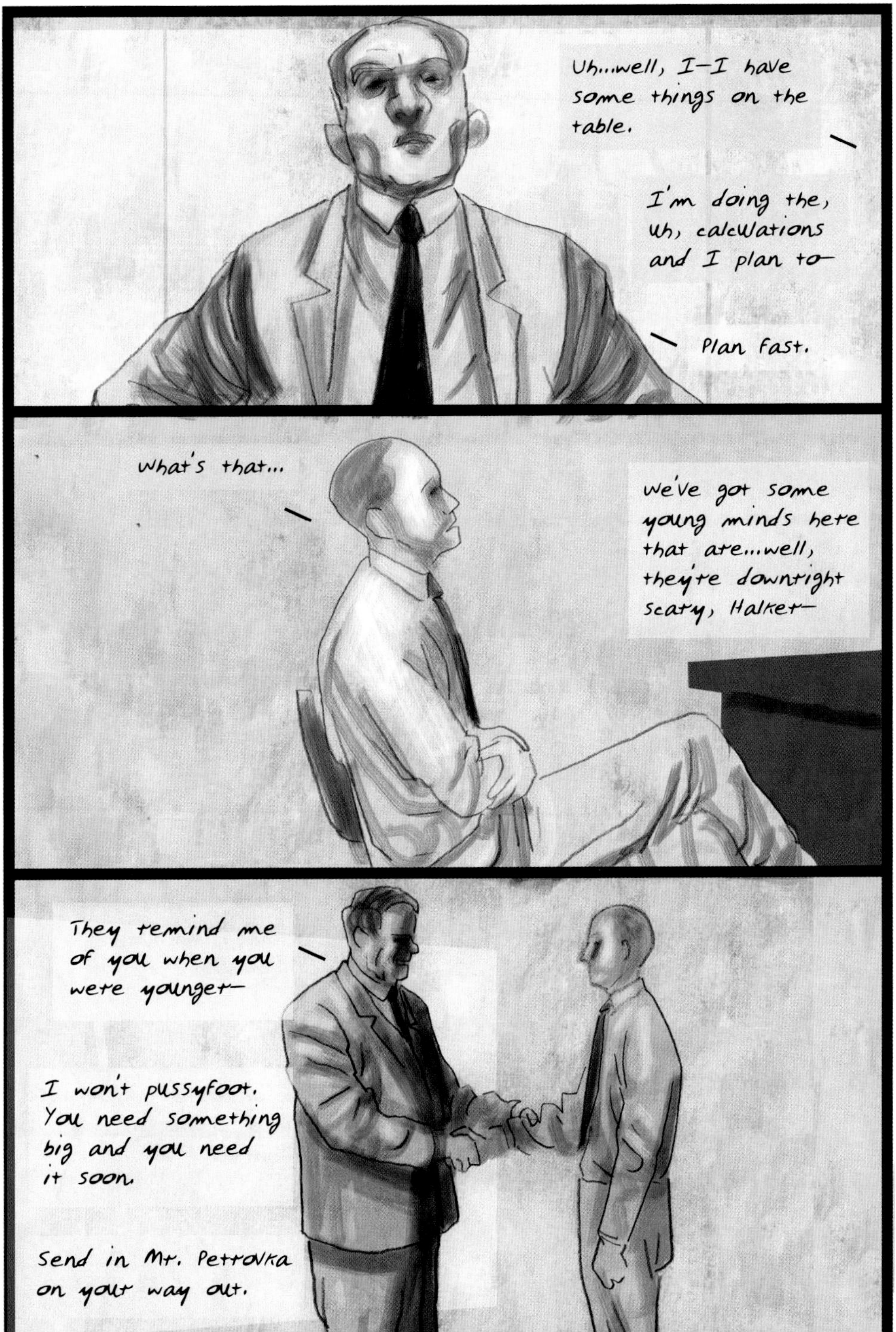
Uh...well, I—I have some things on the table.
I'm doing the, uh, calculations and I plan to—
Plan fast.
what's that...
we've got some young minds here that are...well, they're downright scary, Halker—
They remind me of you when you were younger—
I won't pussyfoot. You need something big and you need it soon.
Send in Mr. Petrovka on your way out.

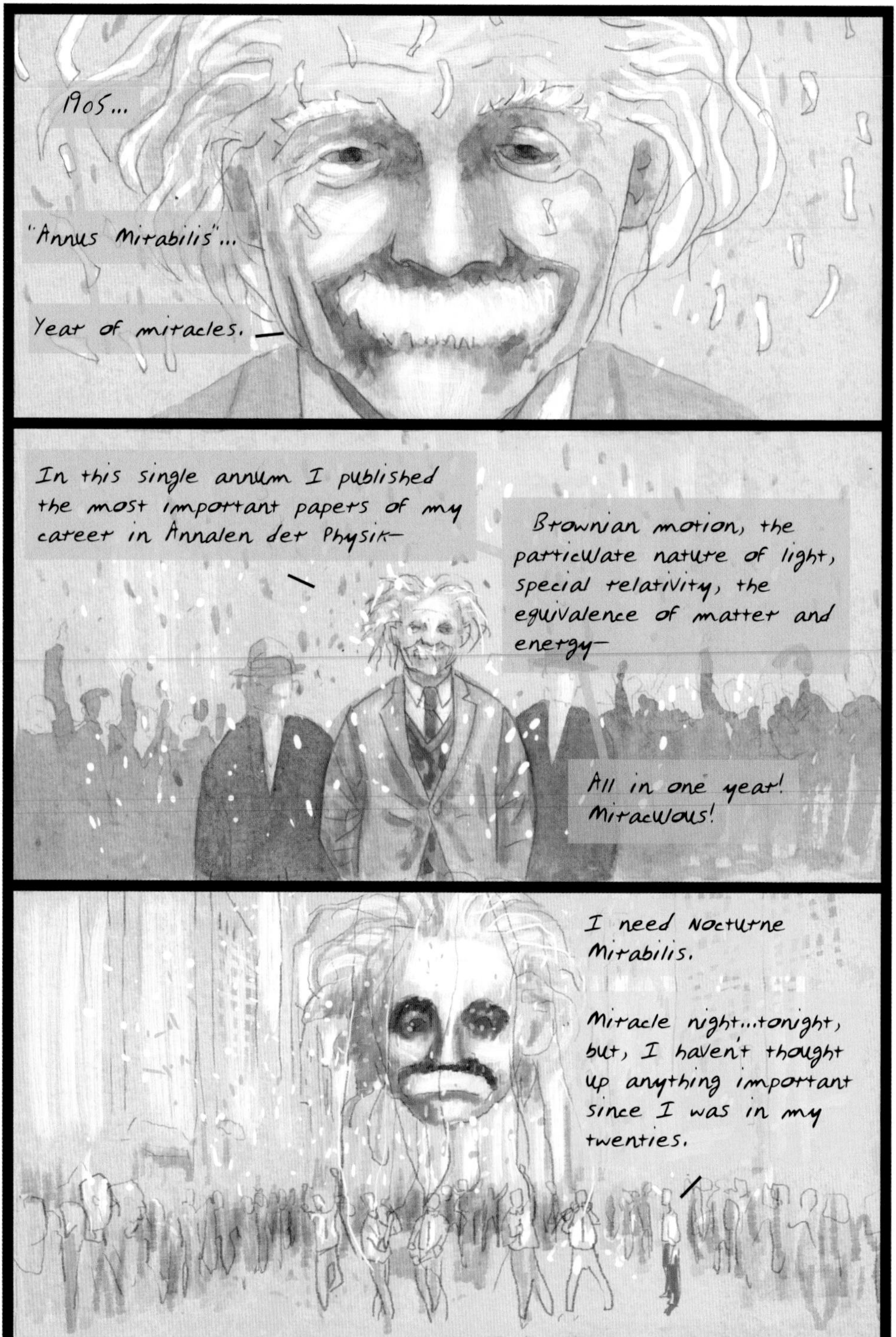
1905...
"Annus Mirabilis"...
Year of miracles.
In this single annum I published the most important papers of my career in Annalen der Physik—
Brownian motion, the particulate nature of light, special relativity, the equivalence of matter and energy—
All in one year! Miraculous!
I need Nocturne Mirabilis.
Miracle night...tonight, but, I haven't thought up anything important since I was in my twenties.

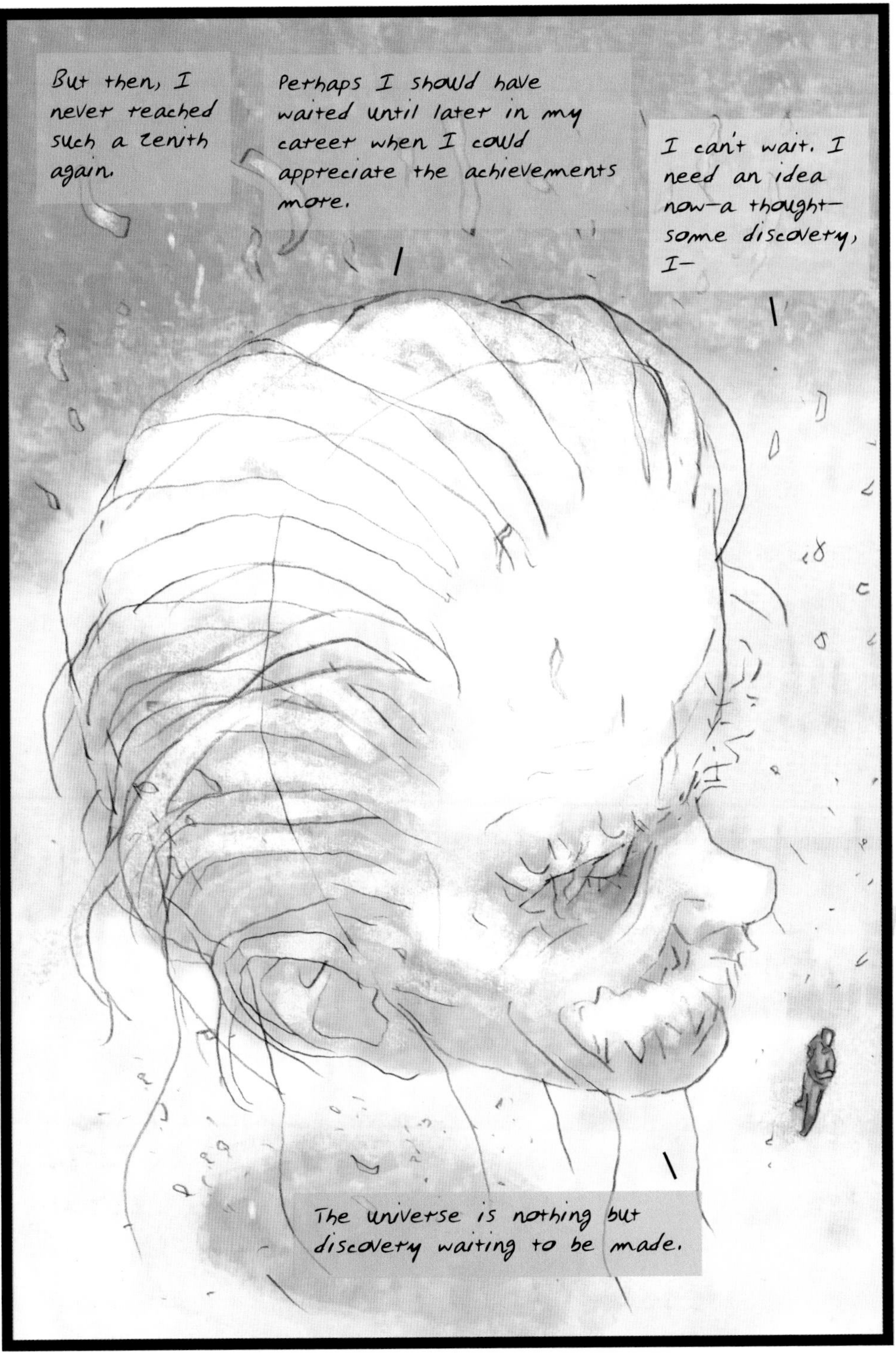
But then, I never reached such a zenith again.
Perhaps I should have waited until later in my career when I could appreciate the achievements more.
I can't wait. I need an idea now—a thought—some discovery, I—
The universe is nothing but discovery waiting to be made.

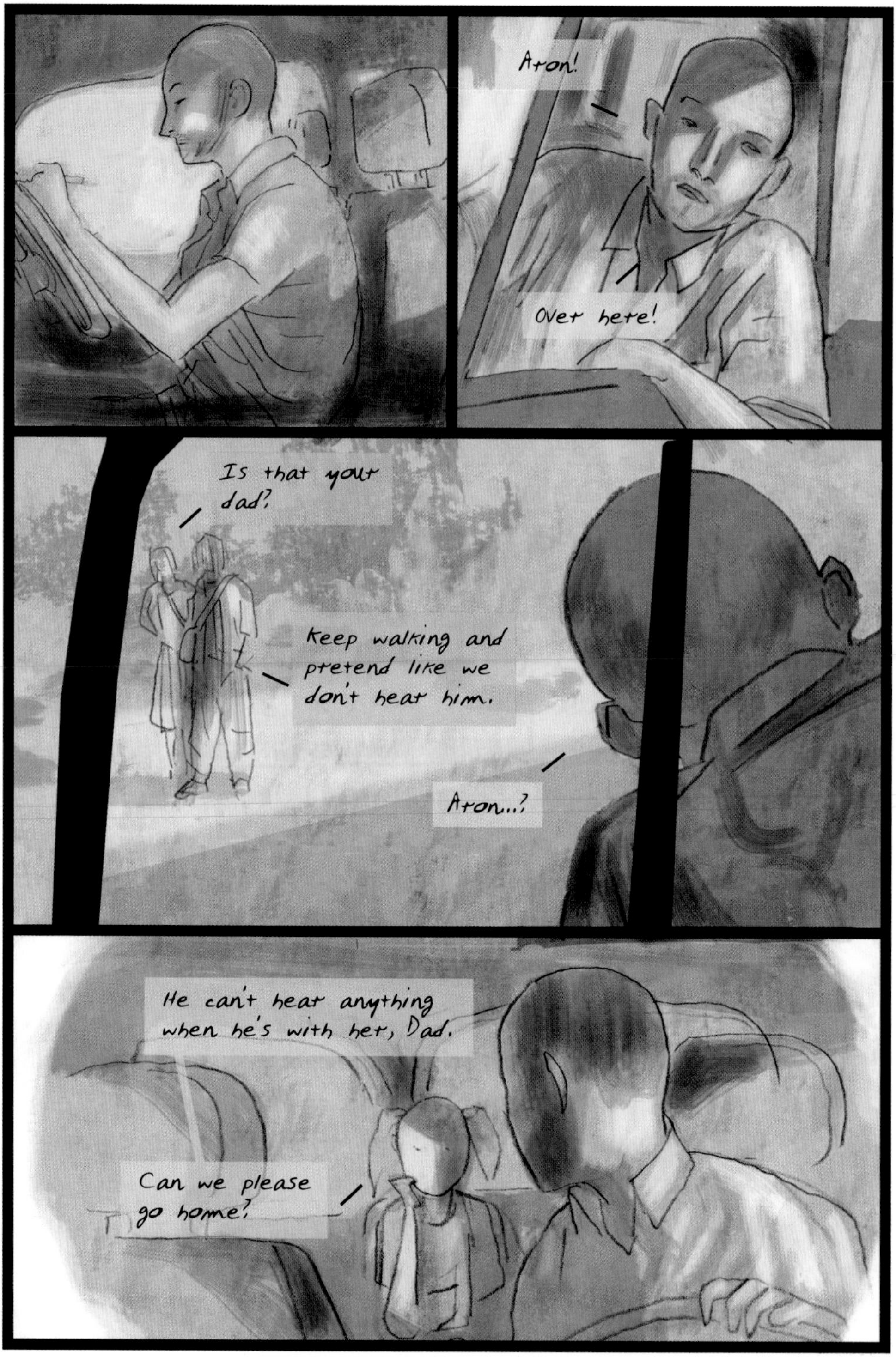
Aron!
Over here!
Is that your dad?
Keep walking and pretend like we don't hear him.
Aron...?
He can't hear anything when he's with her, Dad.
Can we please go home?

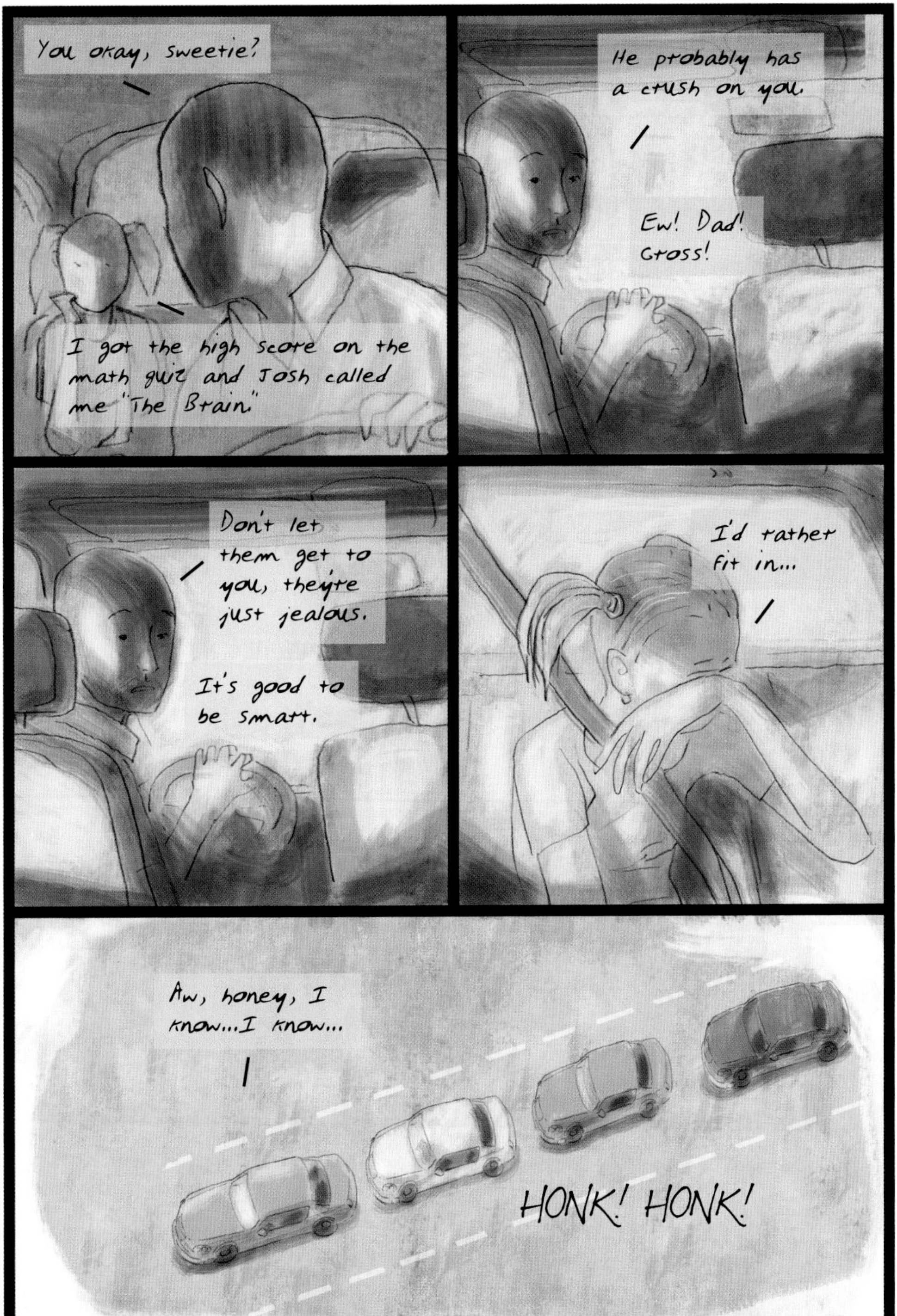
You okay, sweetie?
I got the high score on the math quiz and Josh called me "The Brain."
He probably has a crush on you.
Ew! Dad! Gross!
Don't let them get to you, they're just jealous.
It's good to be smart.
I'd rather fit in...
Aw, honey, I know...I know...
HONK! HONK!

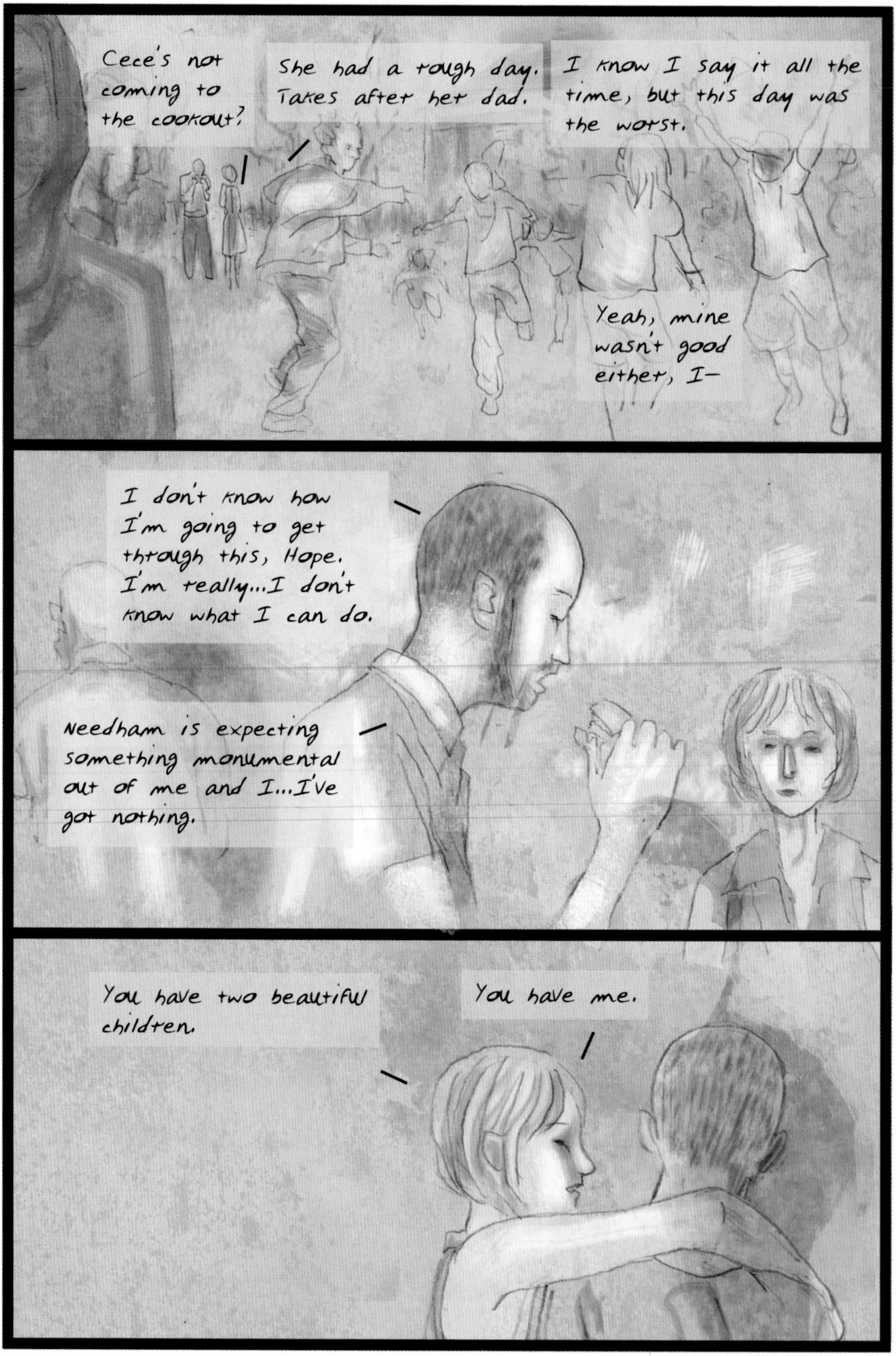

Cece's not coming to the cookout?
She had a tough day. Takes after her dad.
I know I say it all the time, but this day was the worst.
Yeah, mine wasn't good either, I—
I don't know how I'm going to get through this, Hope. I'm really...I don't know what I can do.
Needham is expecting something monumental out of me and I...I've got nothing.
You have two beautiful children.
You have me.

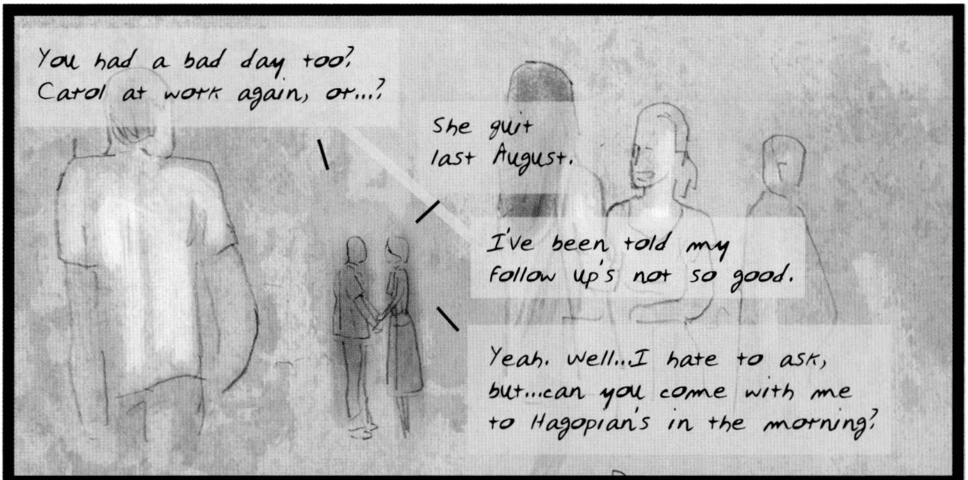
You had a bad day too? Carol at work again, or...?
She quit last August.
I've been told my follow up's not so good.
Yeah. Well...I hate to ask, but...can you come with me to Hagopian's in the morning?

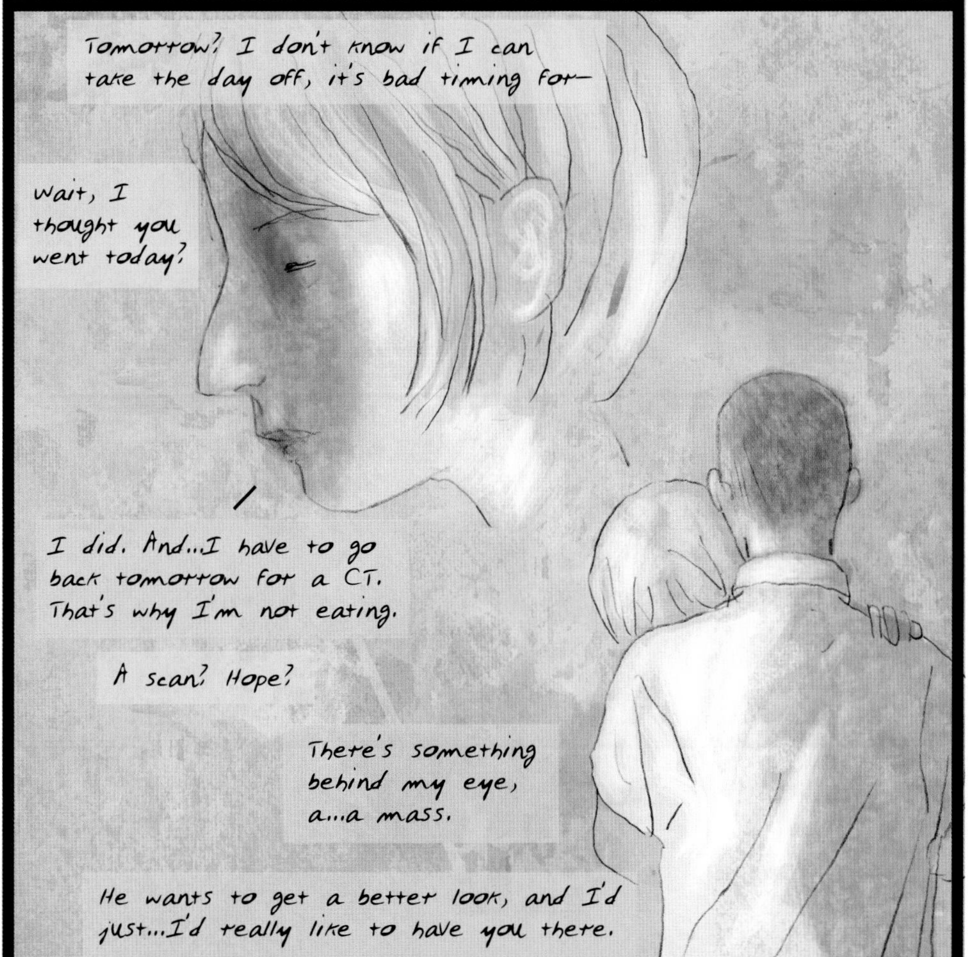
Tomorrow? I don't know if I can take the day off, it's bad timing for—
wait, I thought you went today?
I did. And...I have to go back tomorrow for a CT. That's why I'm not eating.
A scan? Hope?
There's something behind my eye, a...a mass.
He wants to get a better look, and I'd just...I'd really like to have you there.

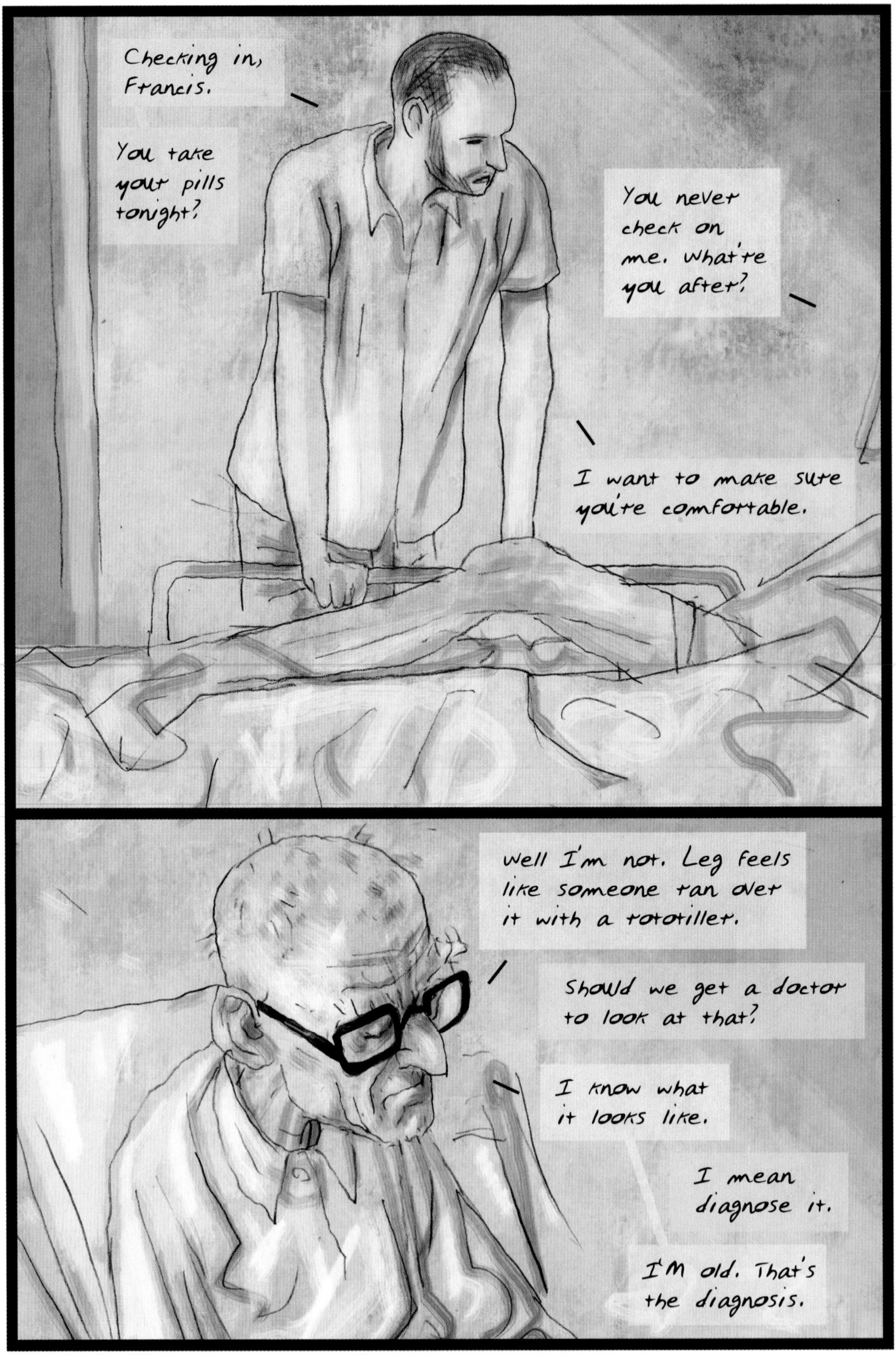
Checking in, Francis.
You take your pills tonight?
You never check on me. What're you after?
I want to make sure you're comfortable.
Well I'm not. Leg feels like someone ran over it with a rototiller.
Should we get a doctor to look at that?
I know what it looks like.
I mean diagnose it.
I'M old. That's the diagnosis.

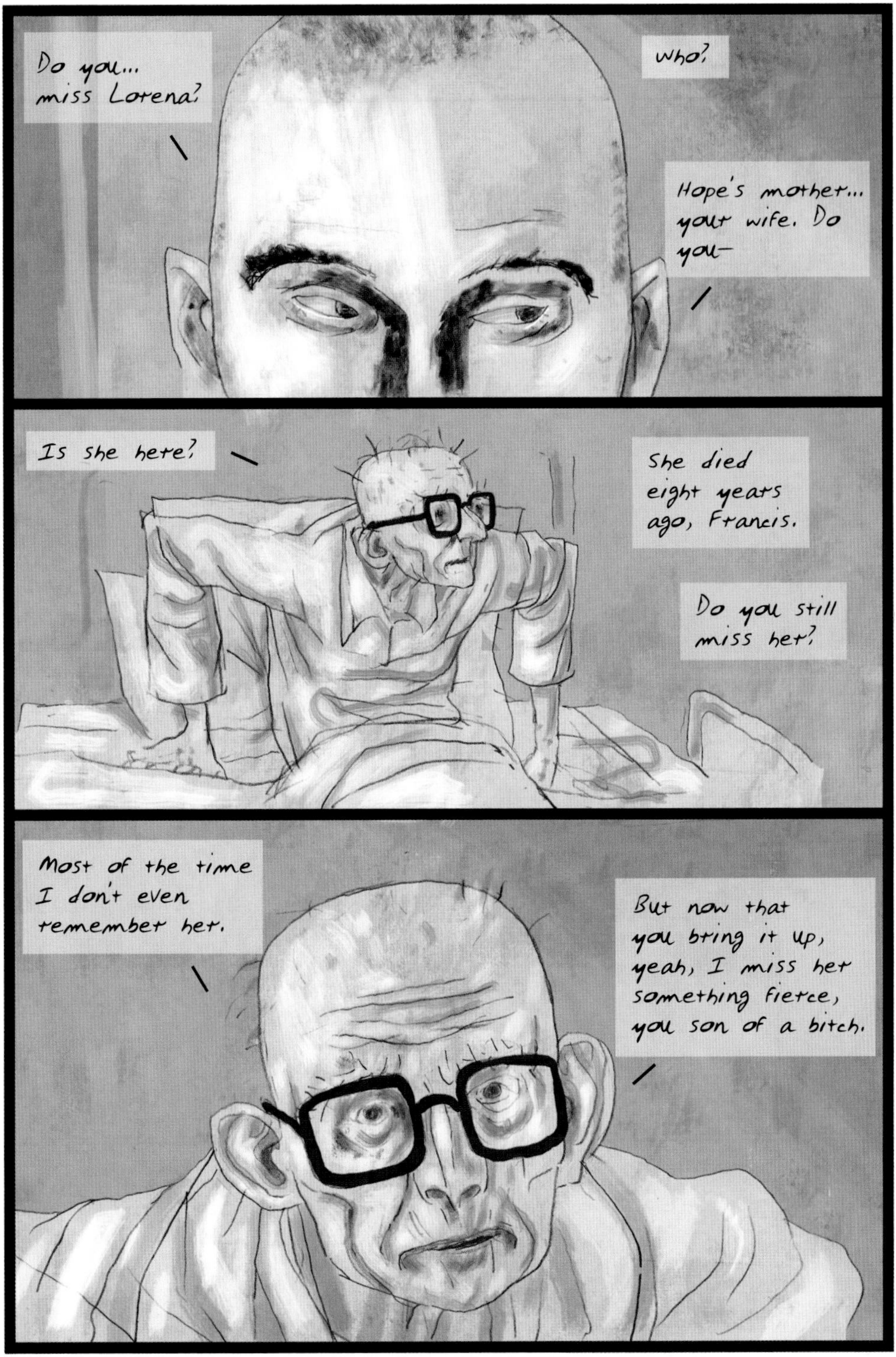
Do you...
miss Lorena?
Who?
Hope's mother...
your wife. Do
you—
Is she here?
She died
eight years
ago, Francis.
Do you still
miss her?
Most of the time
I don't even
remember her.
But now that
you bring it up,
yeah, I miss her
something fierce,
you son of a bitch.

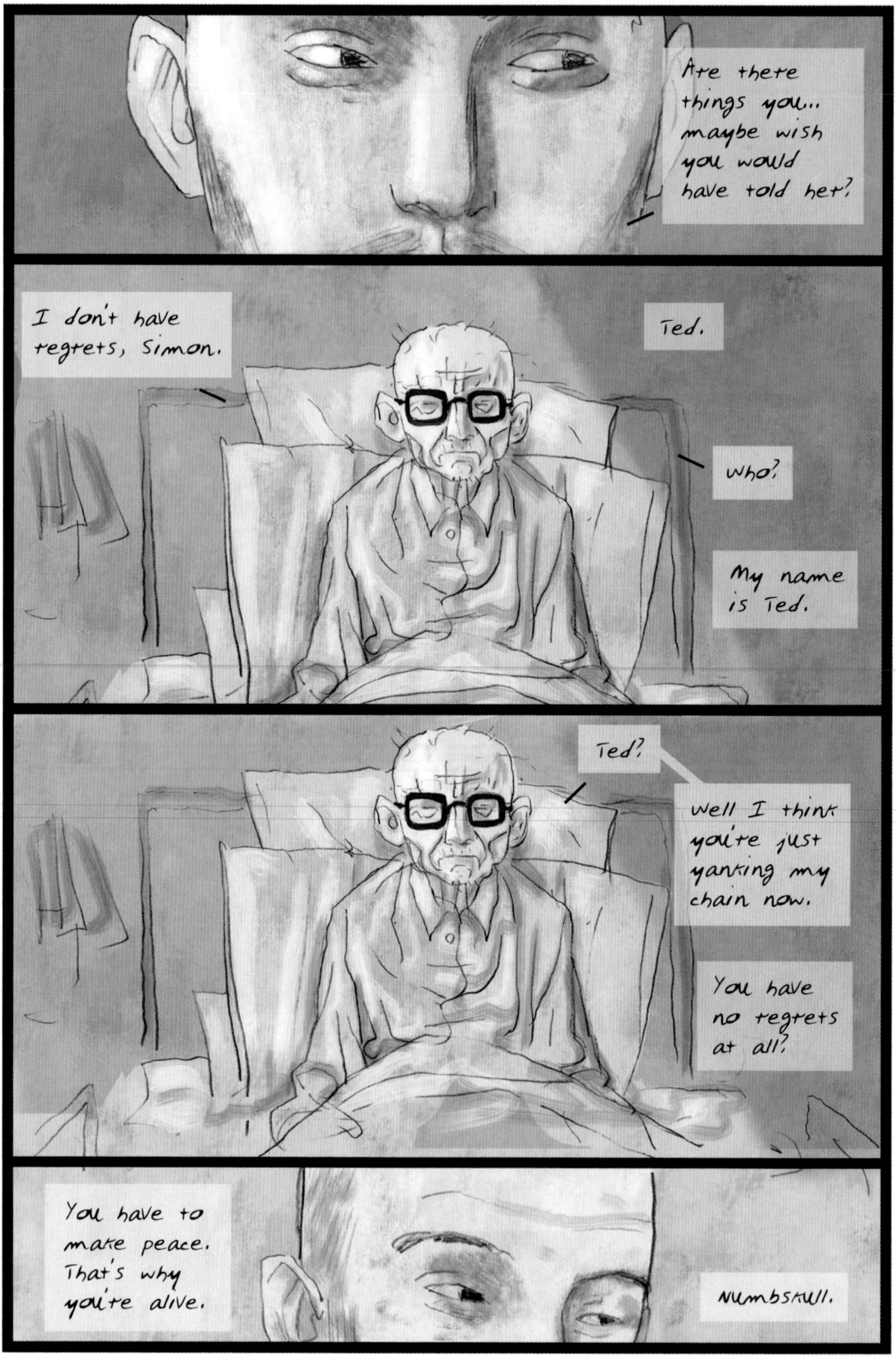
Are there things you... maybe wish you would have told her?
I don't have regrets, Simon.
Ted.
Who?
My name is Ted.
Ted?
Well I think you're just yanking my chain now.
You have no regrets at all?
You have to make peace. That's why you're alive.
Numbskull.

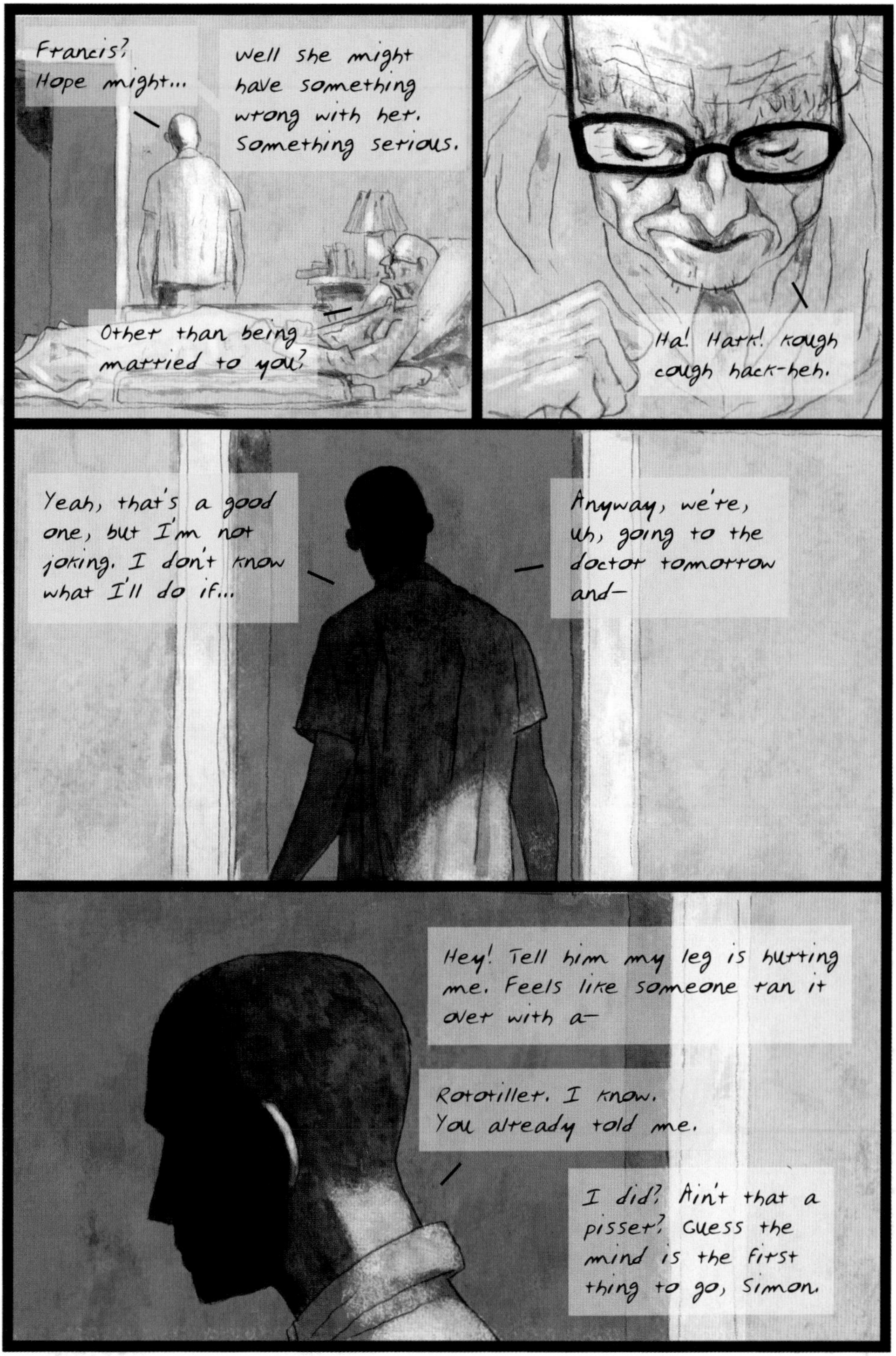
Francis? Hope might...
Well she might have something wrong with her. Something serious.
Other than being married to you?
Ha! Hark! kough cough hack-heh.
Yeah, that's a good one, but I'm not joking. I don't know what I'll do if...
Anyway, we're, uh, going to the doctor tomorrow and—
Hey! Tell him my leg is hurting me. Feels like someone ran it over with a—
Rototiller. I know. You already told me.
I did? Ain't that a pisser? Guess the mind is the first thing to go, Simon.

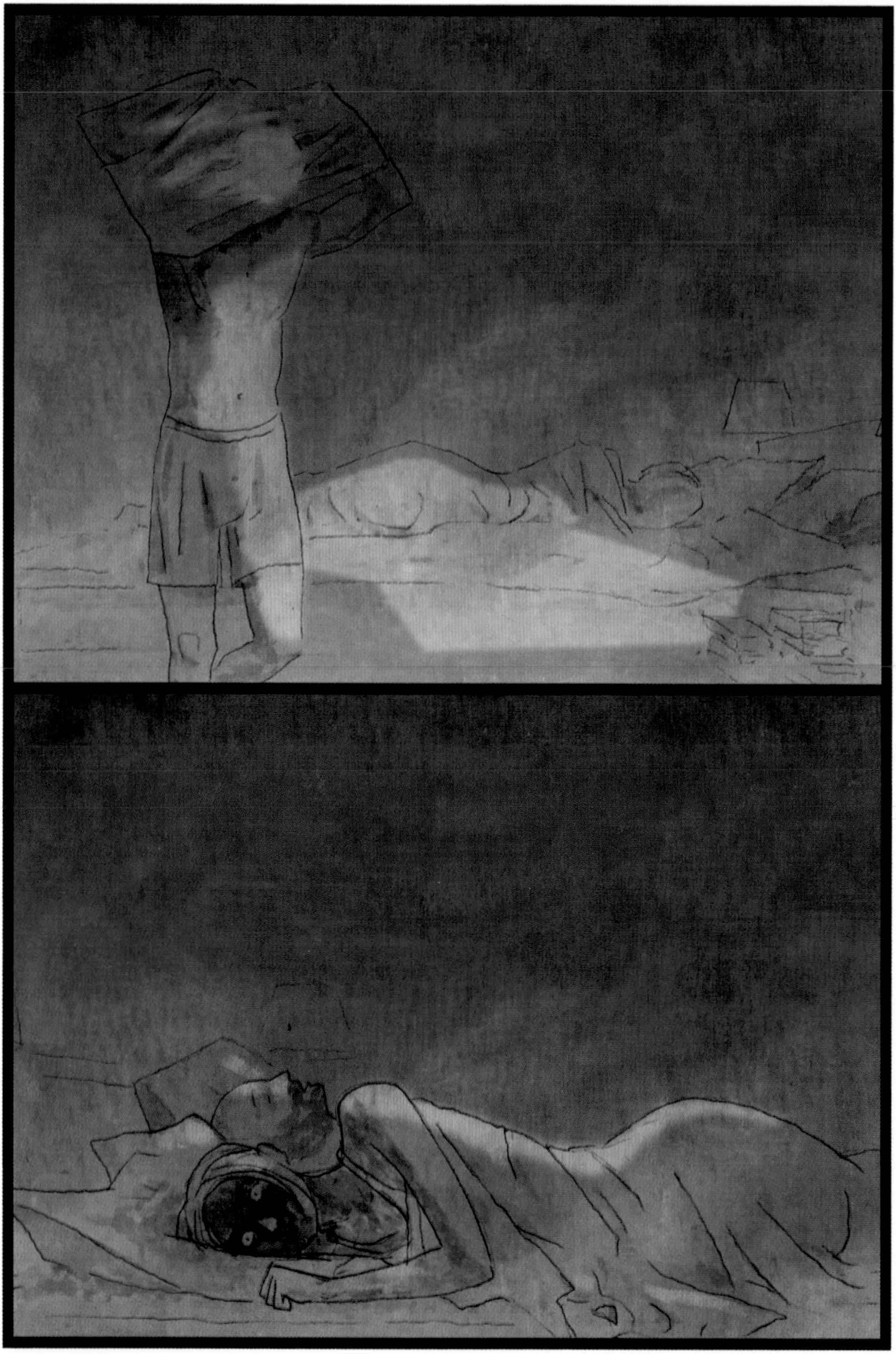

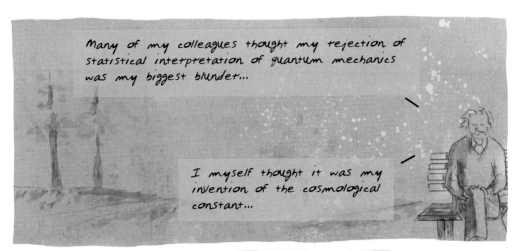

Many of my colleagues thought my rejection of statistical interpretation of quantum mechanics was my biggest blunder...

I myself thought it was my invention of the cosmological constant...

But in actuality, I would say my greatest intellectual shortfalls were in my dealings with the beautiful ladies who kept my company.

I had a daughter I never even saw, you know.

She died.

Are you...talking to me...?

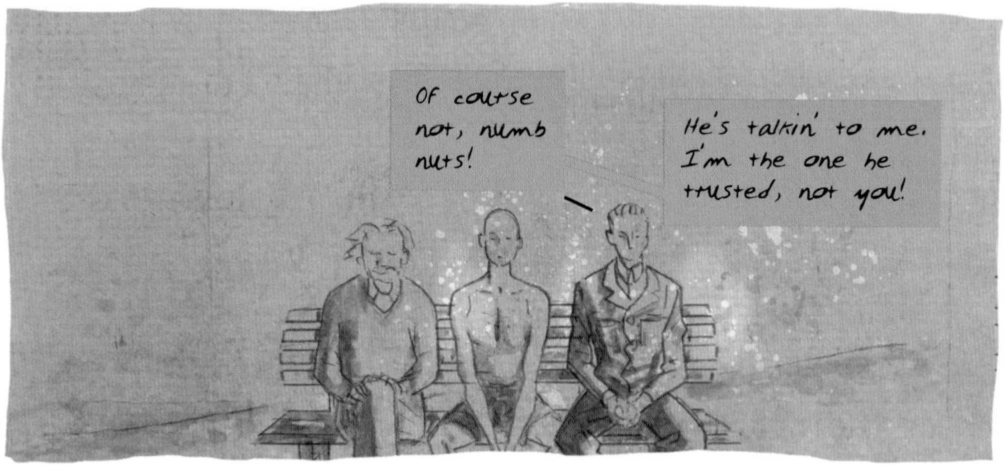
Of course not, numb nuts!
He's talkin' to me. I'm the one he trusted, not you!

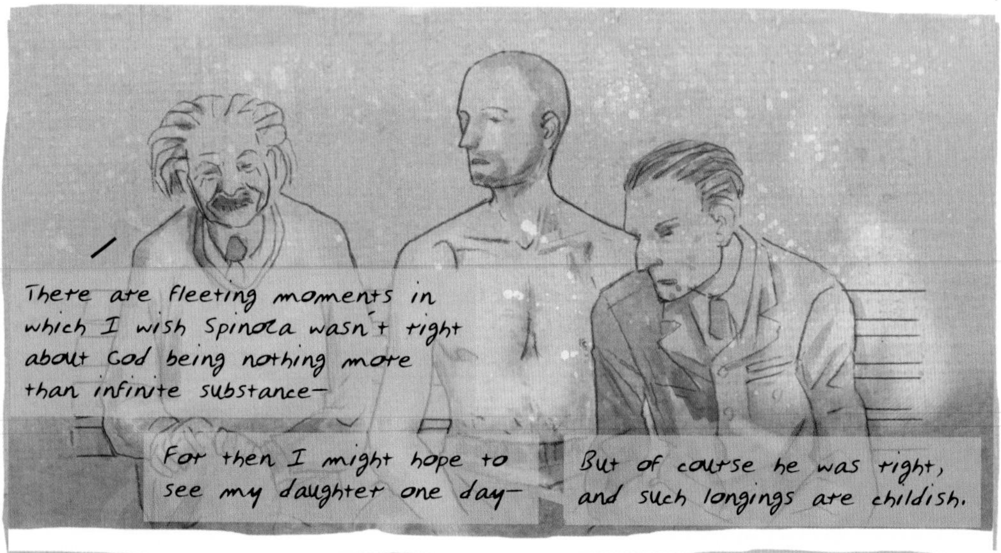
There are fleeting moments in which I wish Spinoza wasn't right about God being nothing more than infinite substance—
For then I might hope to see my daughter one day—
But of course he was right, and such longings are childish.

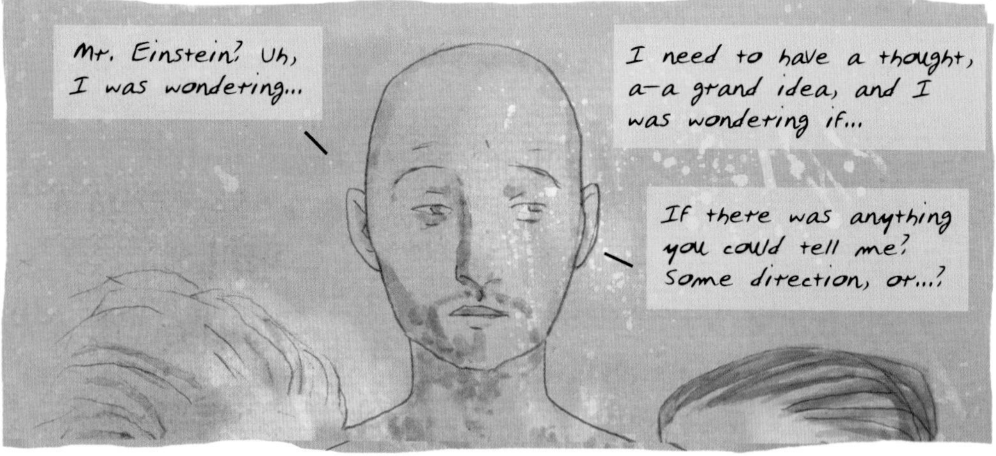
Mr. Einstein? Uh, I was wondering...
I need to have a thought, a-a grand idea, and I was wondering if...
If there was anything you could tell me? Some direction, or...?

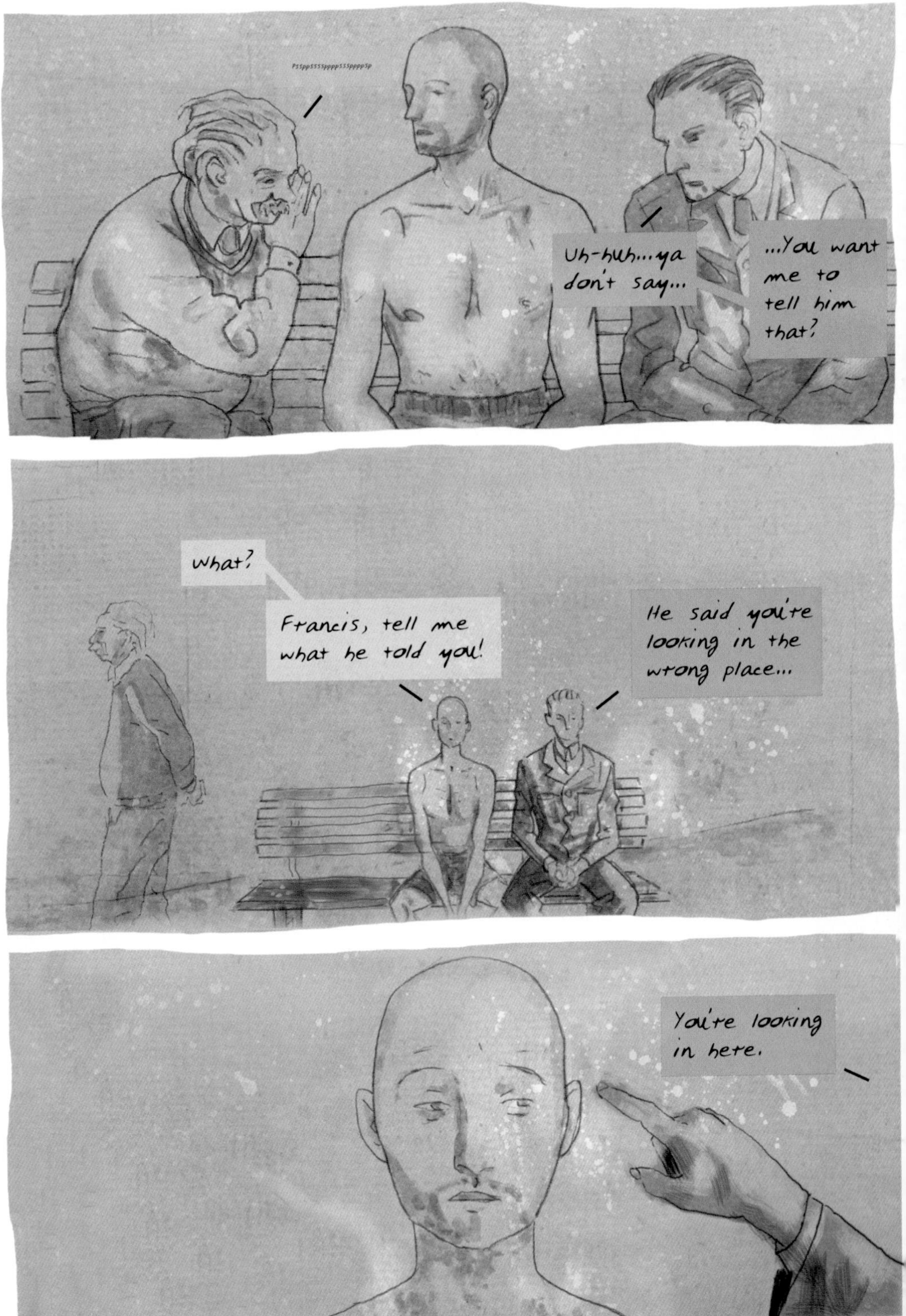
Psspppssssppppsssppppsp
Uh-huh...ya don't say...
...You want me to tell him that?
What?
Francis, tell me what he told you!
He said you're looking in the wrong place...
You're looking in here.

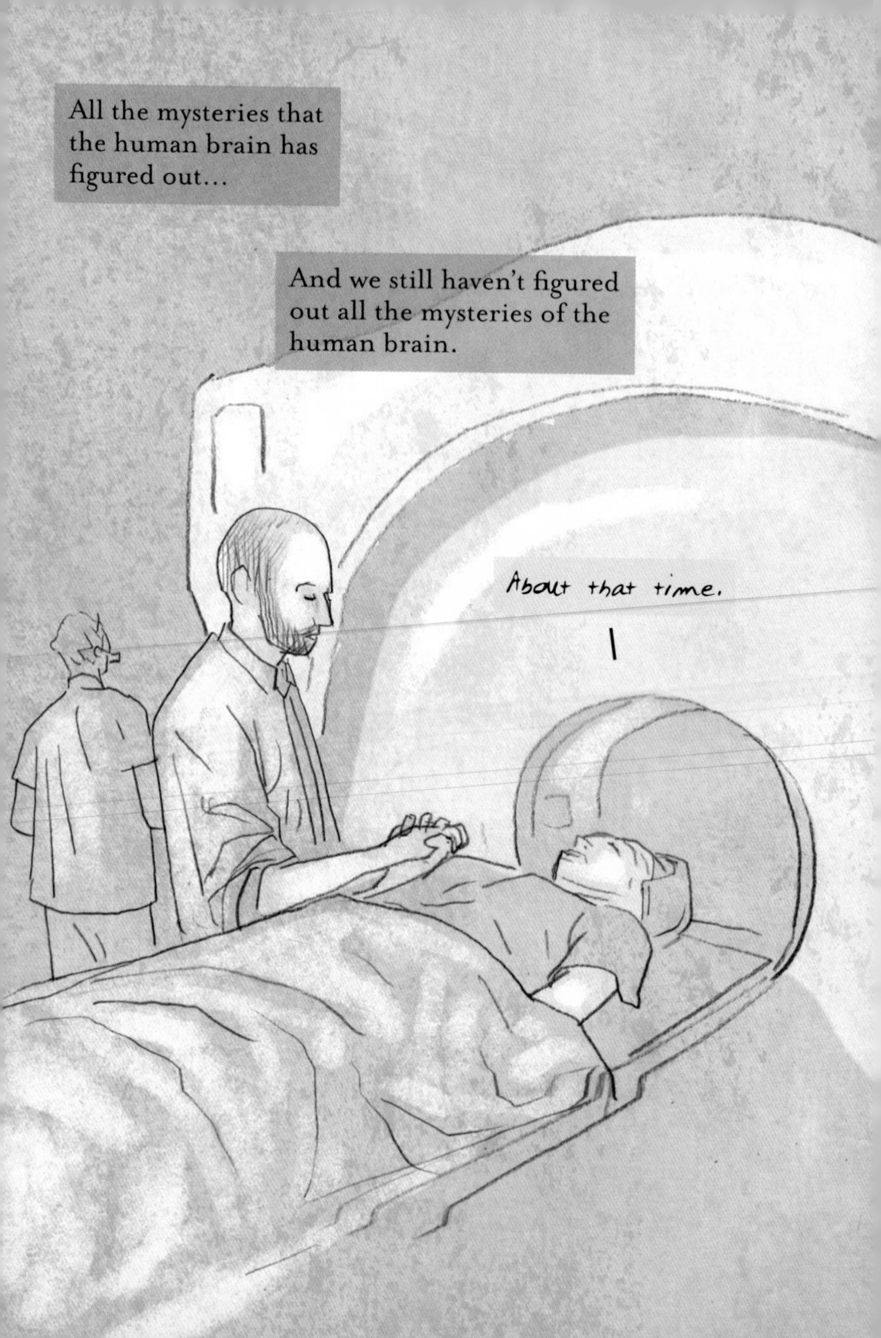
All the mysteries that the human brain has figured out...
And we still haven't figured out all the mysteries of the human brain.
About that time.

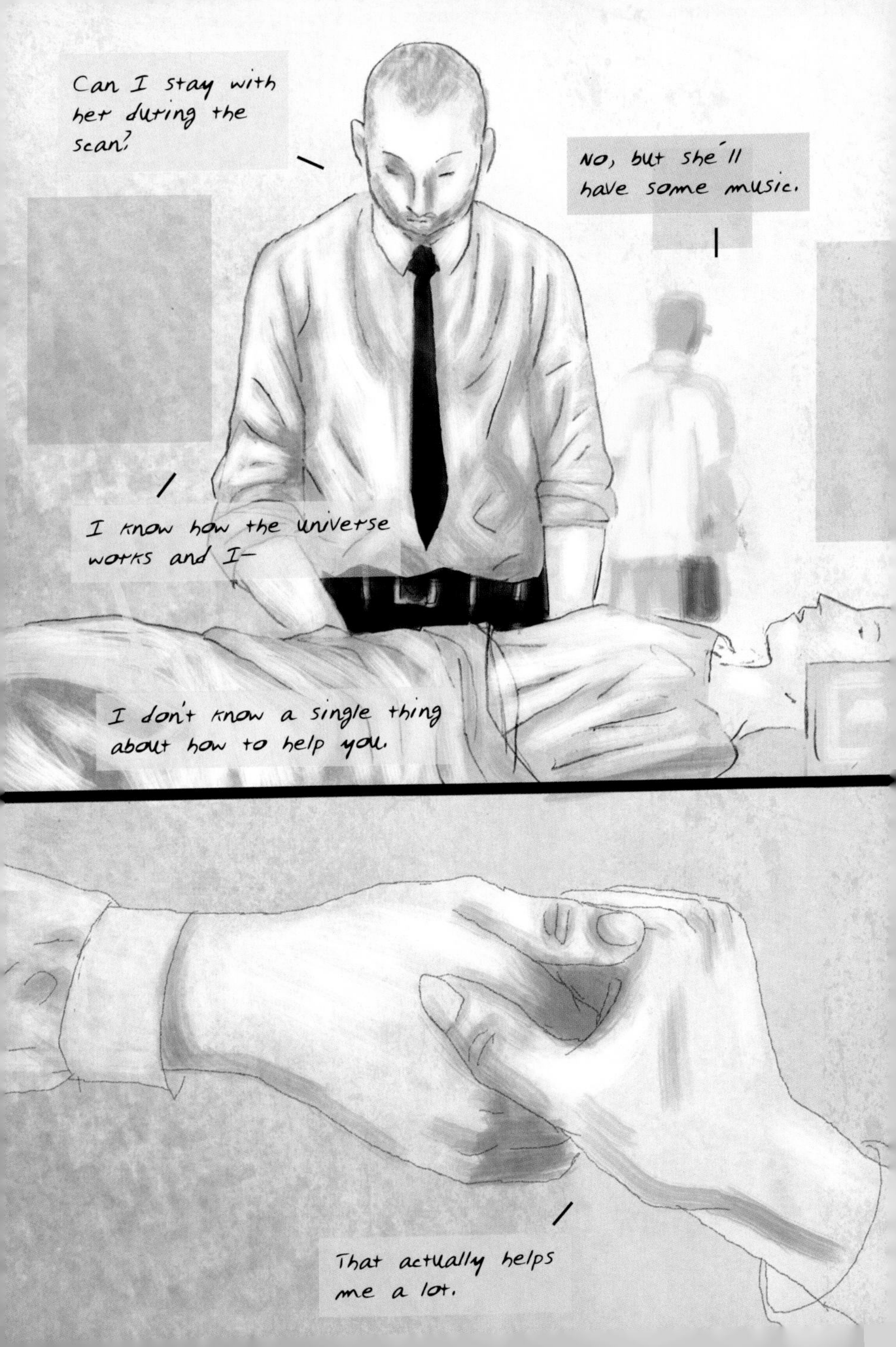
Can I stay with her during the scan?
No, but she'll have some music.
I know how the universe works and I—
I don't know a single thing about how to help you.
That actually helps me a lot.

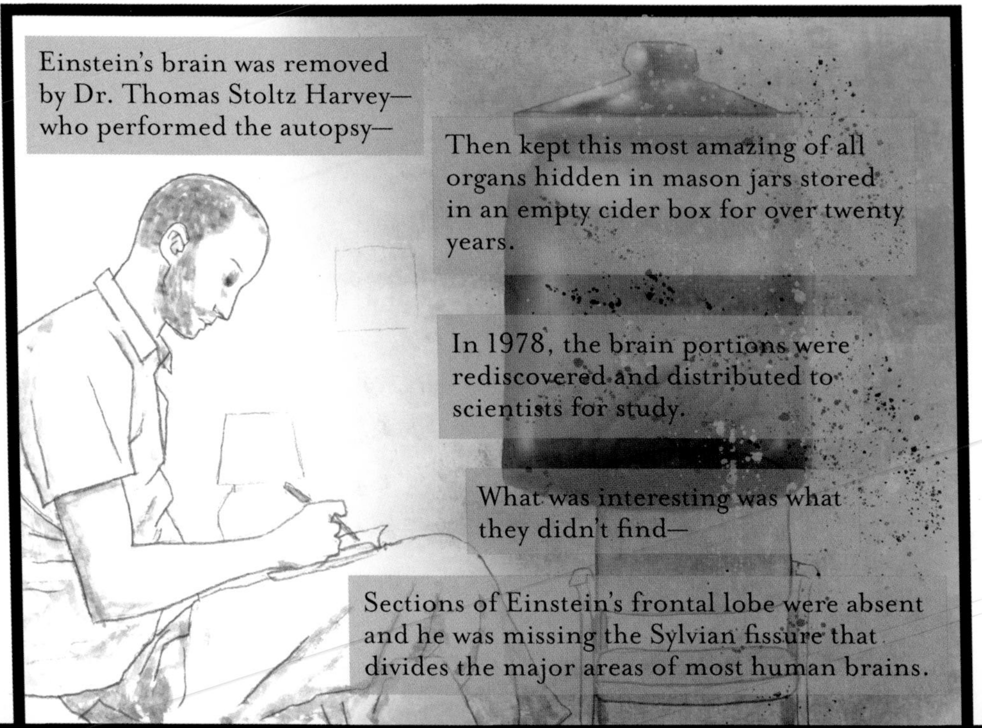
Einstein's brain was removed by Dr. Thomas Stoltz Harvey—who performed the autopsy—
Then kept this most amazing of all organs hidden in mason jars stored in an empty cider box for over twenty years.
In 1978, the brain portions were rediscovered and distributed to scientists for study.
What was interesting was what they didn't find—
Sections of Einstein's frontal lobe were absent and he was missing the Sylvian fissure that divides the major areas of most human brains.

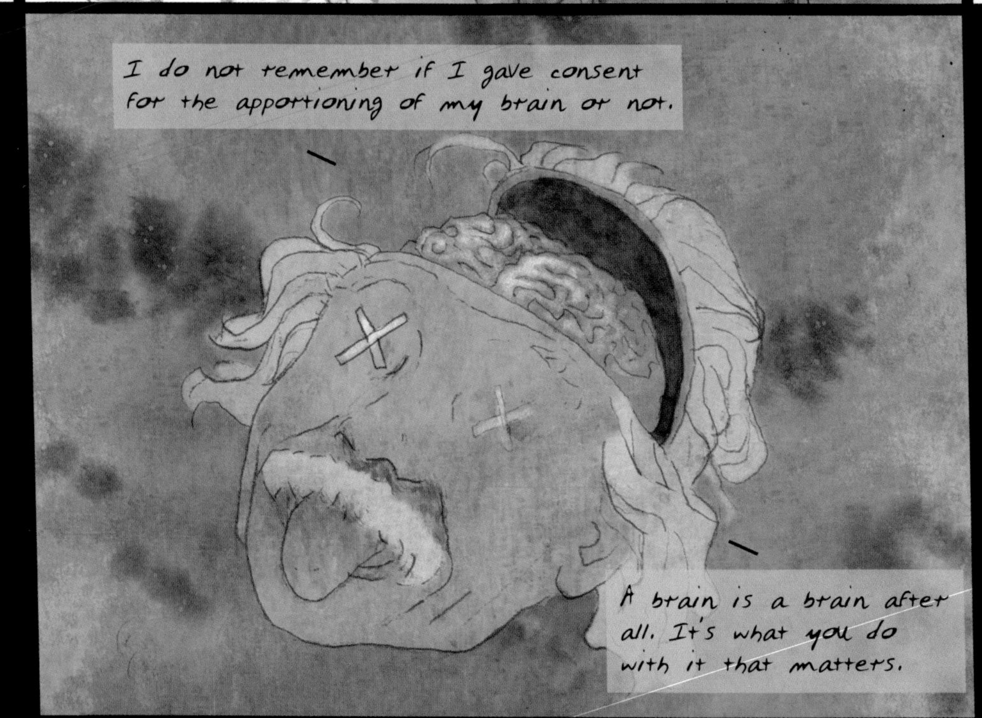
I do not remember if I gave consent for the apportioning of my brain or not.
A brain is a brain after all. It's what you do with it that matters.

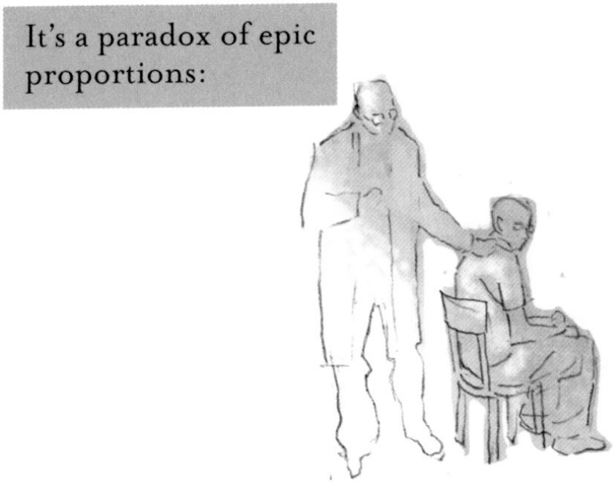
It's a paradox of epic proportions:

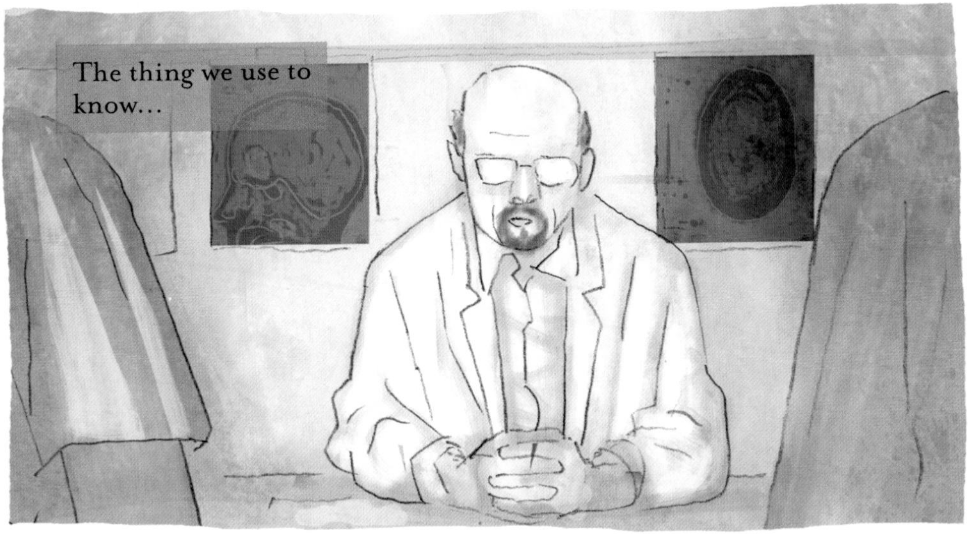
The thing we use to know...

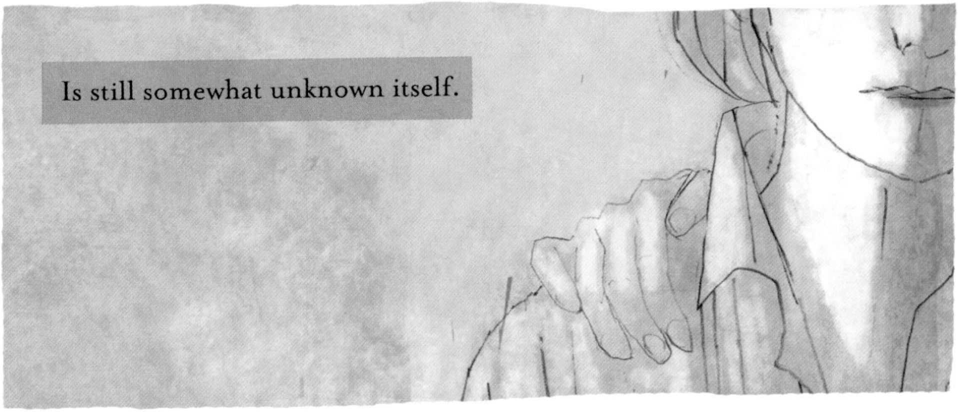
Is still somewhat unknown itself.

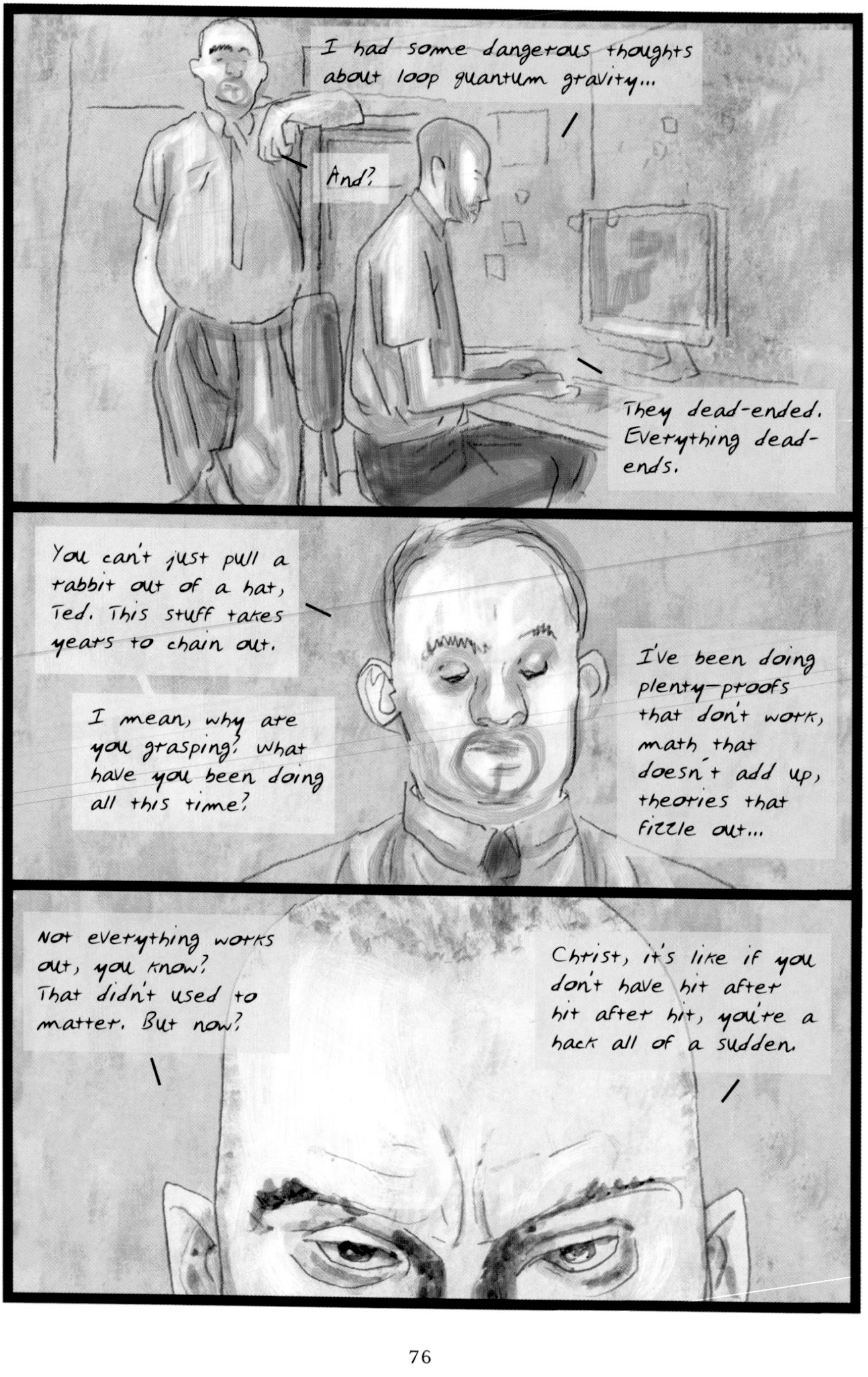
I had some dangerous thoughts about loop quantum gravity...
And?
They dead-ended. Everything dead-ends.
You can't just pull a rabbit out of a hat, Ted. This stuff takes years to chain out.
I mean, why are you grasping? What have you been doing all this time?
I've been doing plenty—proofs that don't work, math that doesn't add up, theories that fizzle out...
Not everything works out, you know? That didn't used to matter. But now?
Christ, it's like if you don't have hit after hit, you're a hack all of a sudden.

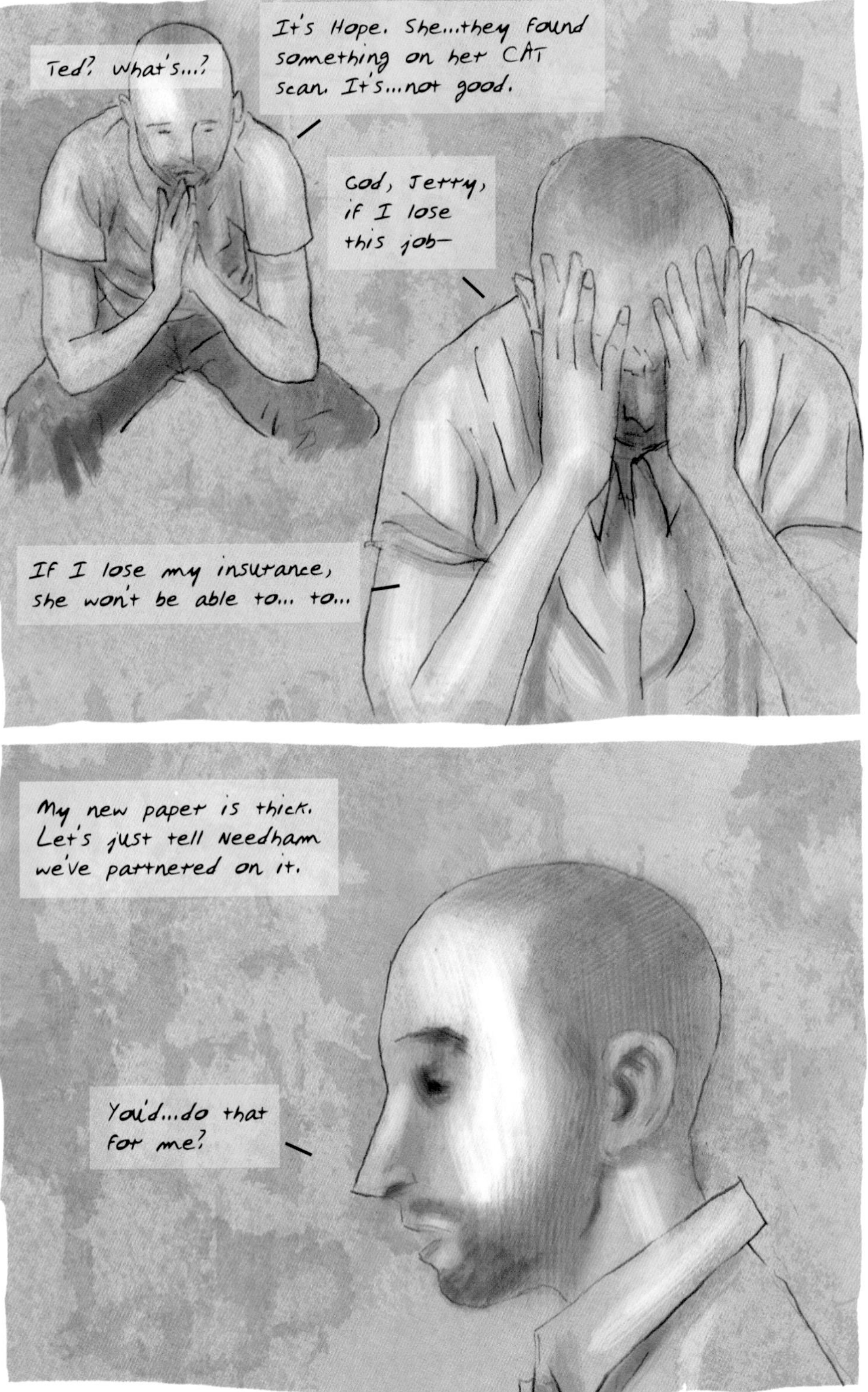

Ted? What's...?
It's Hope. She...they found something on her CAT scan. It's...not good.
God, Jerry, if I lose this job—
If I lose my insurance, she won't be able to... to...
My new paper is thick. Let's just tell Needham we've partnered on it.
You'd...do that for me?

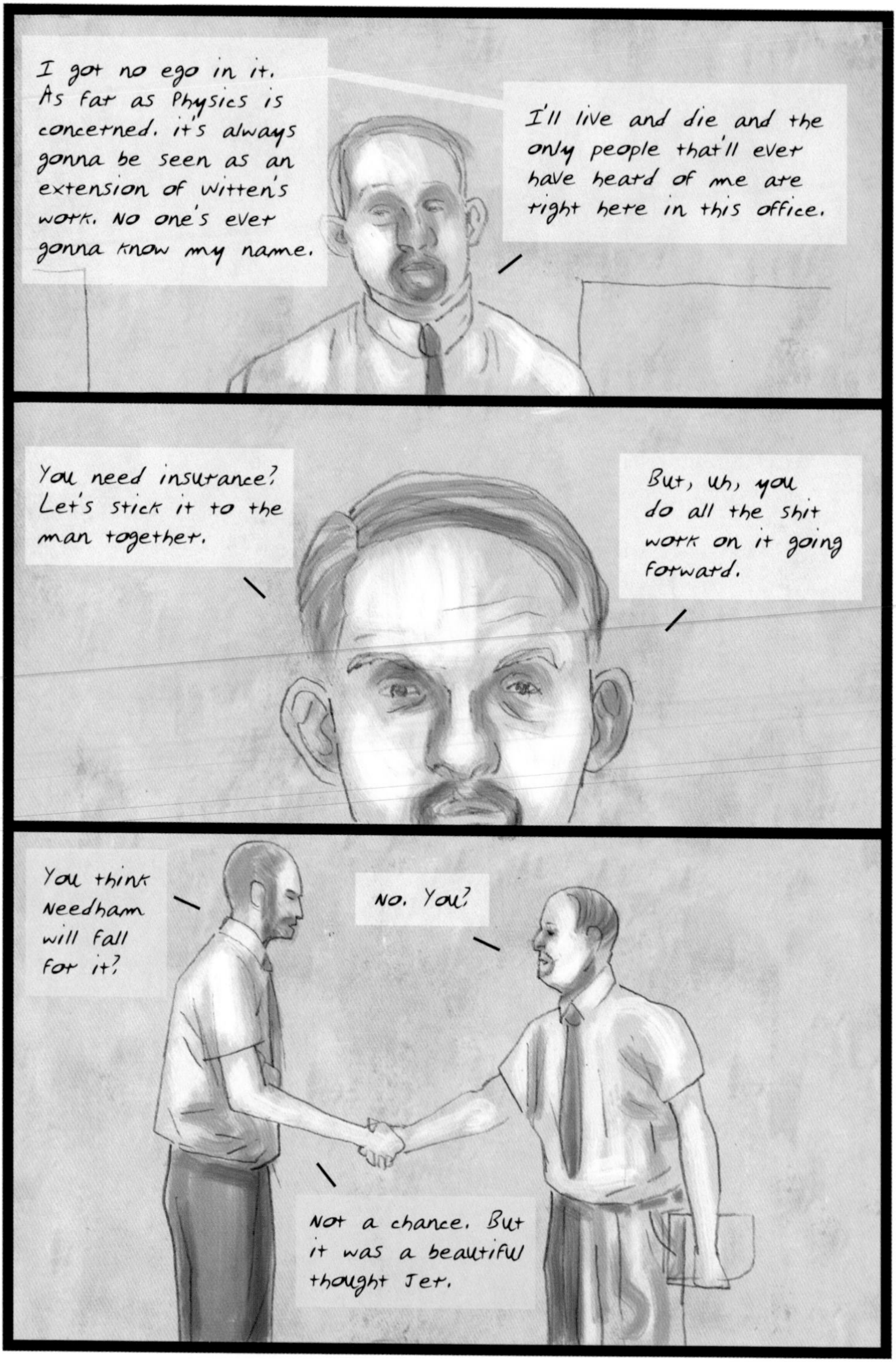
I got no ego in it. As far as Physics is concerned, it's always gonna be seen as an extension of Witten's work. No one's ever gonna know my name.
I'll live and die and the only people that'll ever have heard of me are right here in this office.
You need insurance? Let's stick it to the man together.
But, uh, you do all the shit work on it going forward.
You think Needham will fall for it?
No. You?
Not a chance. But it was a beautiful thought Jer.

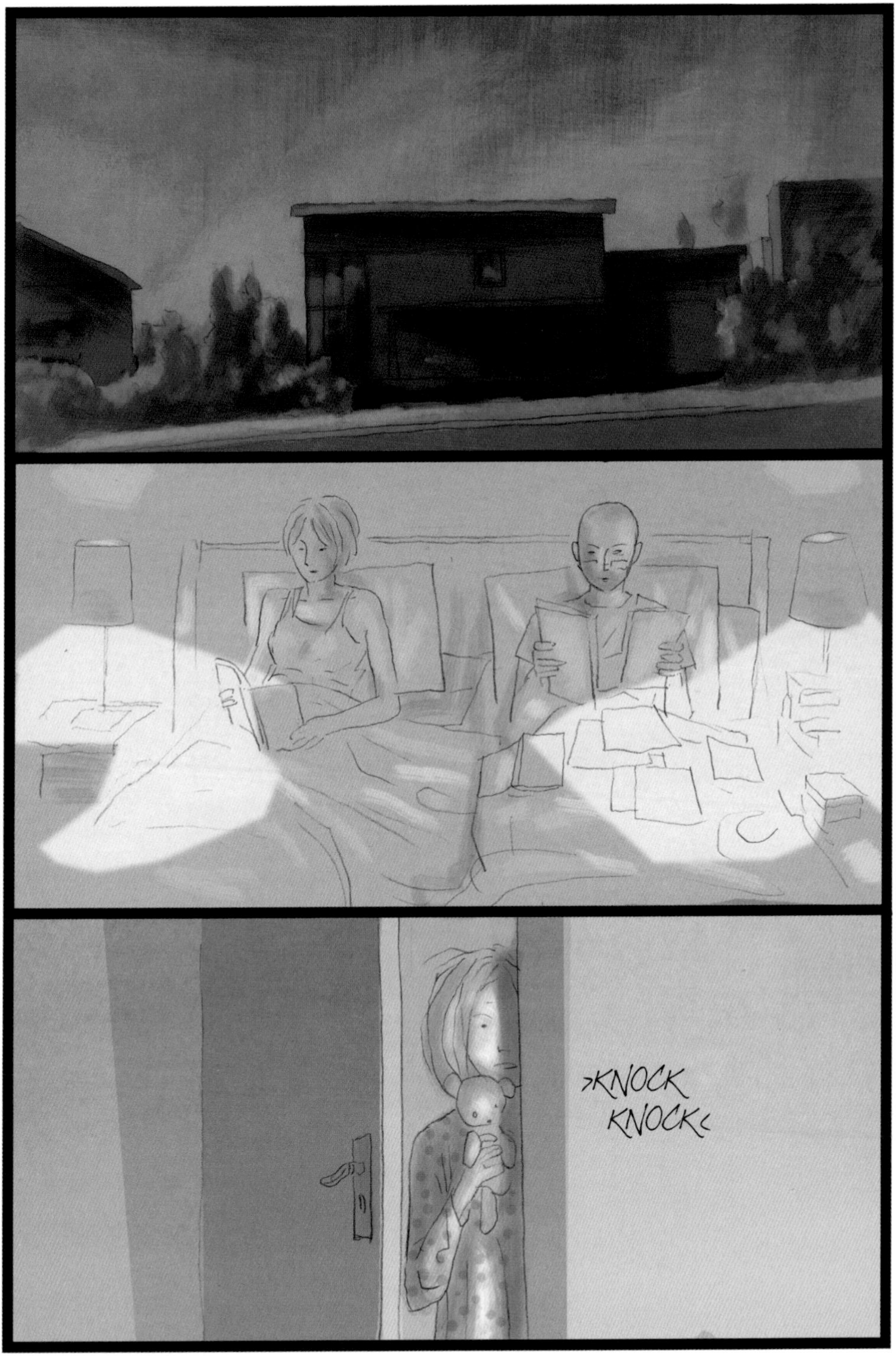
>KNOCK
KNOCK<

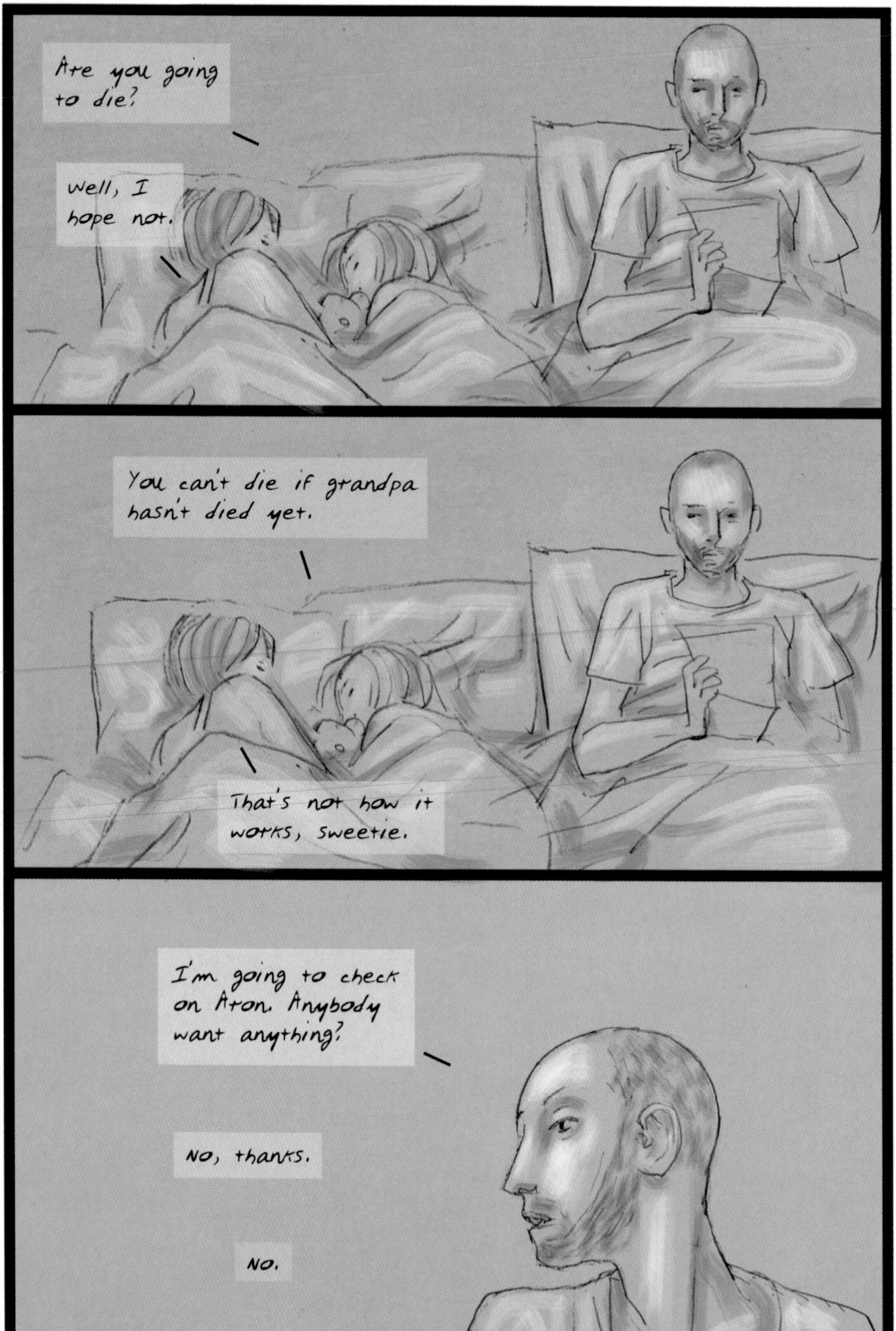
Are you going to die?
Well, I hope not.
You can't die if grandpa hasn't died yet.
That's not how it works, sweetie.
I'm going to check on Aron. Anybody want anything?
No, thanks.
No.

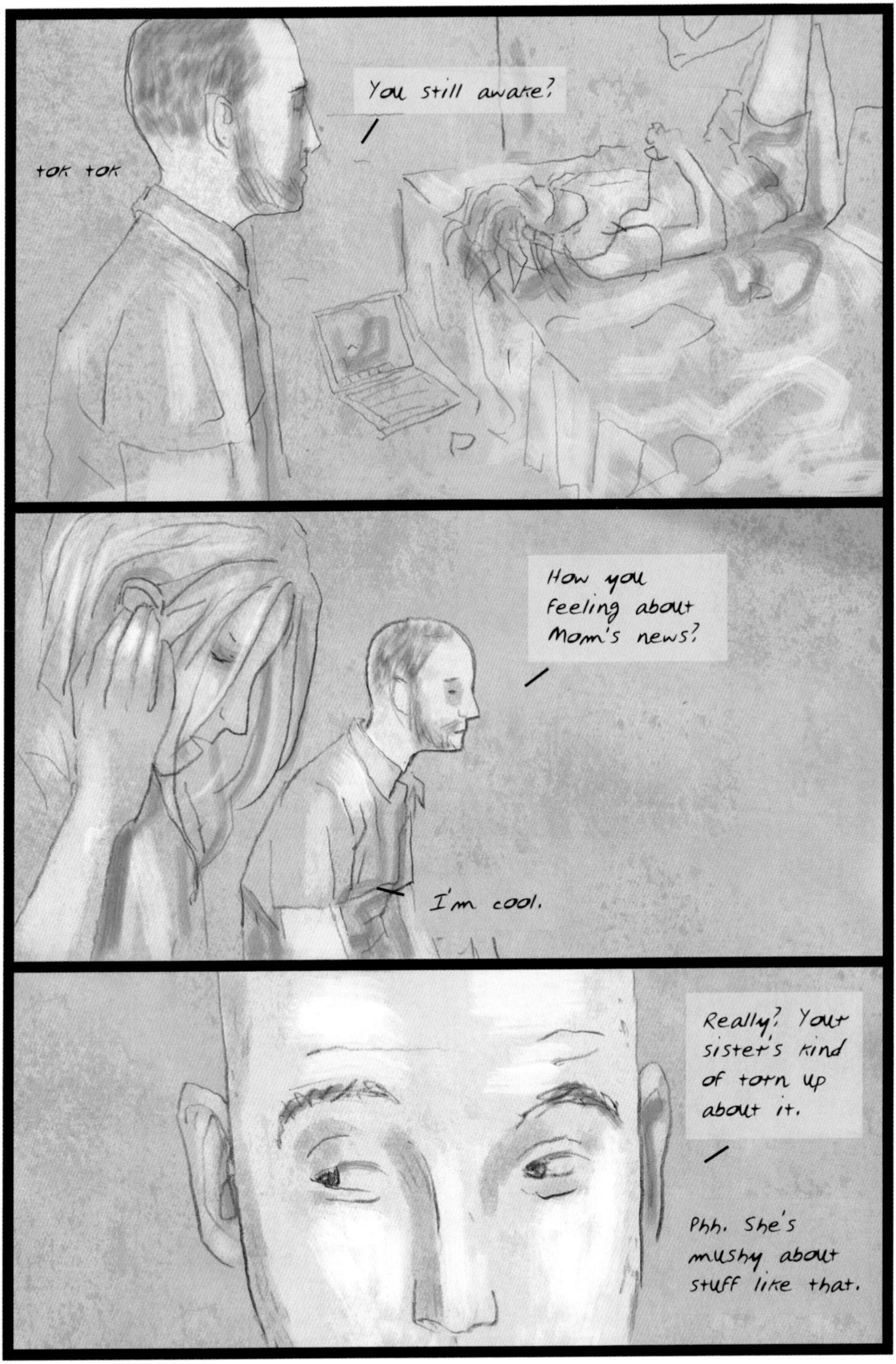
tok tok
You still awake?
How you feeling about Mom's news?
I'm cool.
Really? Your sister's kind of torn up about it.
Phh. She's mushy about stuff like that.

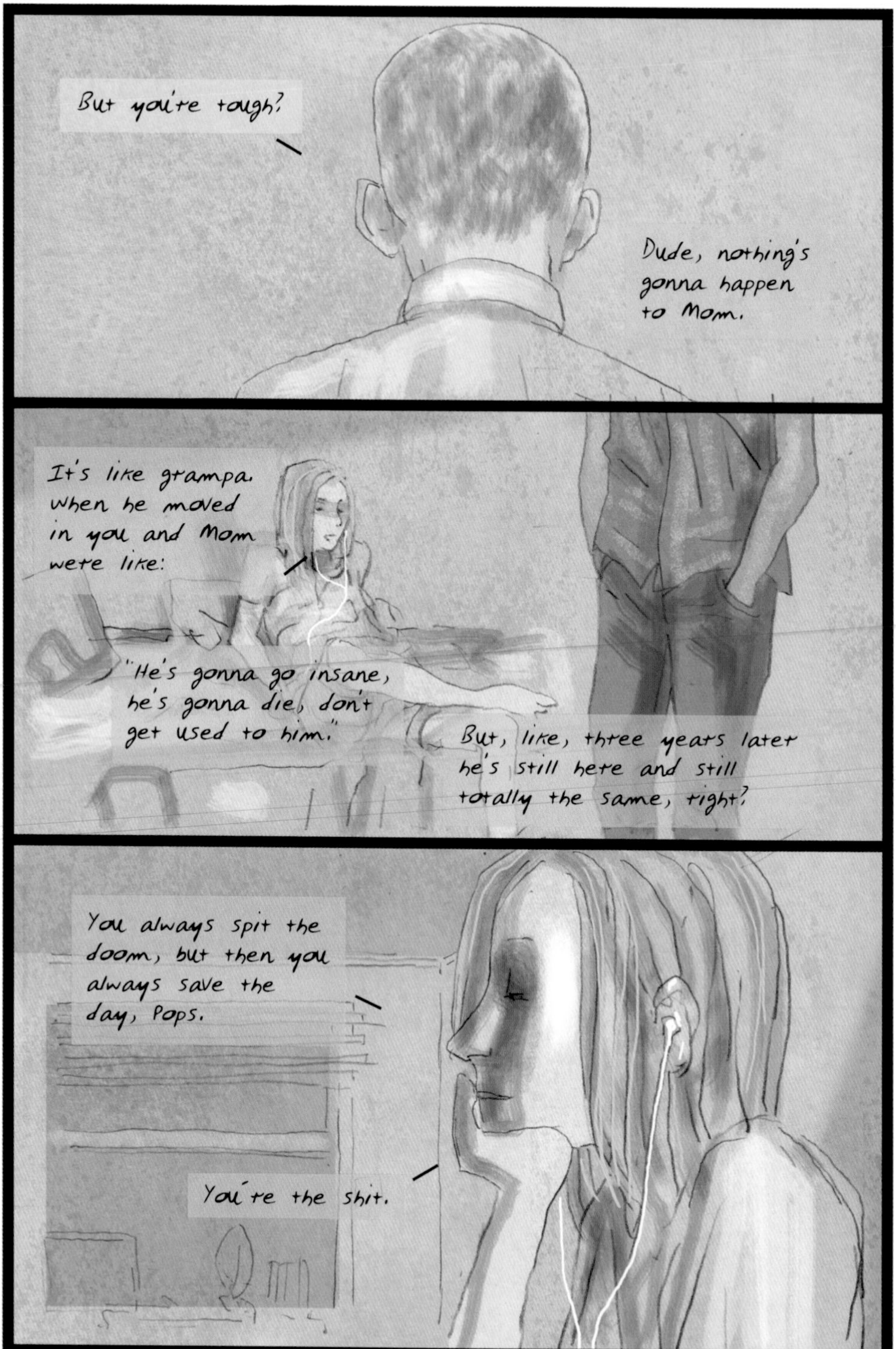

But you're tough?
Dude, nothing's gonna happen to Mom.
It's like grampa. When he moved in you and Mom were like:
"He's gonna go insane, he's gonna die, don't get used to him."
But, like, three years later he's still here and still totally the same, right?
You always spit the doom, but then you always save the day, Pops.
You're the shit.

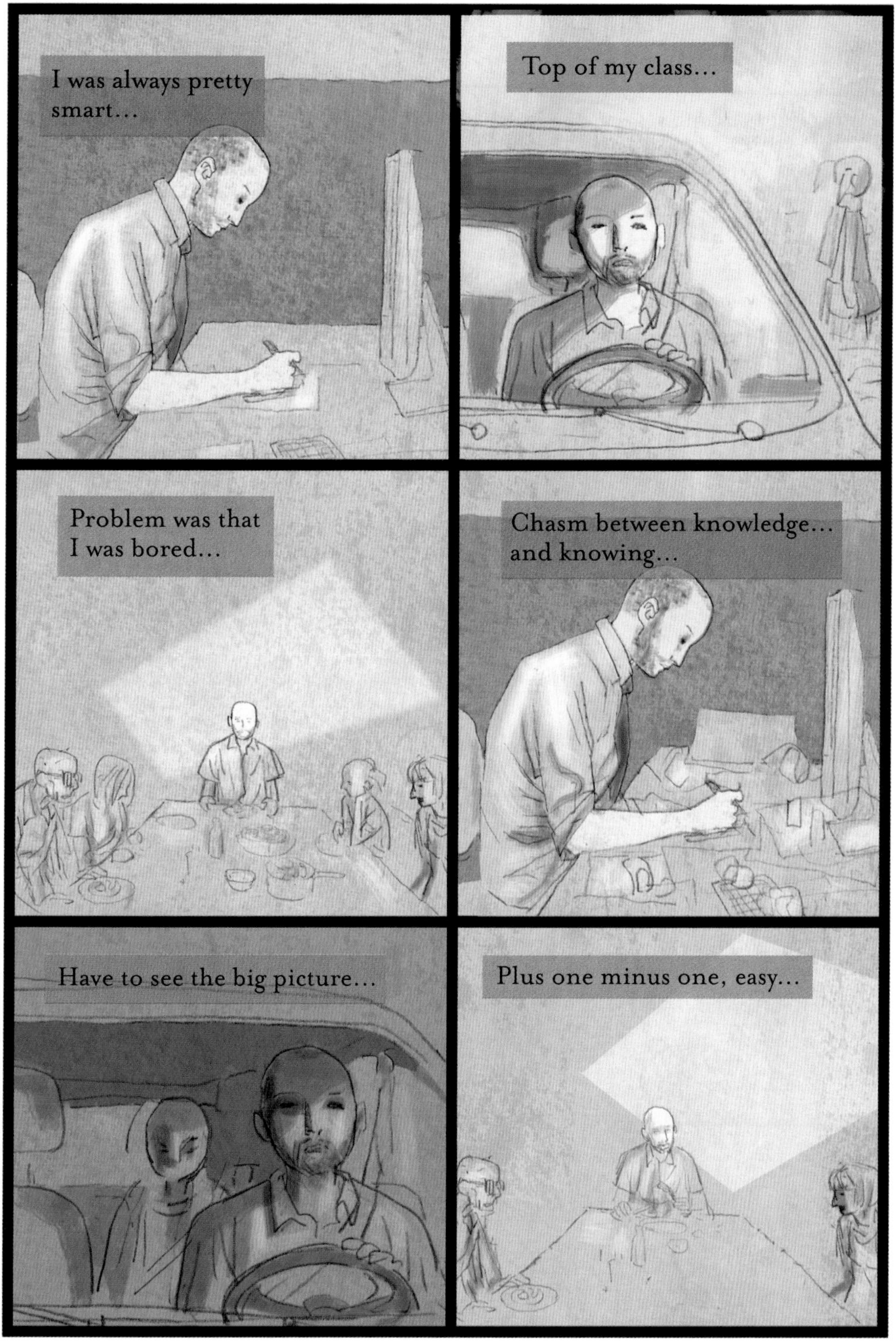
I was always pretty smart...
Top of my class...
Problem was that I was bored...
Chasm between knowledge... and knowing...
Have to see the big picture...
Plus one minus one, easy...

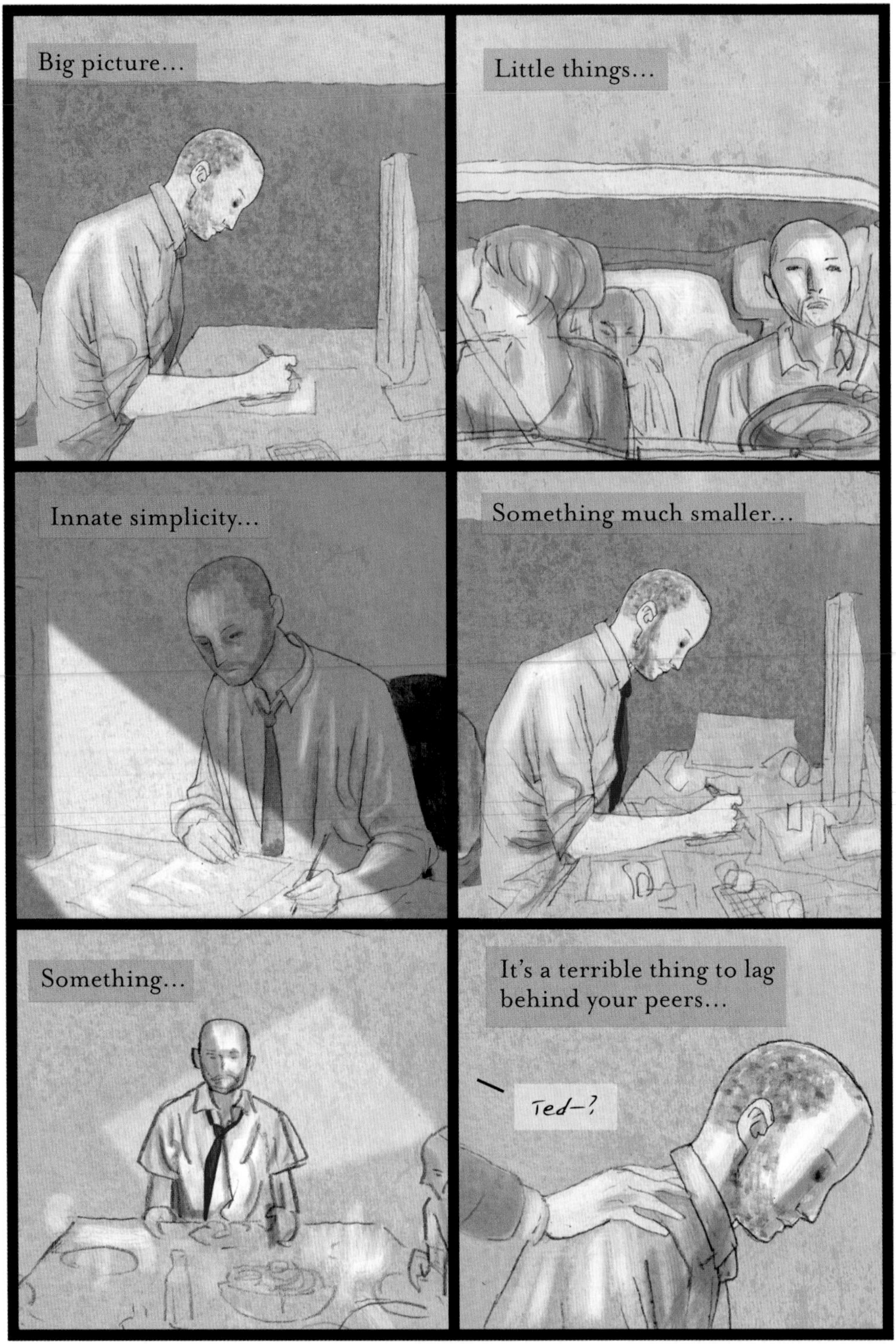
Big picture...
Little things...
Innate simplicity...
Something much smaller...
Something...
It's a terrible thing to lag behind your peers...
Ted—?

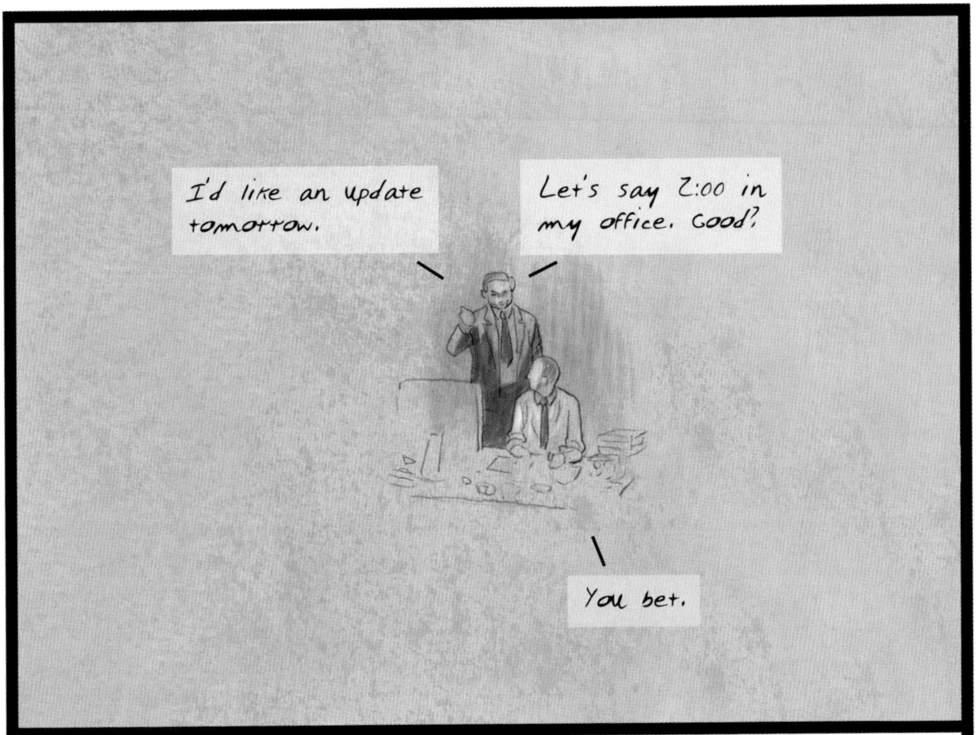
I'd like an update tomorrow.
Let's say 2:00 in my office. Good?
You bet.
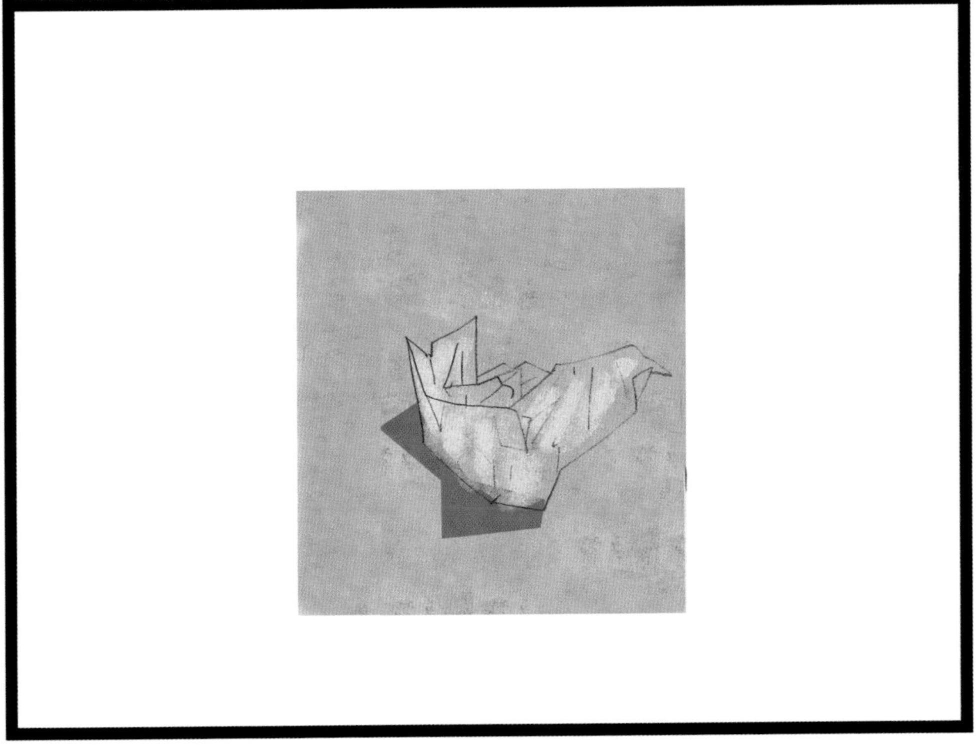

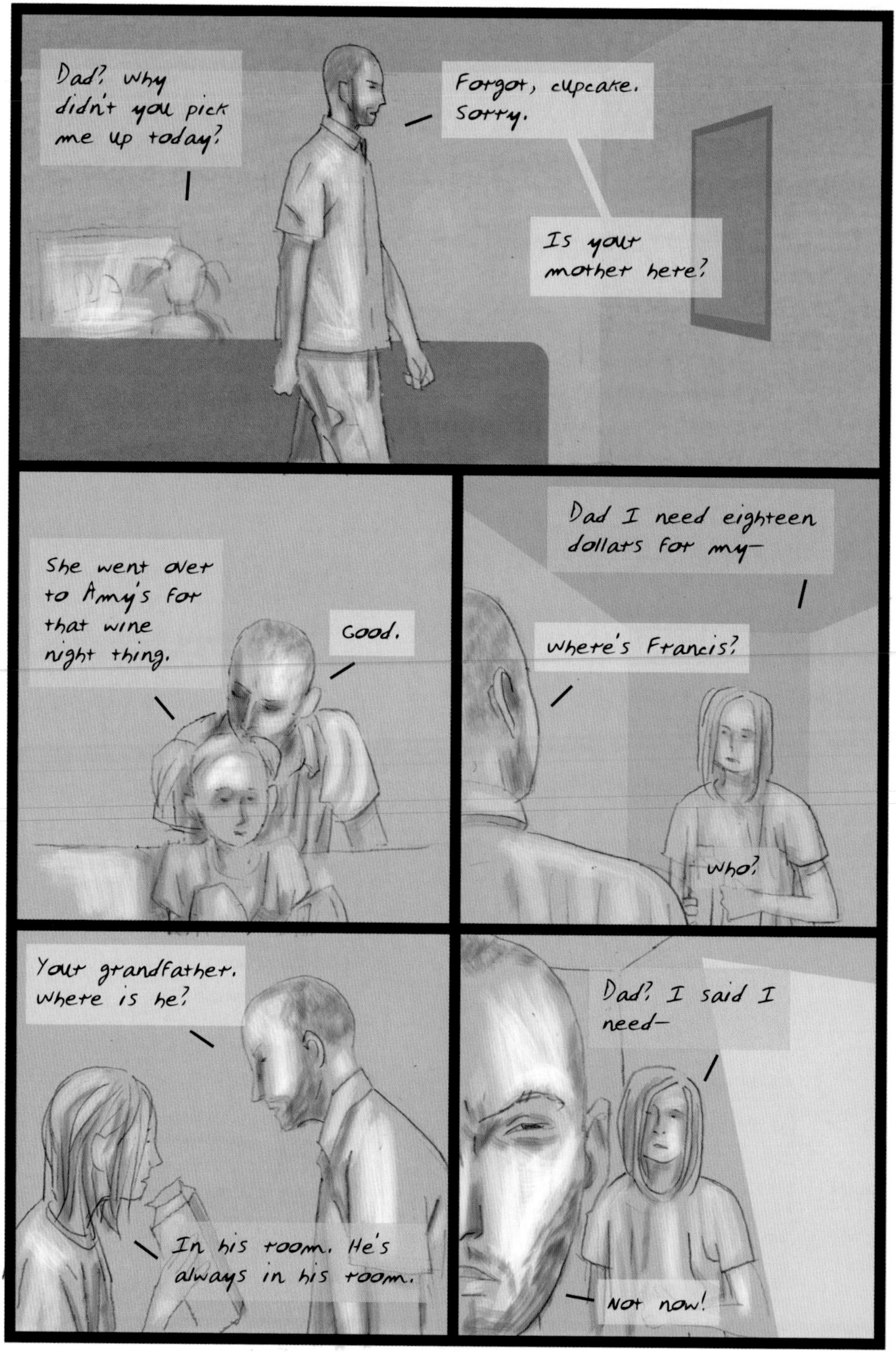
Dad? why didn't you pick me up today?
Forgot, cupcake. Sorry.
Is your mother here?
She went over to Amy's for that wine night thing.
Good.
Dad I need eighteen dollars for my—
Where's Francis?
Who?
Your grandfather. Where is he?
In his room. He's always in his room.
Dad? I said I need—
Not now!

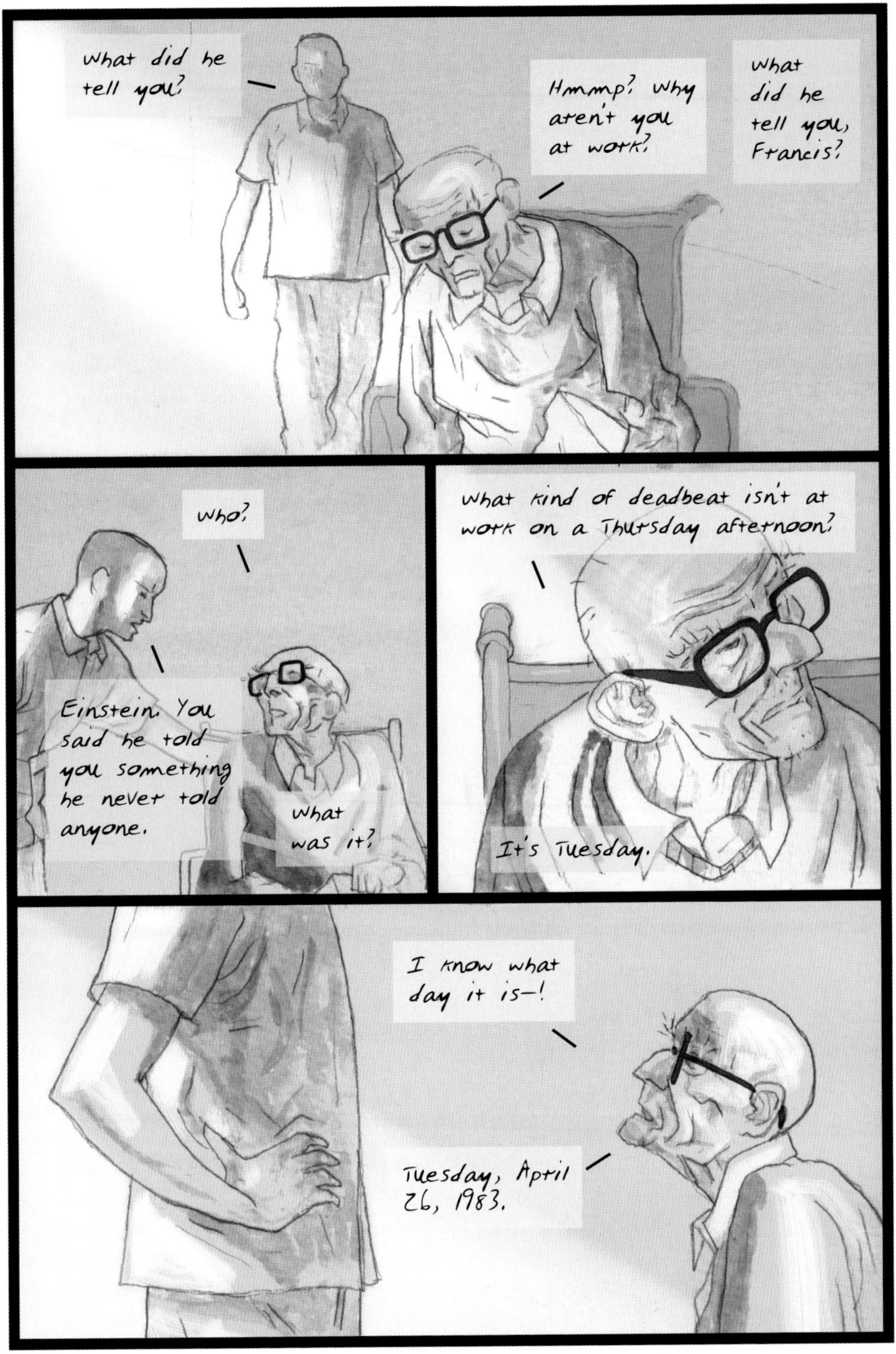
What did he tell you?
Hmmp? Why aren't you at work?
What did he tell you, Francis?
Who?
Einstein. You said he told you something he never told anyone.
What was it?
What kind of deadbeat isn't at work on a Thursday afternoon?
It's Tuesday.
I know what day it is—!
Tuesday, April 26, 1983.

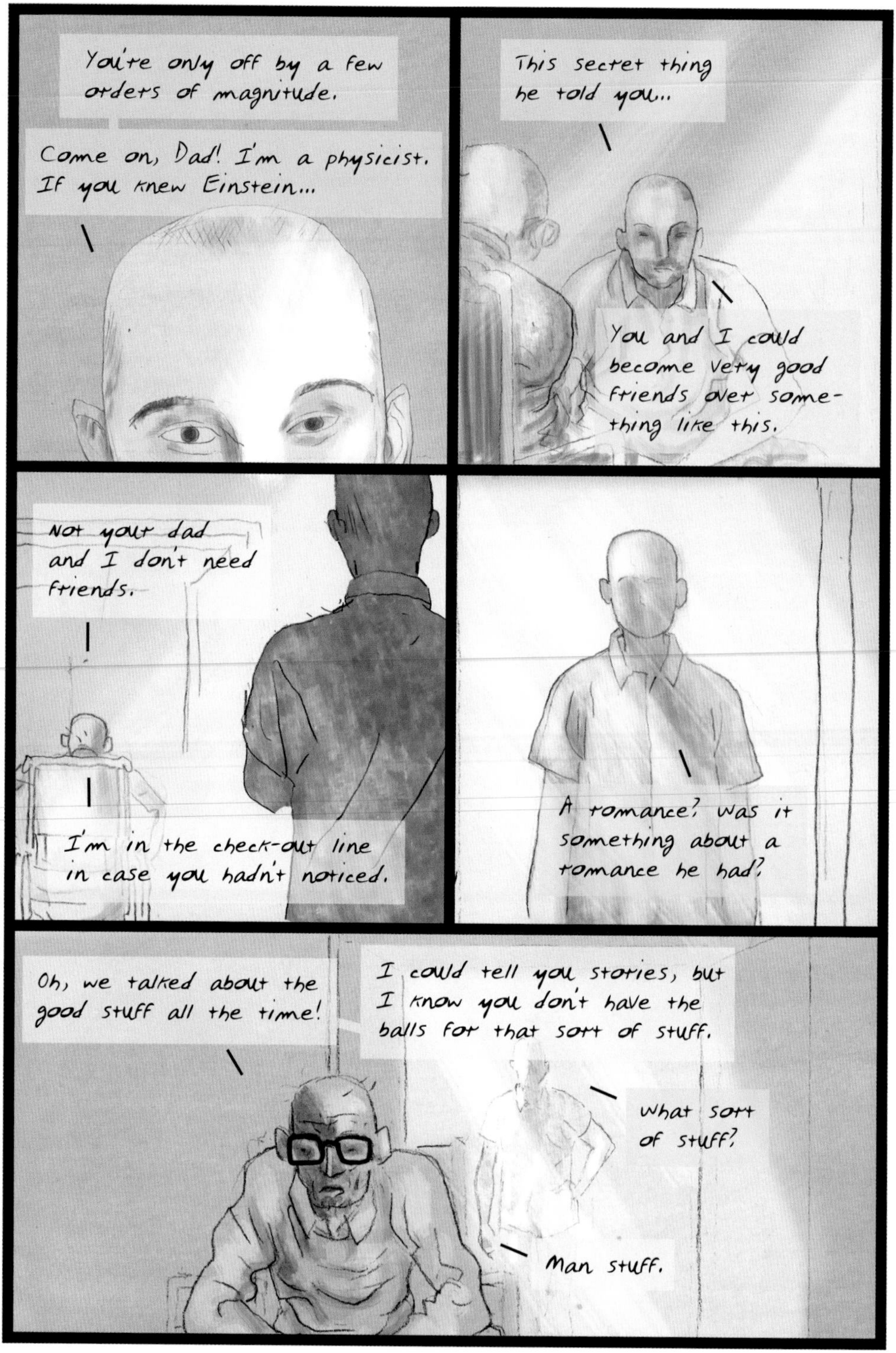
You're only off by a few orders of magnitude.
Come on, Dad! I'm a physicist. If you knew Einstein...
This secret thing he told you...
You and I could become very good friends over something like this.
Not your dad and I don't need friends.
I'm in the check-out line in case you hadn't noticed.
A romance? Was it something about a romance he had?
Oh, we talked about the good stuff all the time!
I could tell you stories, but I know you don't have the balls for that sort of stuff.
What sort of stuff?
Man stuff.

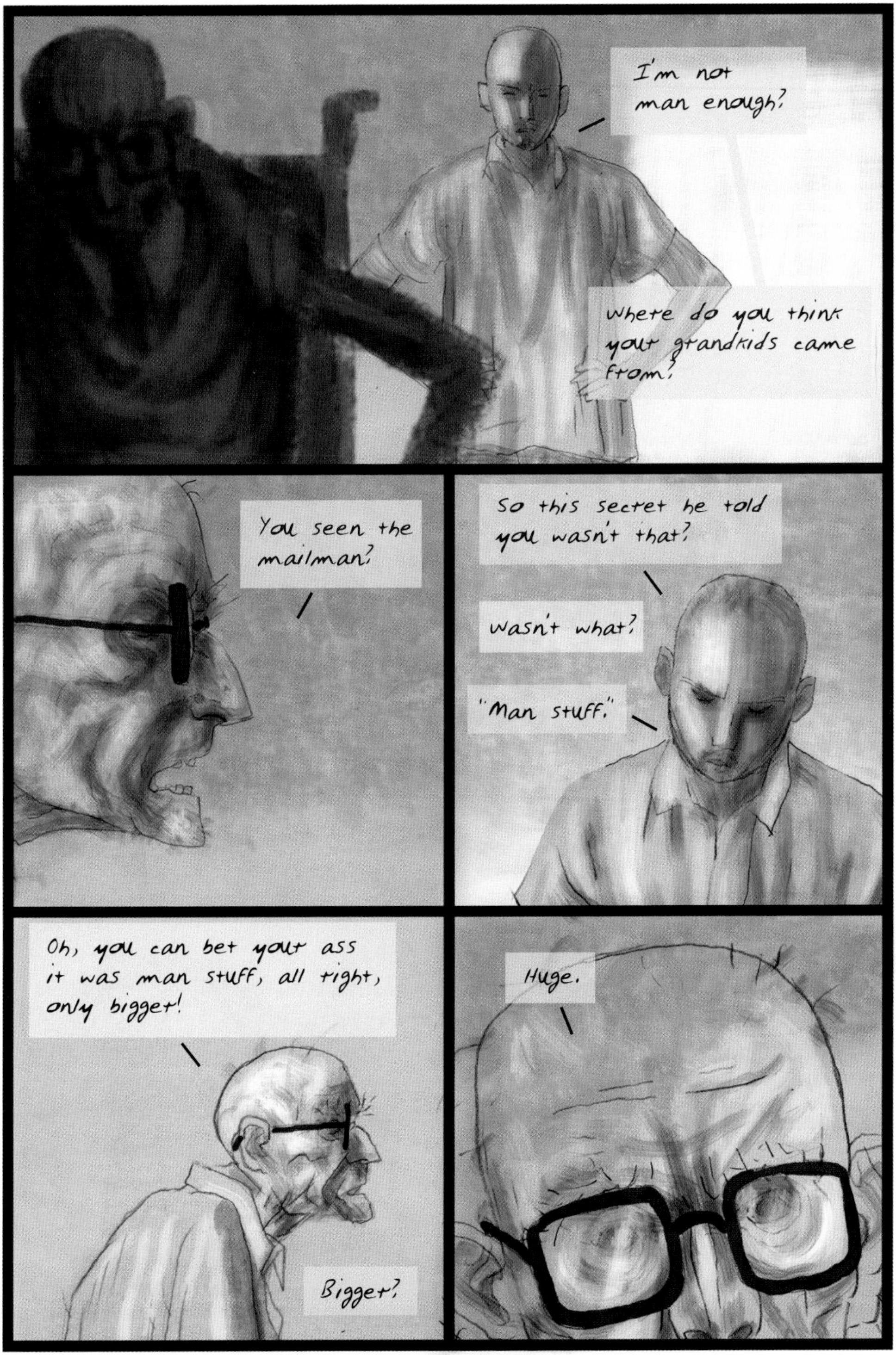
I'm not man enough?
Where do you think your grandkids came from?
You seen the mailman?
So this secret he told you wasn't that?
Wasn't what?
"Man stuff."
Oh, you can bet your ass it was man stuff, all right, only bigger!
Bigger?
Huge.

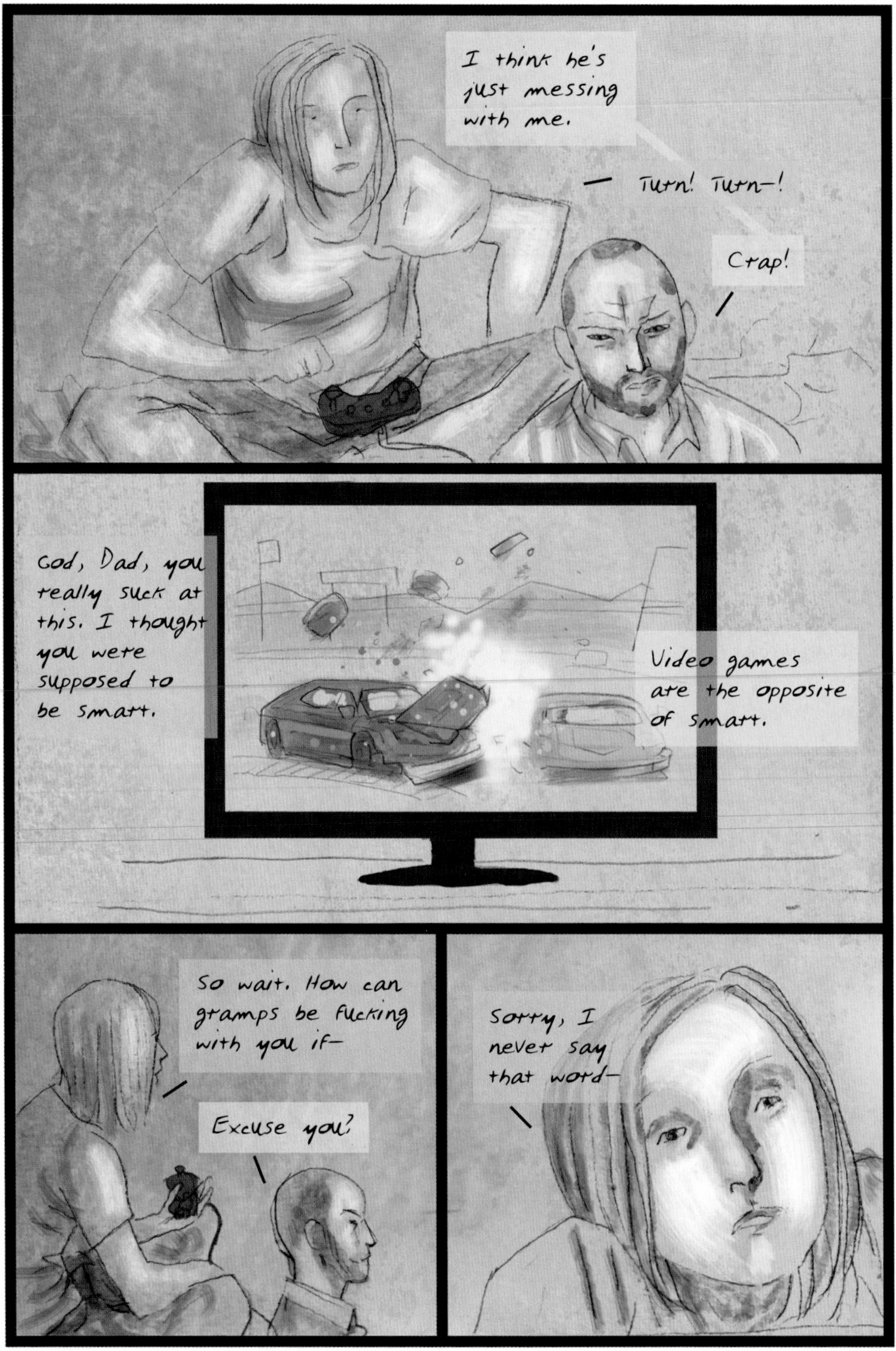
I think he's just messing with me.
— Turn! Turn—!
Crap!
God, Dad, you really suck at this. I thought you were supposed to be smart.
Video games are the opposite of smart.
So wait. How can gramps be fucking with you if—
Excuse you?
Sorry, I never say that word—

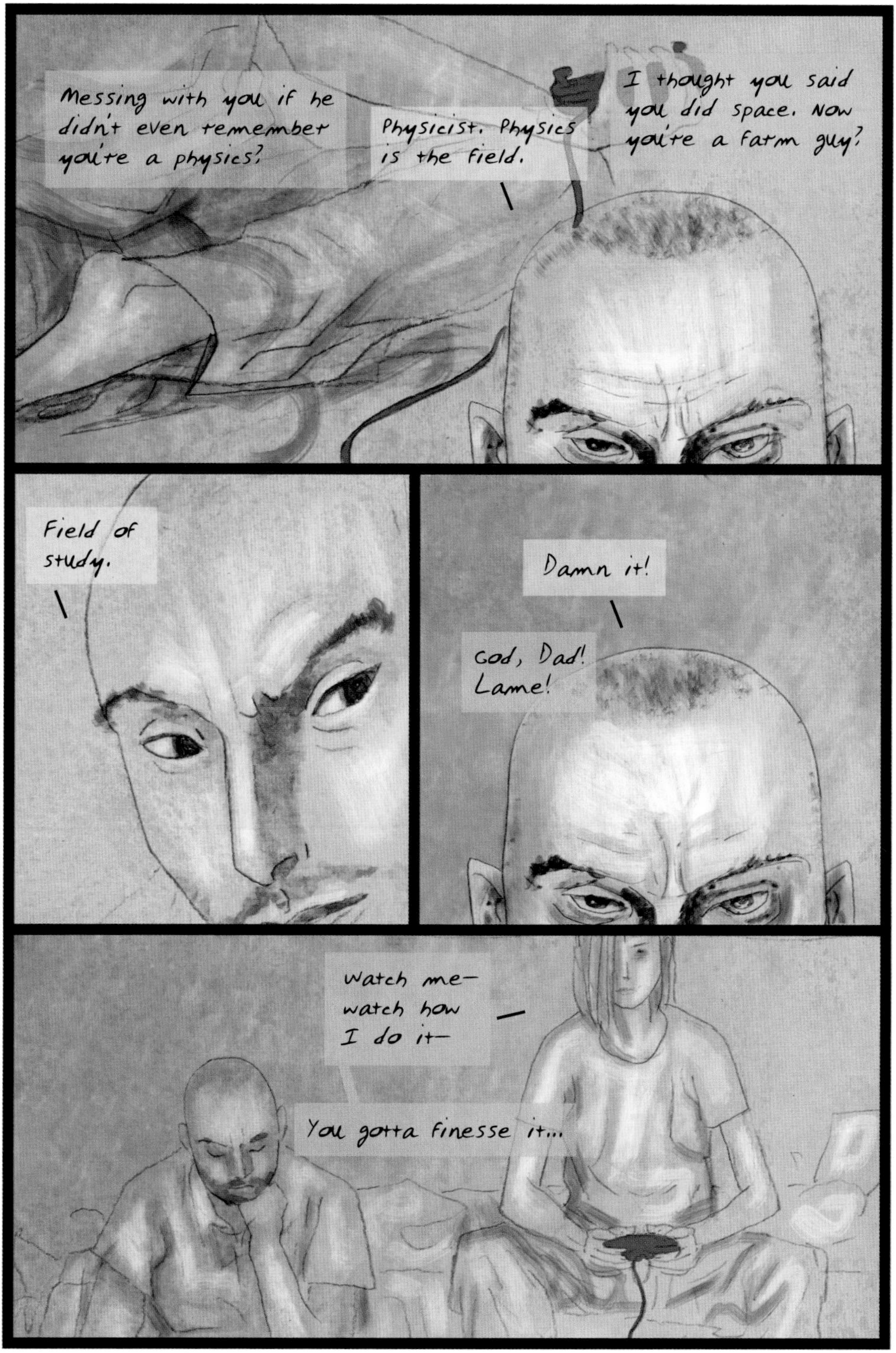

Messing with you if he didn't even remember you're a physics?
Physicist. Physics is the field.
I thought you said you did space. Now you're a farm guy?
Field of study.
Damn it!
God, Dad! Lame!
Watch me— watch how I do it—
You gotta finesse it...

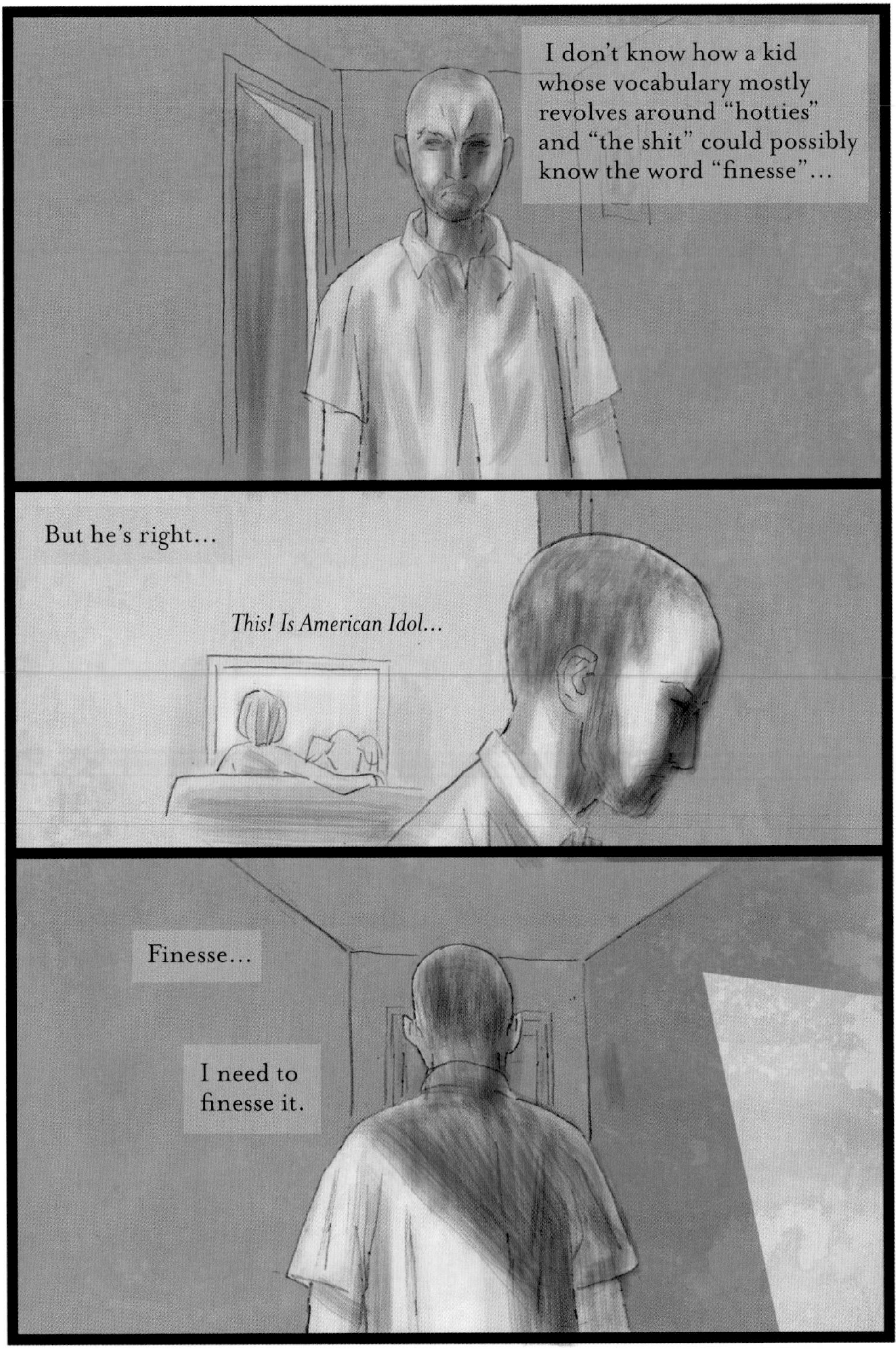
I don't know how a kid whose vocabulary mostly revolves around "hotties" and "the shit" could possibly know the word "finesse"...
But he's right...
This! Is American Idol...
Finesse...
I need to finesse it.

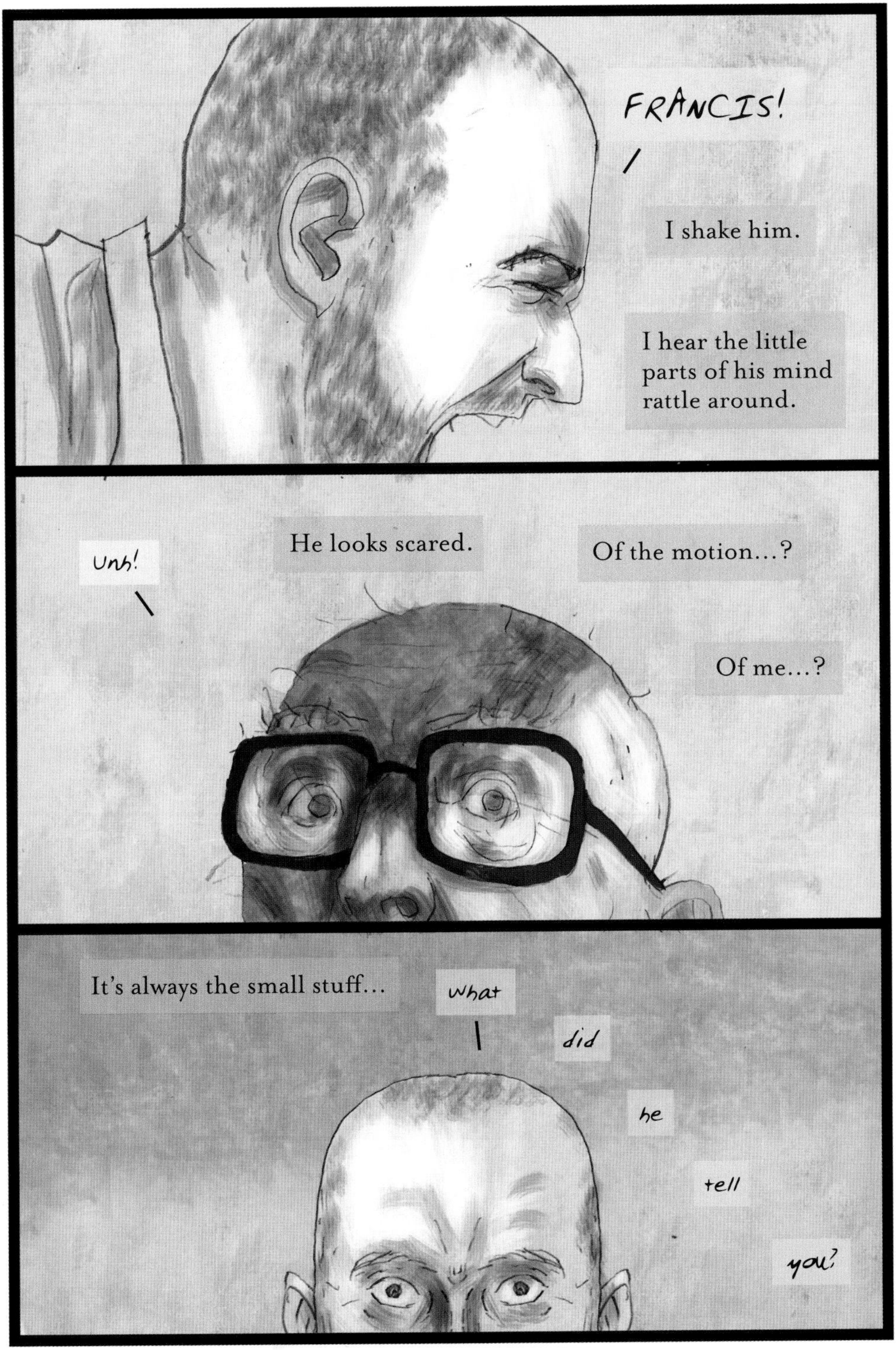
FRANCIS!
I shake him.
I hear the little parts of his mind rattle around.
Unh!
He looks scared.
Of the motion...?
Of me...?
It's always the small stuff...
what
did
he
tell
you?

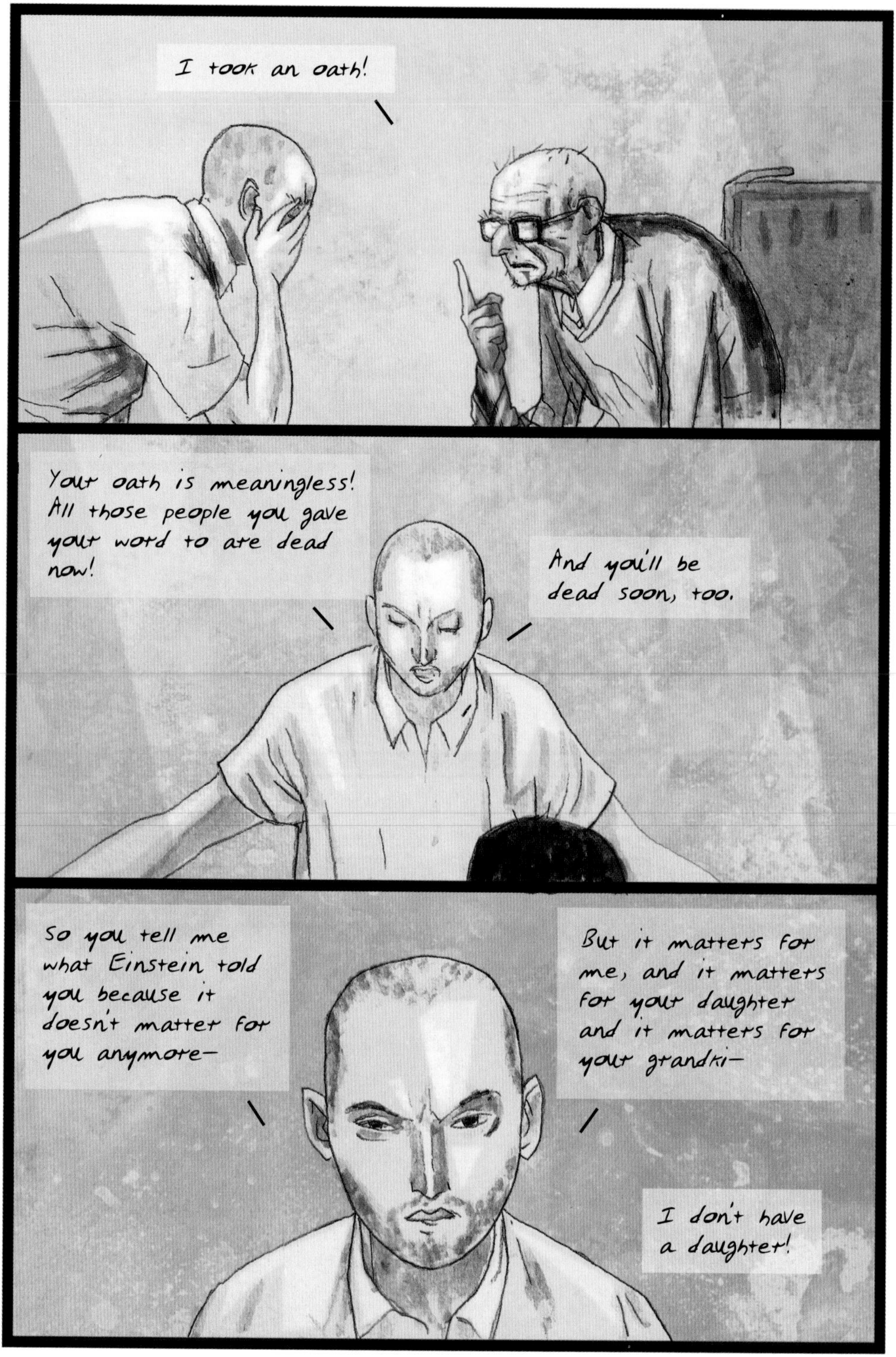
I took an oath!
Your oath is meaningless! All those people you gave your word to are dead now!
And you'll be dead soon, too.
So you tell me what Einstein told you because it doesn't matter for you anymore–
But it matters for me, and it matters for your daughter and it matters for your grandki–
I don't have a daughter!

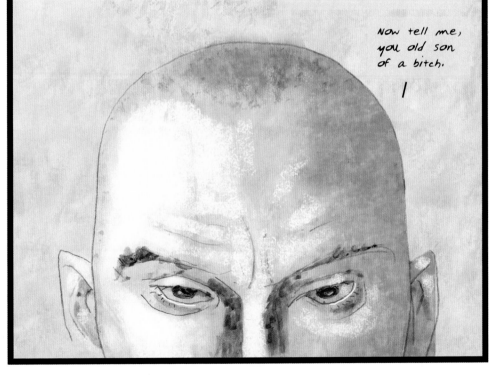

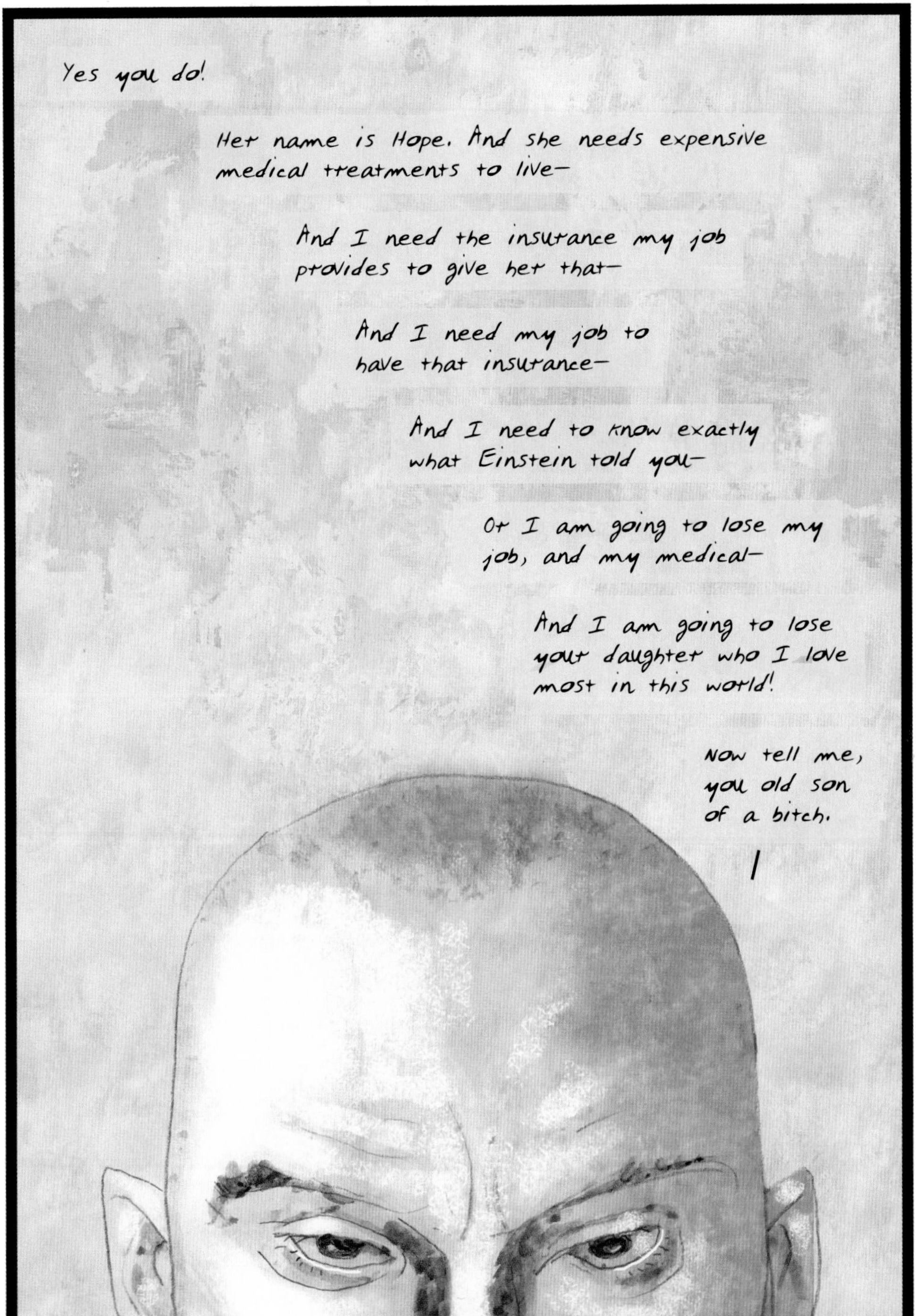

Yes you do!

Her name is Hope. And she needs expensive medical treatments to live—

And I need the insurance my job provides to give her that—

And I need my job to have that insurance—

And I need to know exactly what Einstein told you—

Or I am going to lose my job, and my medical—

And I am going to lose your daughter who I love most in this world!

Now tell me, you old son of a bitch.

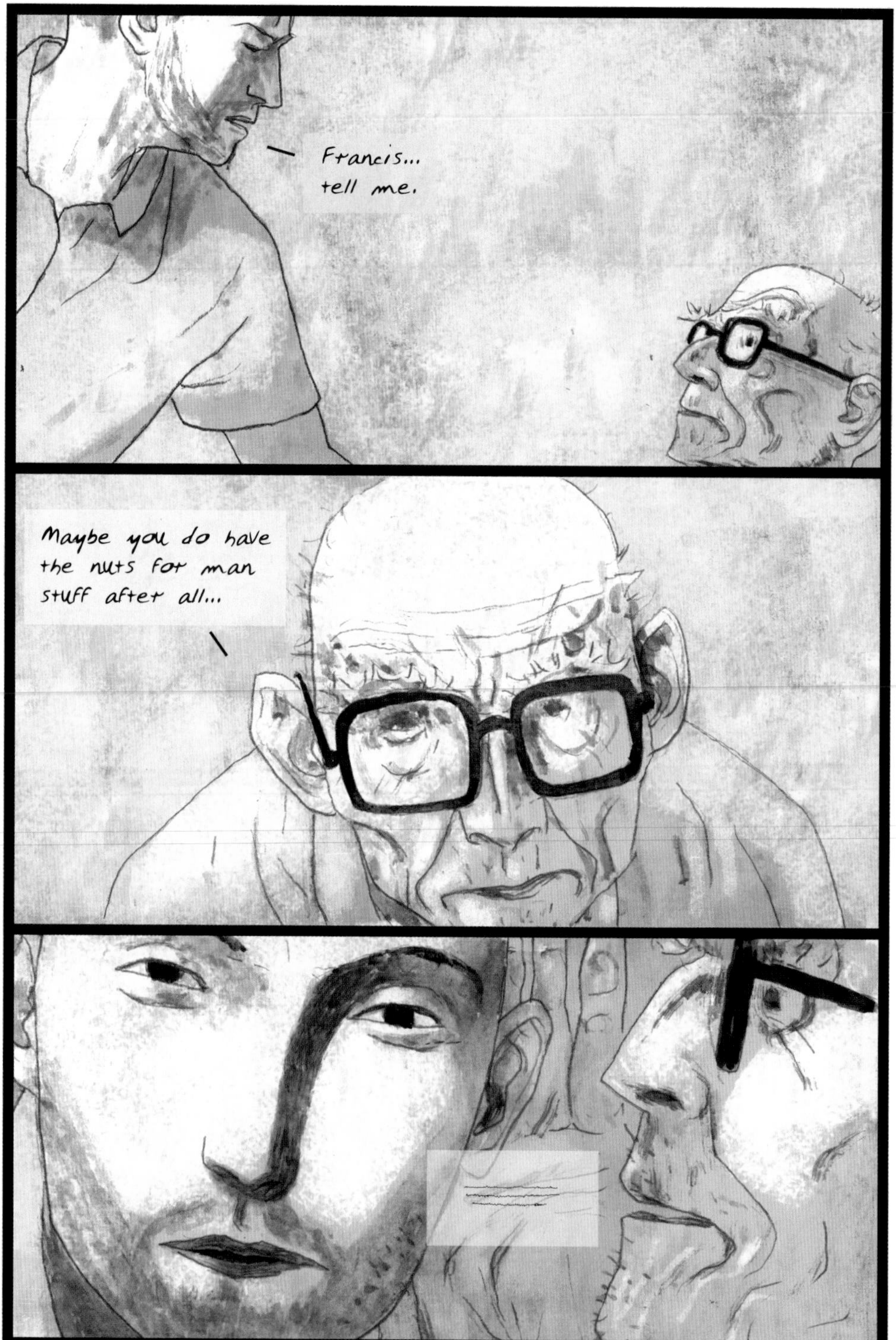
Francis...
tell me.
Maybe you do have the nuts for man stuff after all...

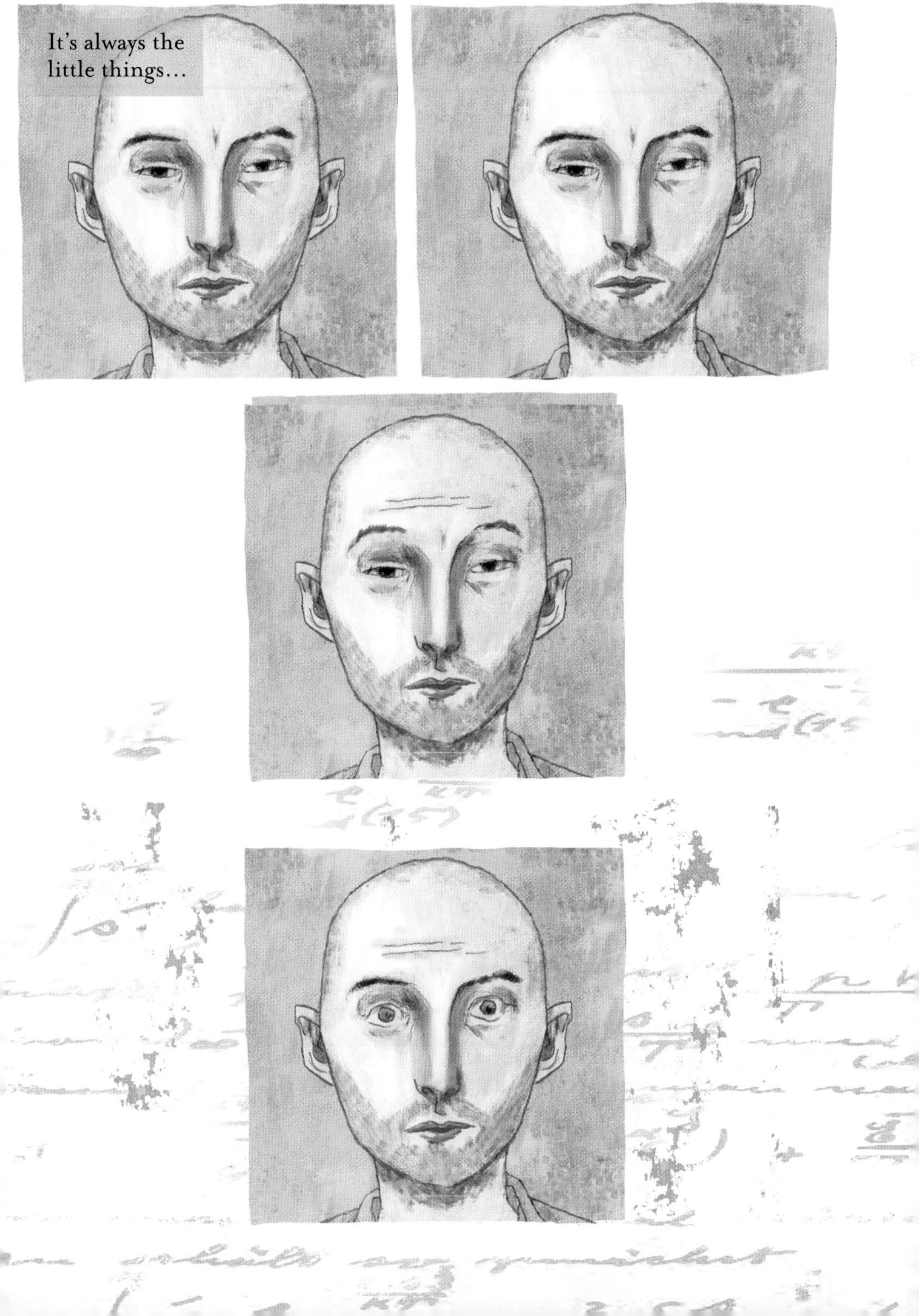
It's always the little things...

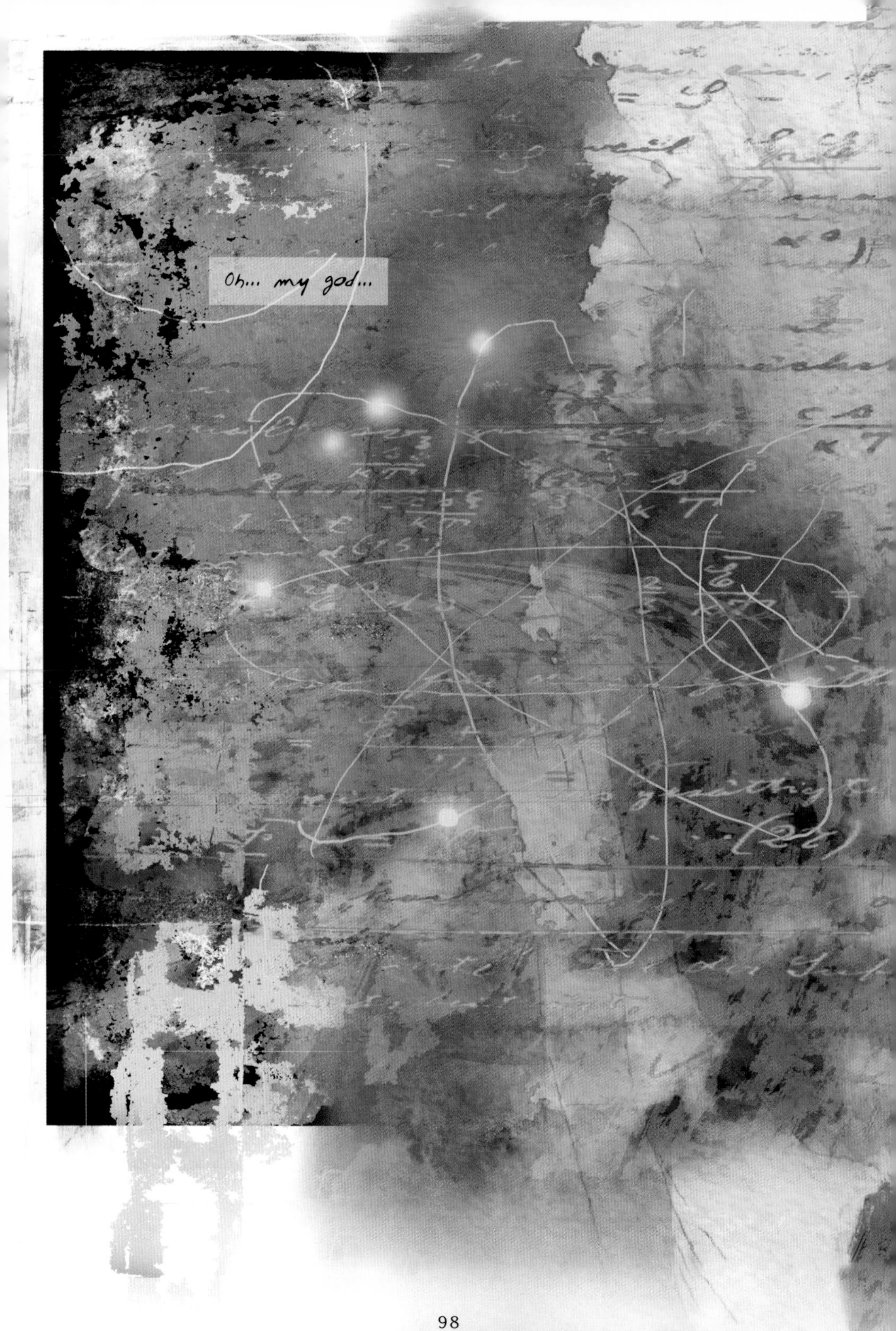
Oh... my god...

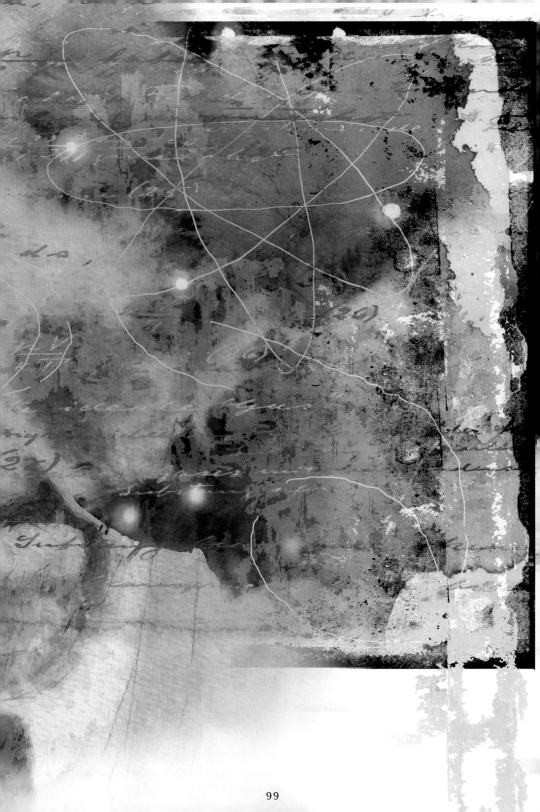

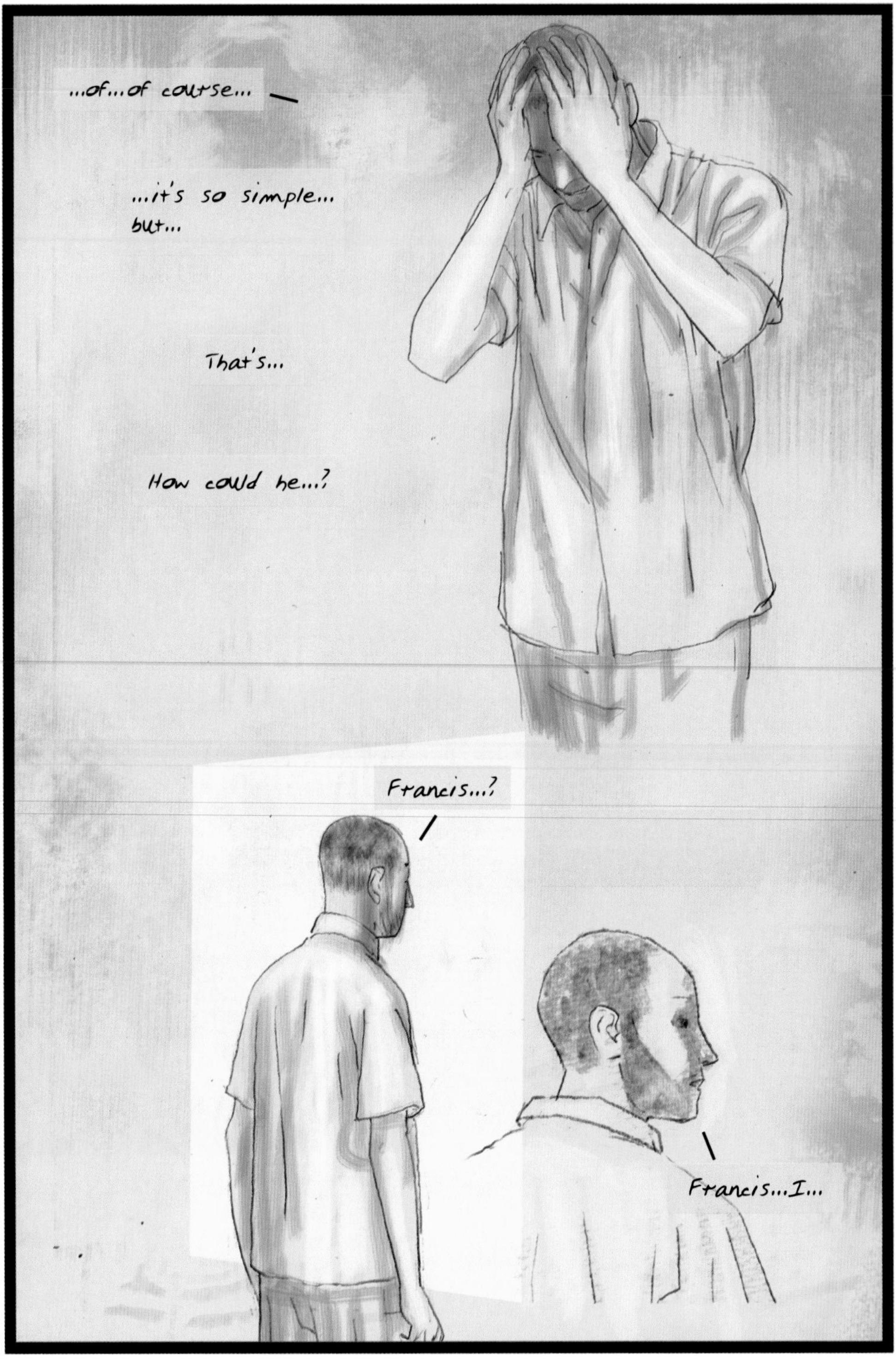
...of...of course...
...it's so simple... but...
That's...
How could he...?
Francis...?
Francis...I...

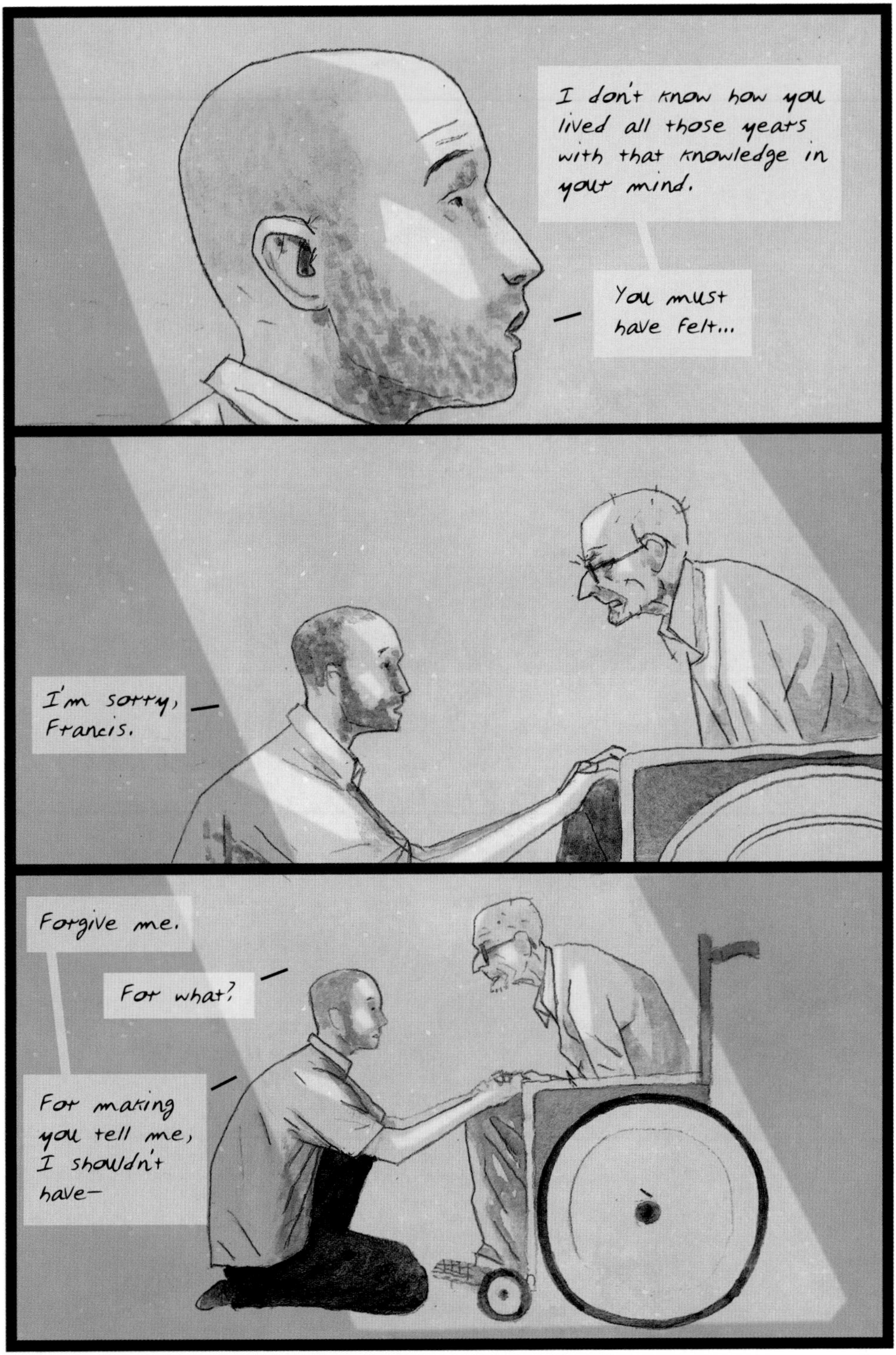
I don't know how you lived all those years with that knowledge in your mind.
You must have felt...
I'm sorry, Francis.
Forgive me.
For what?
For making you tell me, I shouldn't have—

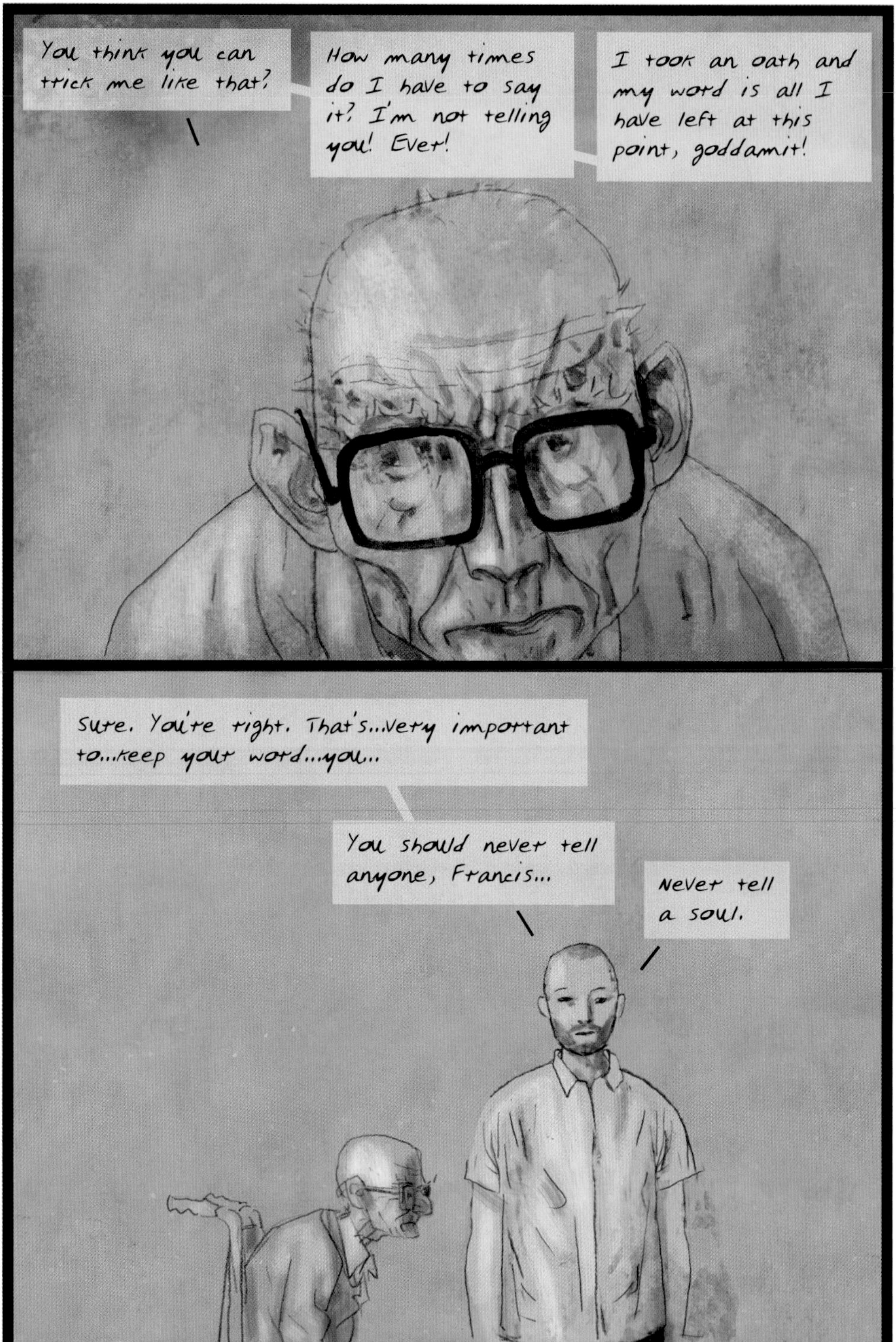
You think you can trick me like that?
How many times do I have to say it? I'm not telling you! Ever!
I took an oath and my word is all I have left at this point, goddamit!
Sure. You're right. That's...very important to...keep your word...you..
You should never tell anyone, Francis...
Never tell a soul.

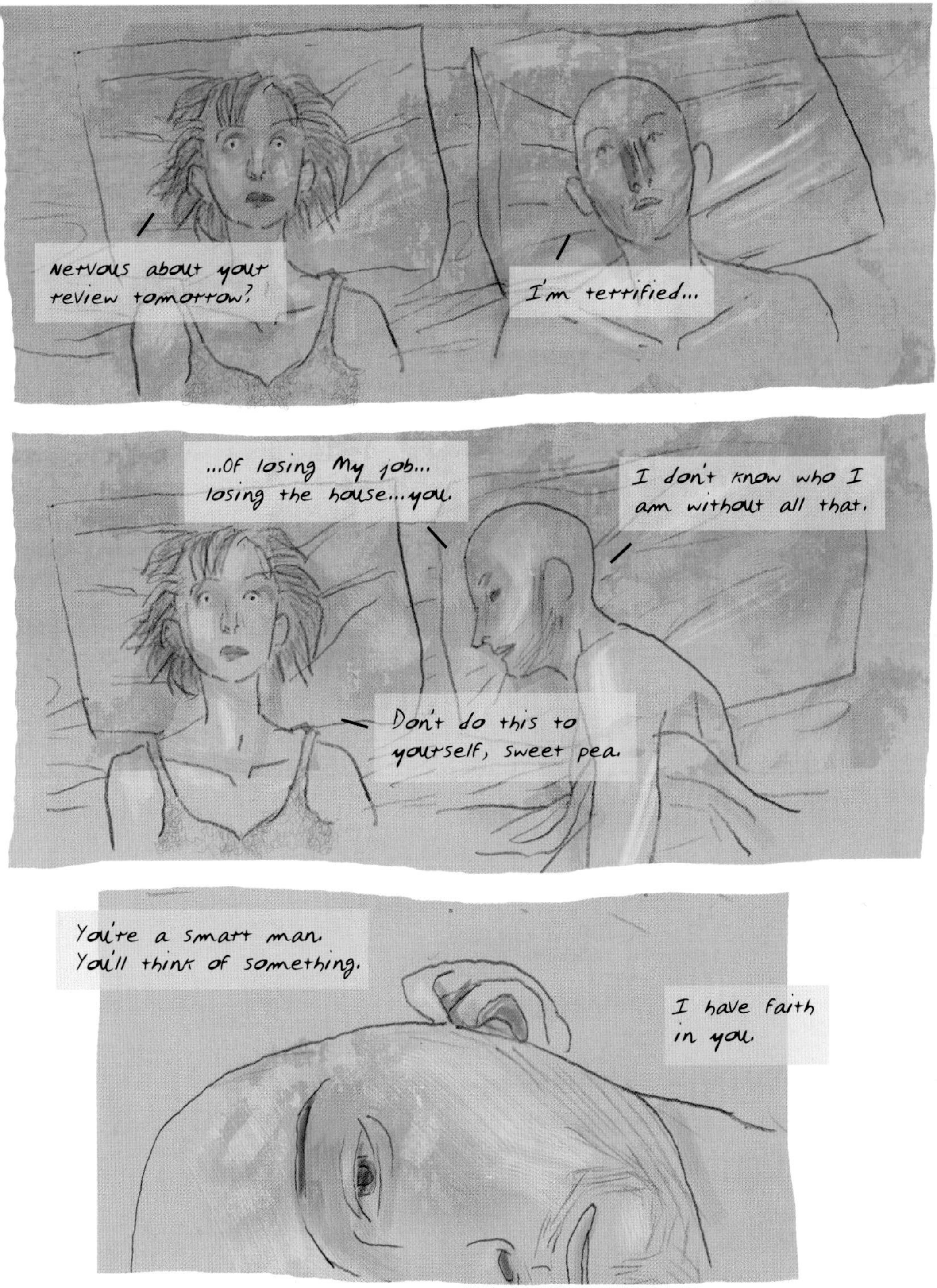
Nervous about your review tomorrow?
I'm terrified...
...Of losing my job... losing the house...you.
I don't know who I am without all that.
Don't do this to yourself, sweet pea.
You're a smart man. You'll think of something.
I have faith in you.

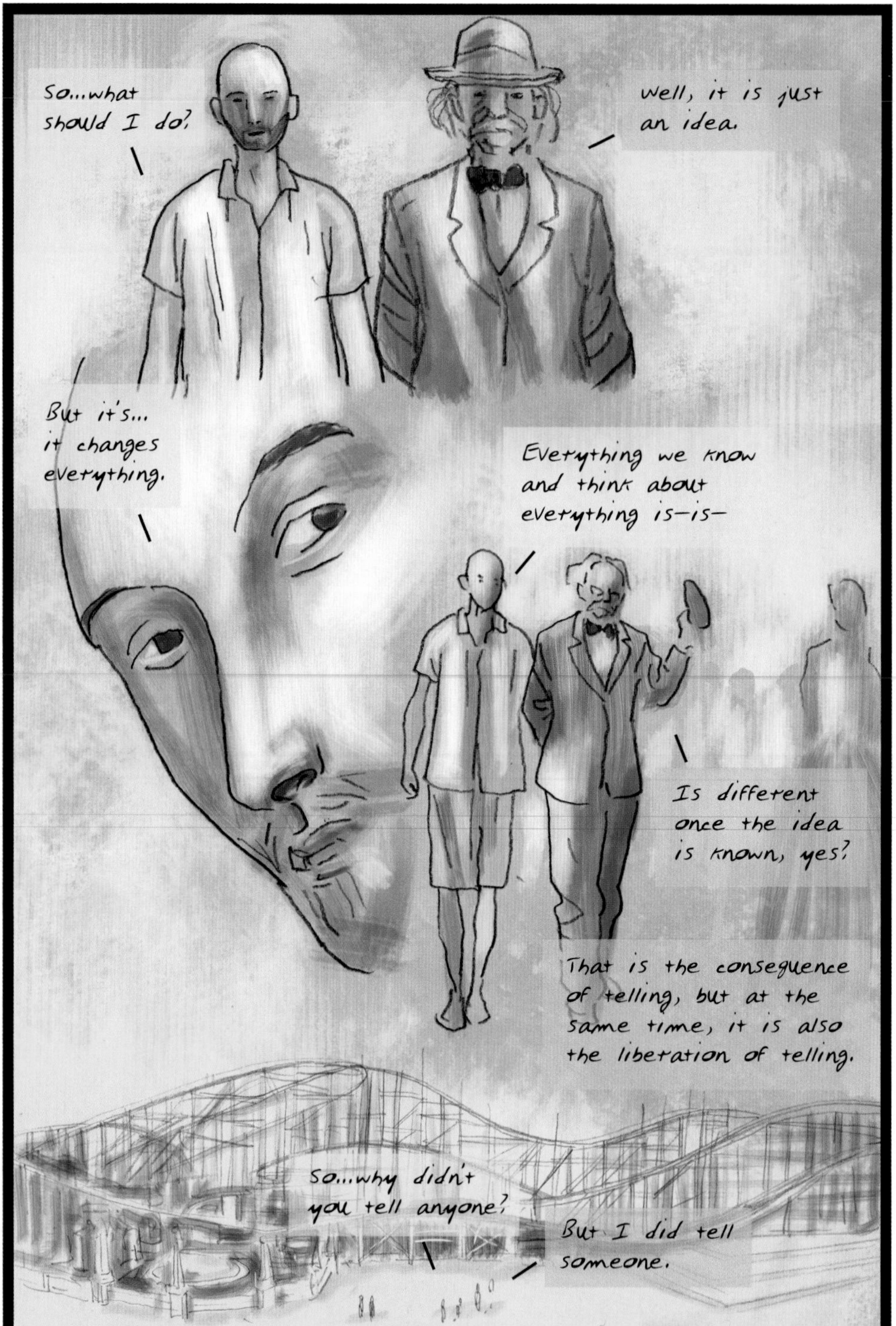

So...what should I do?
Well, it is just an idea.
But it's... it changes everything.
Everything we know and think about everything is—is—
Is different once the idea is known, yes?
That is the consequence of telling, but at the same time, it is also the liberation of telling.
So...why didn't you tell anyone?
But I did tell someone.

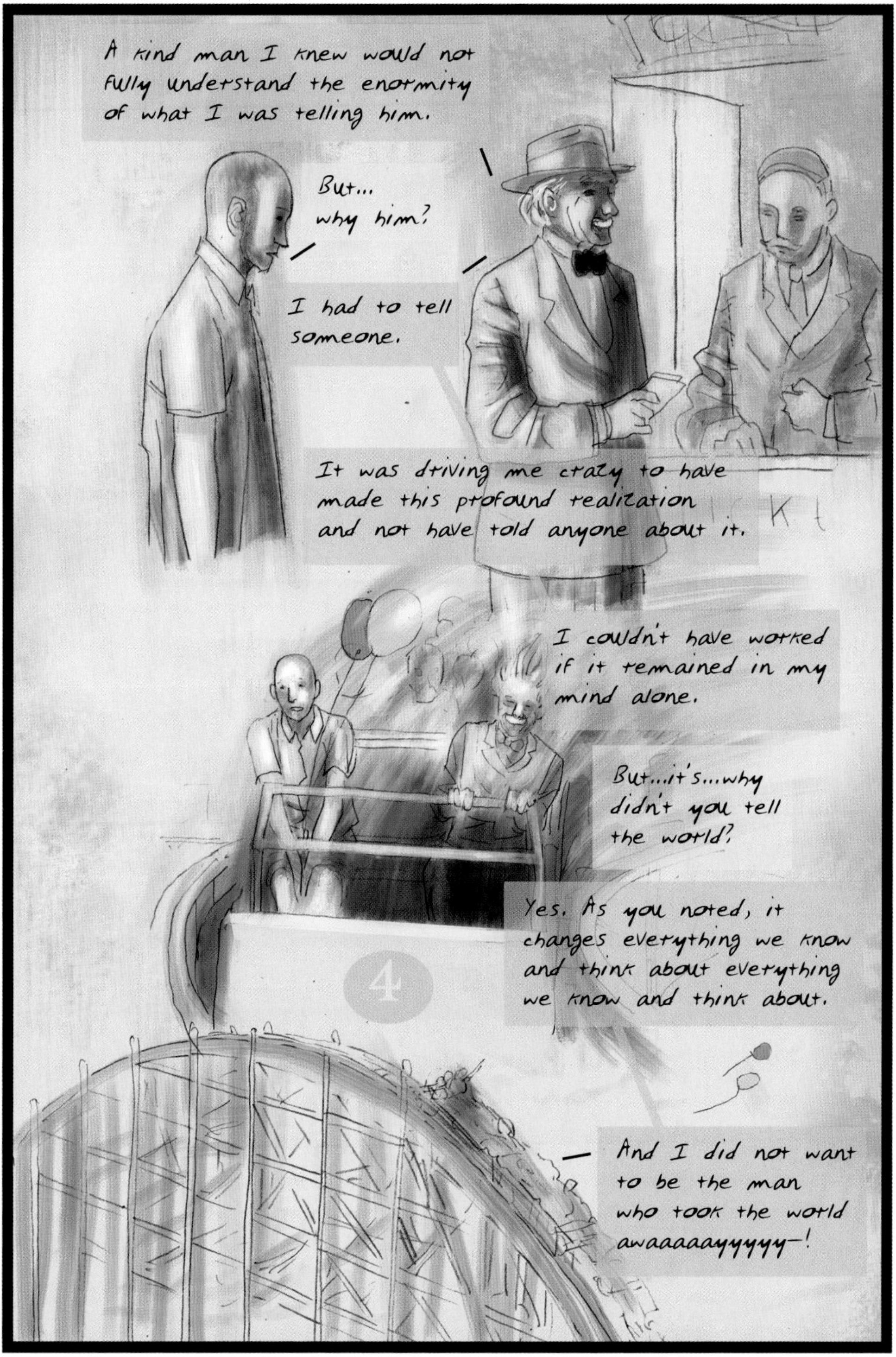

A kind man I knew would not fully understand the enormity of what I was telling him.
But... why him?
I had to tell someone.
It was driving me crazy to have made this profound realization and not have told anyone about it.
I couldn't have worked if it remained in my mind alone.
But...it's...why didn't you tell the world?
Yes. As you noted, it changes everything we know and think about everything we know and think about.
And I did not want to be the man who took the world awaaaaayyyyy—!

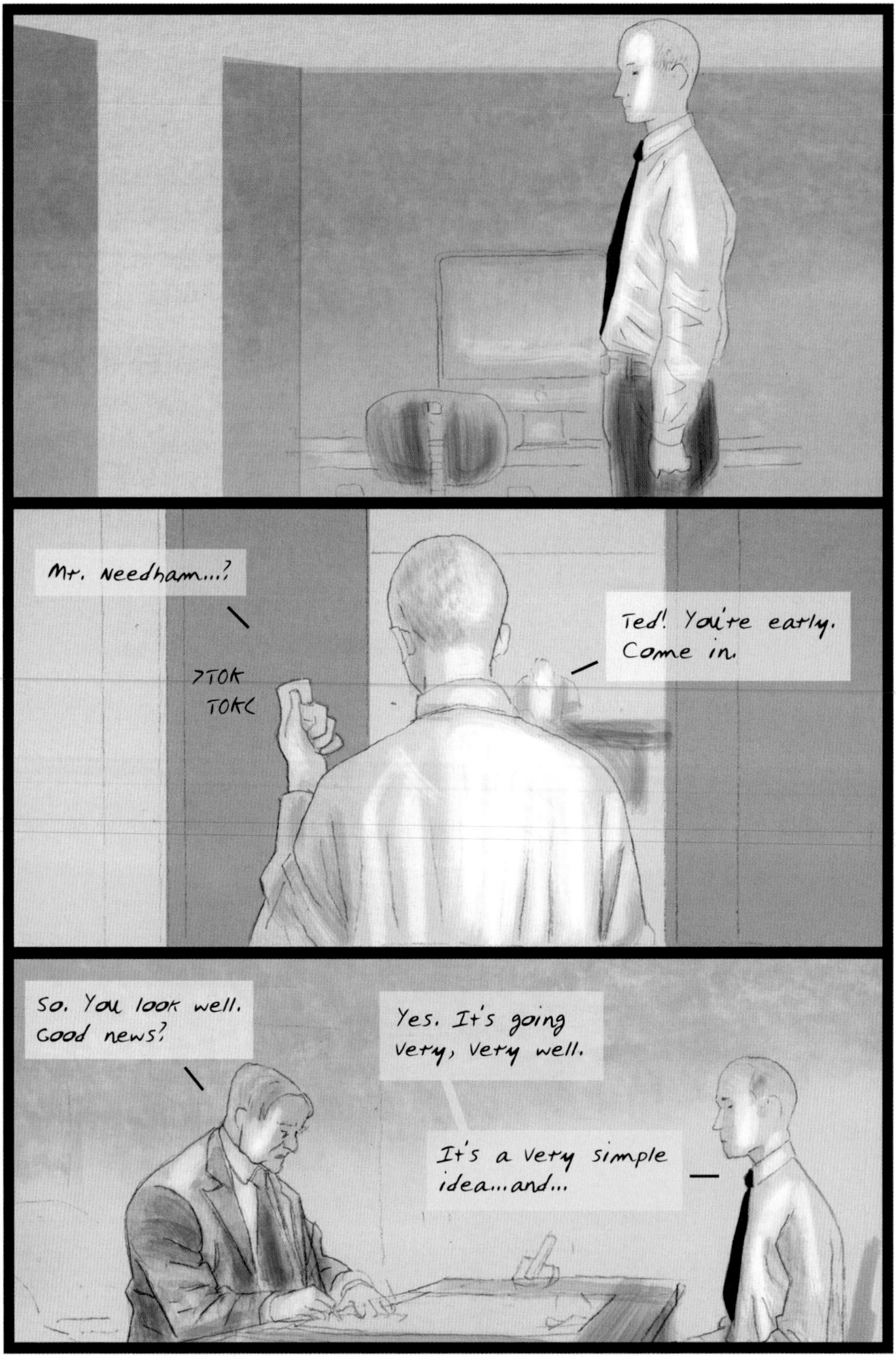
Mr. Needham...?
TOK
TOK
Ted! You're early. Come in.
So. You look well. Good news?
Yes. It's going very, very well.
It's a very simple idea...and...

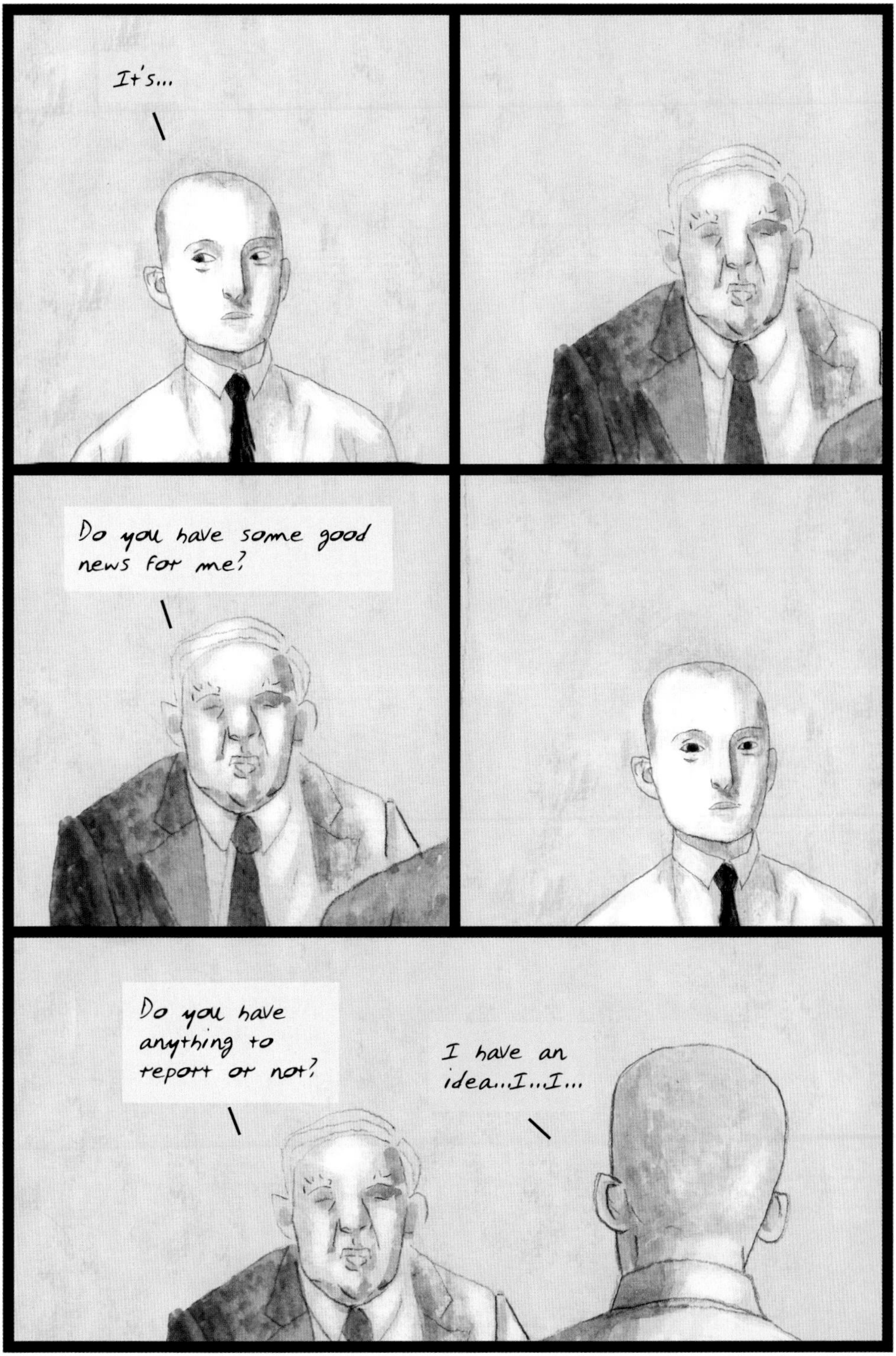
It's...
Do you have some good news for me?
Do you have anything to report or not?
I have an idea...I...I...

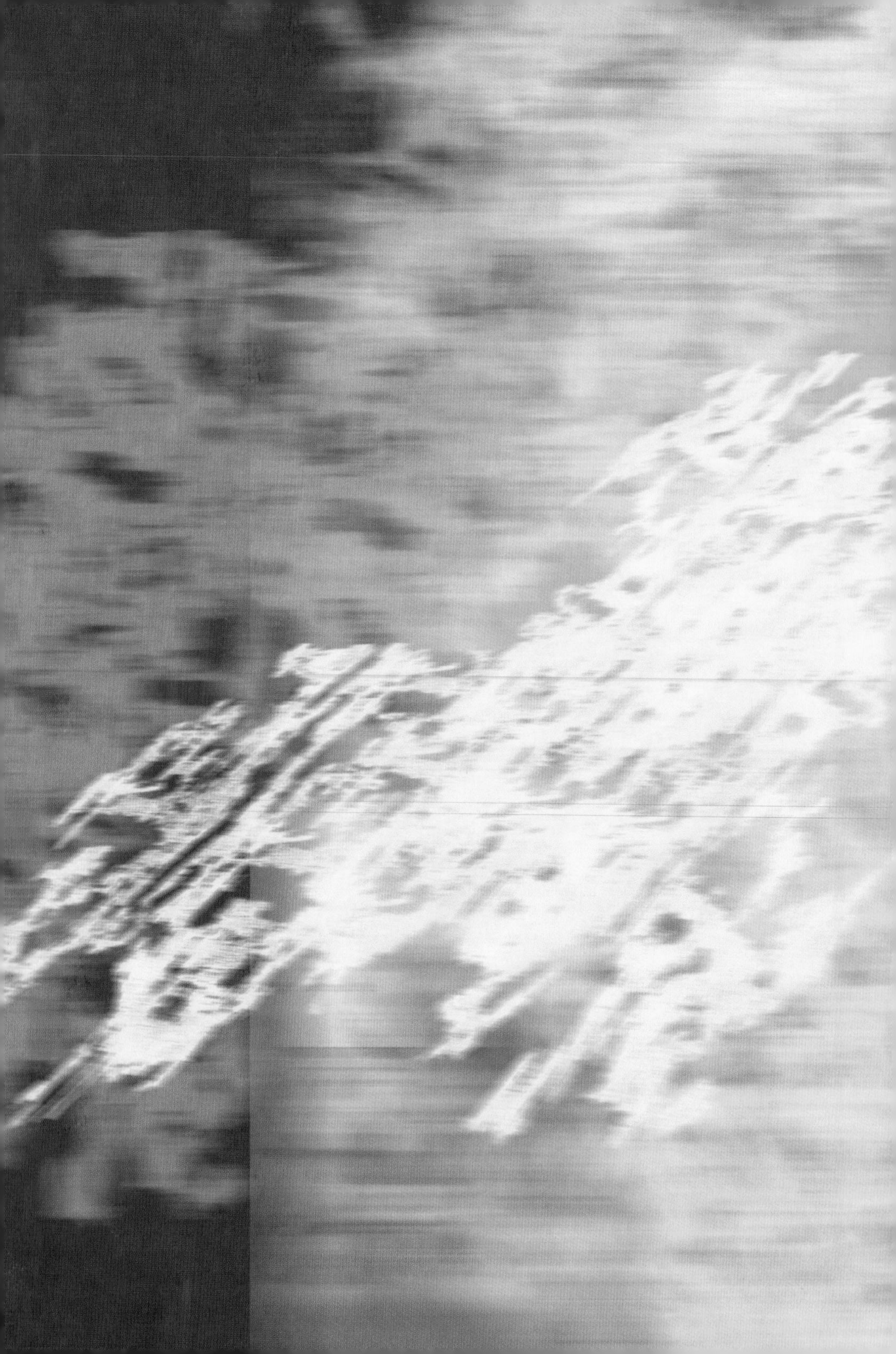

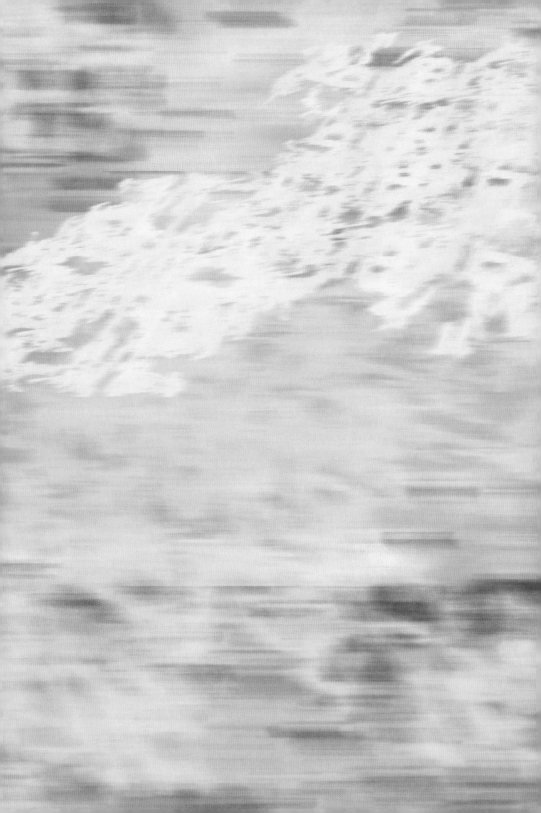

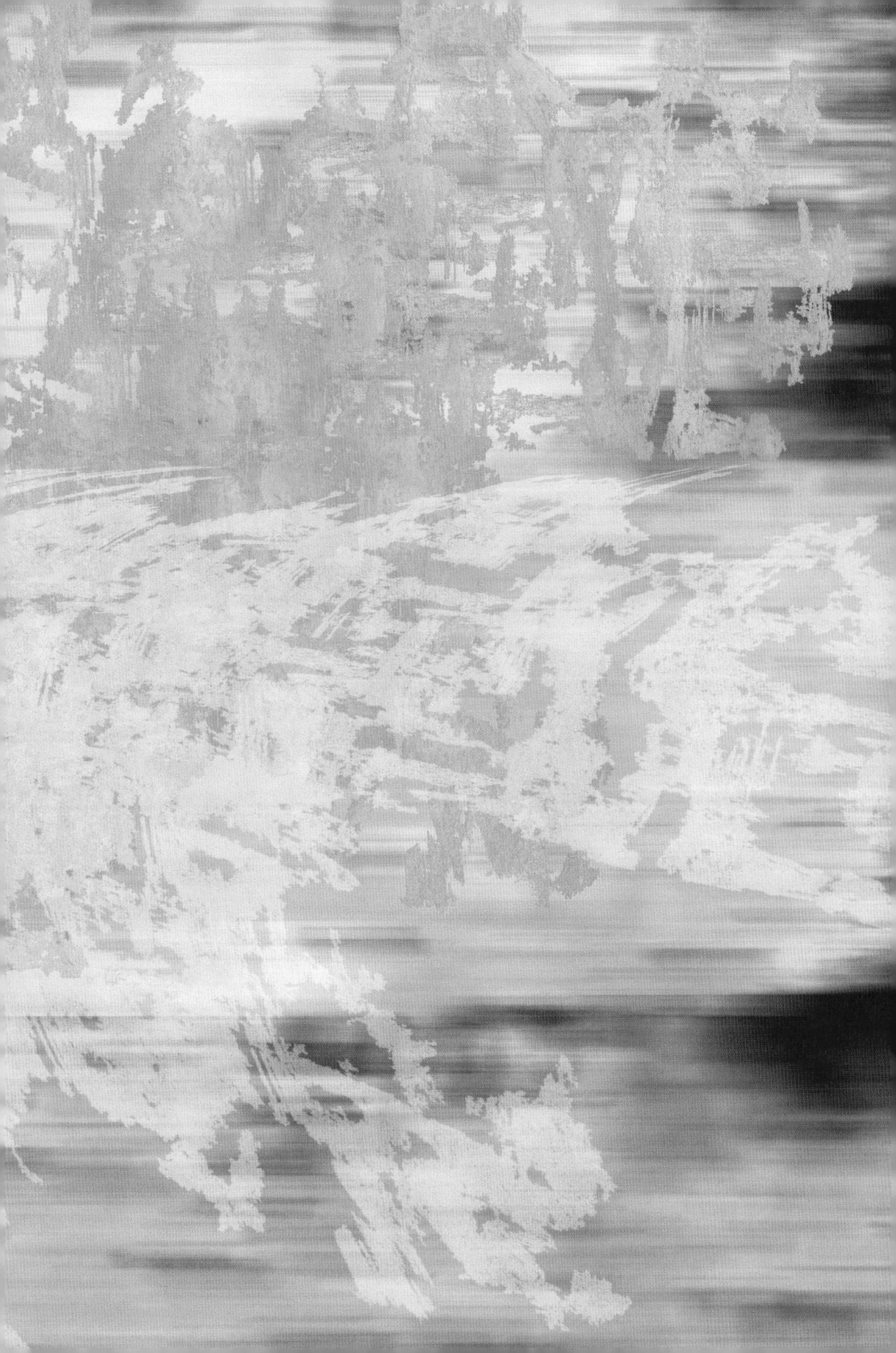

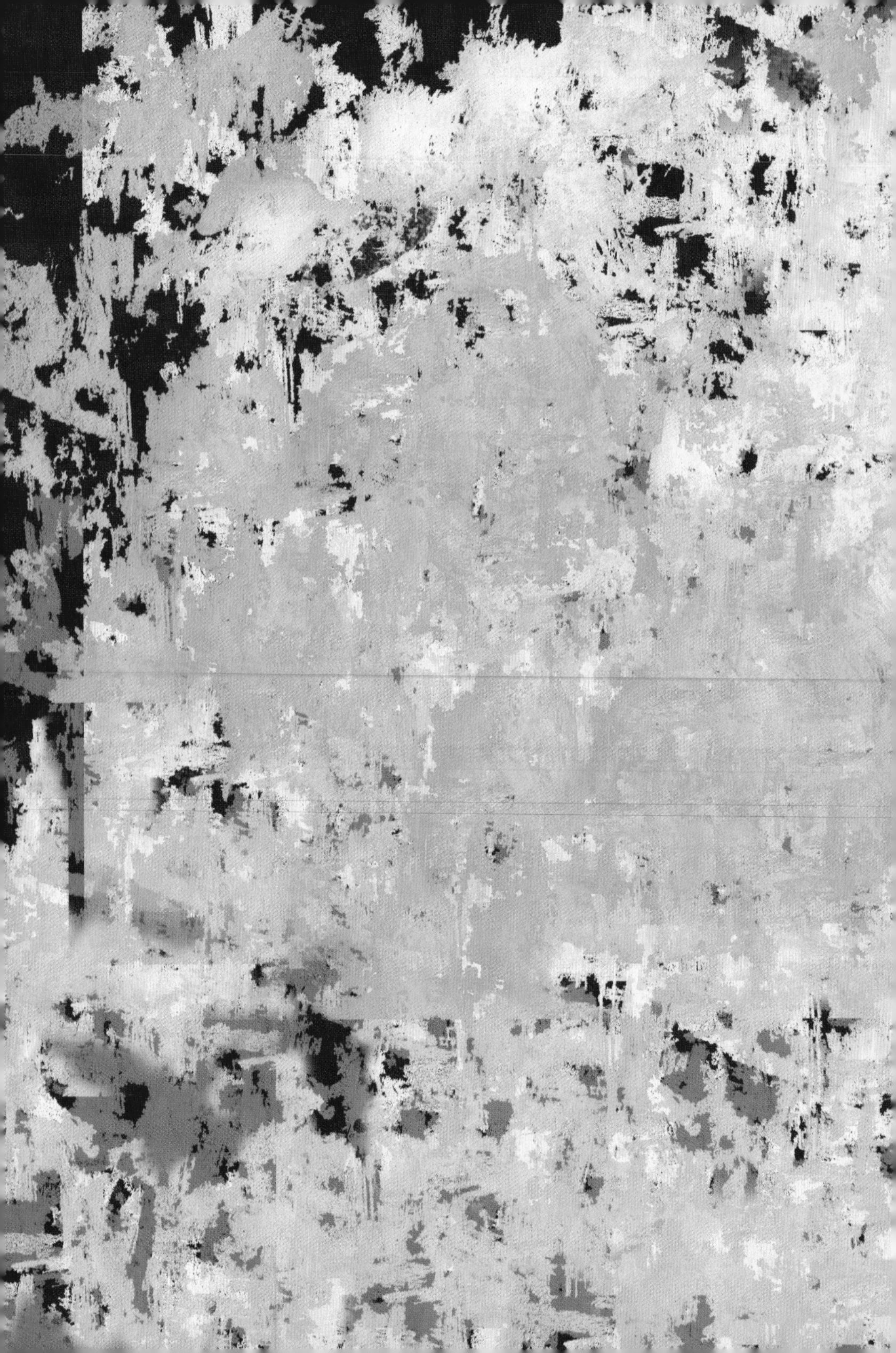

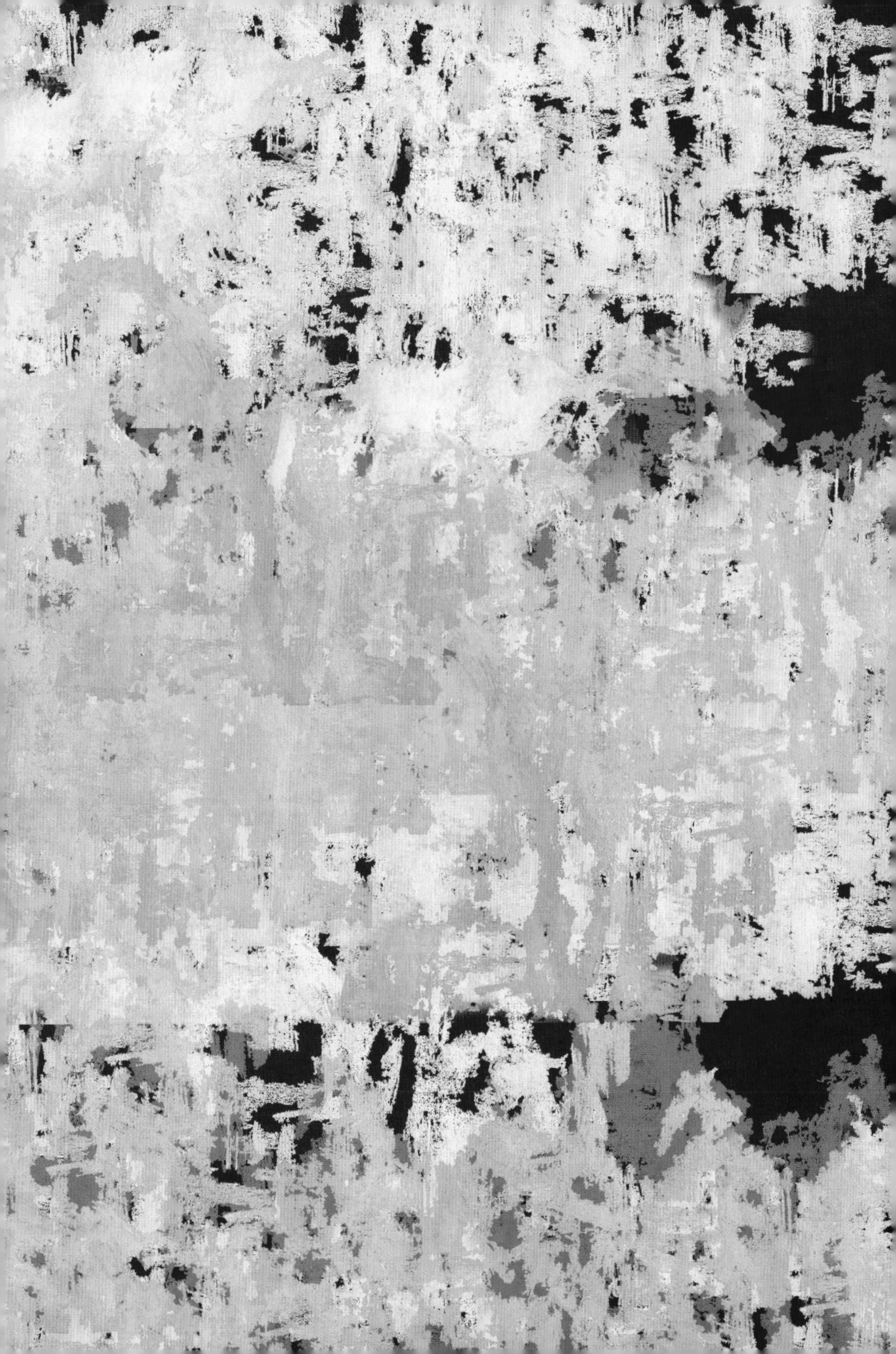

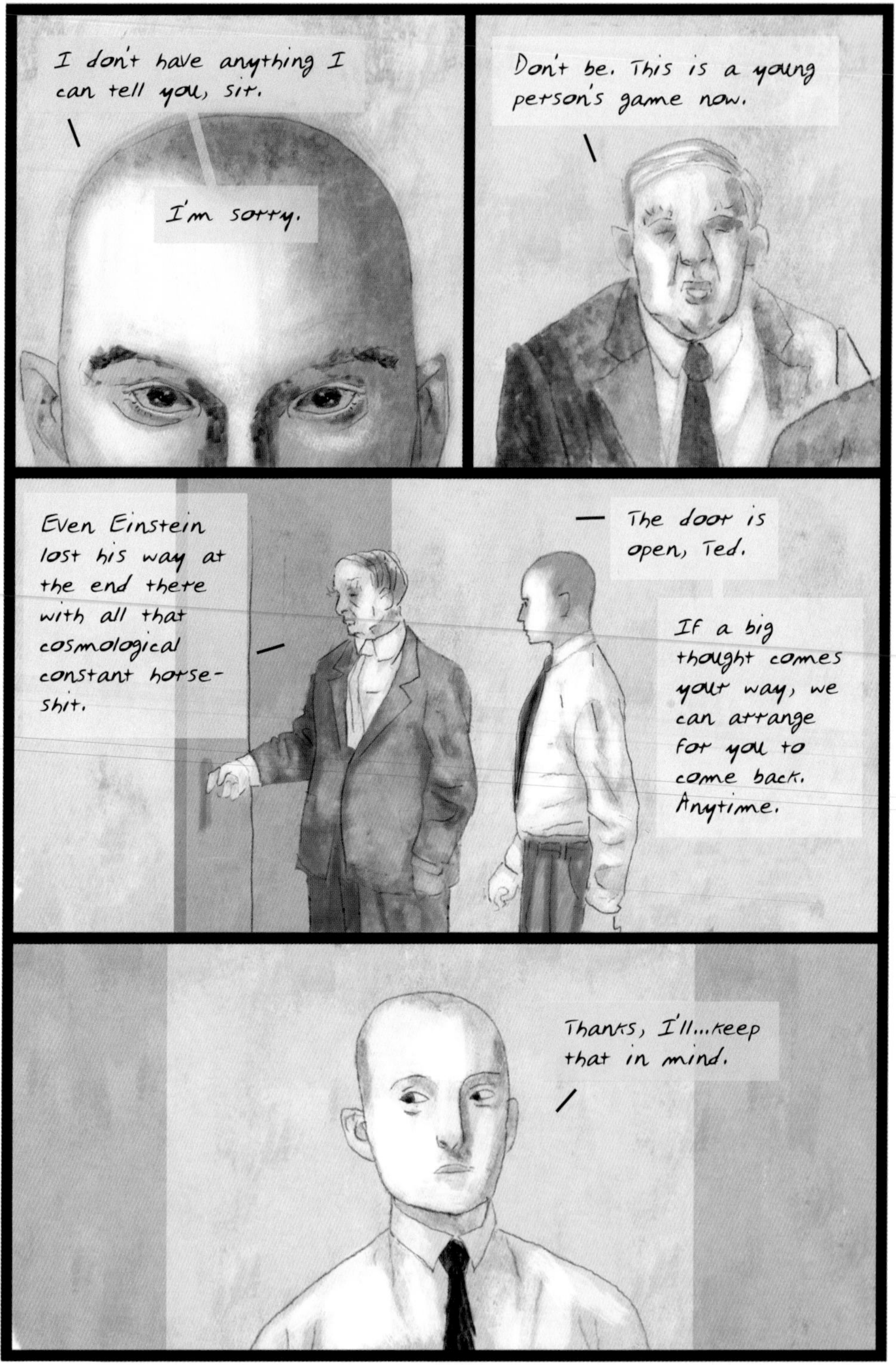
I don't have anything I can tell you, sir.
I'm sorry.
Don't be. This is a young person's game now.
Even Einstein lost his way at the end there with all that cosmological constant horse-shit.
The door is open, Ted.
If a big thought comes your way, we can arrange for you to come back. Anytime.
Thanks, I'll...keep that in mind.

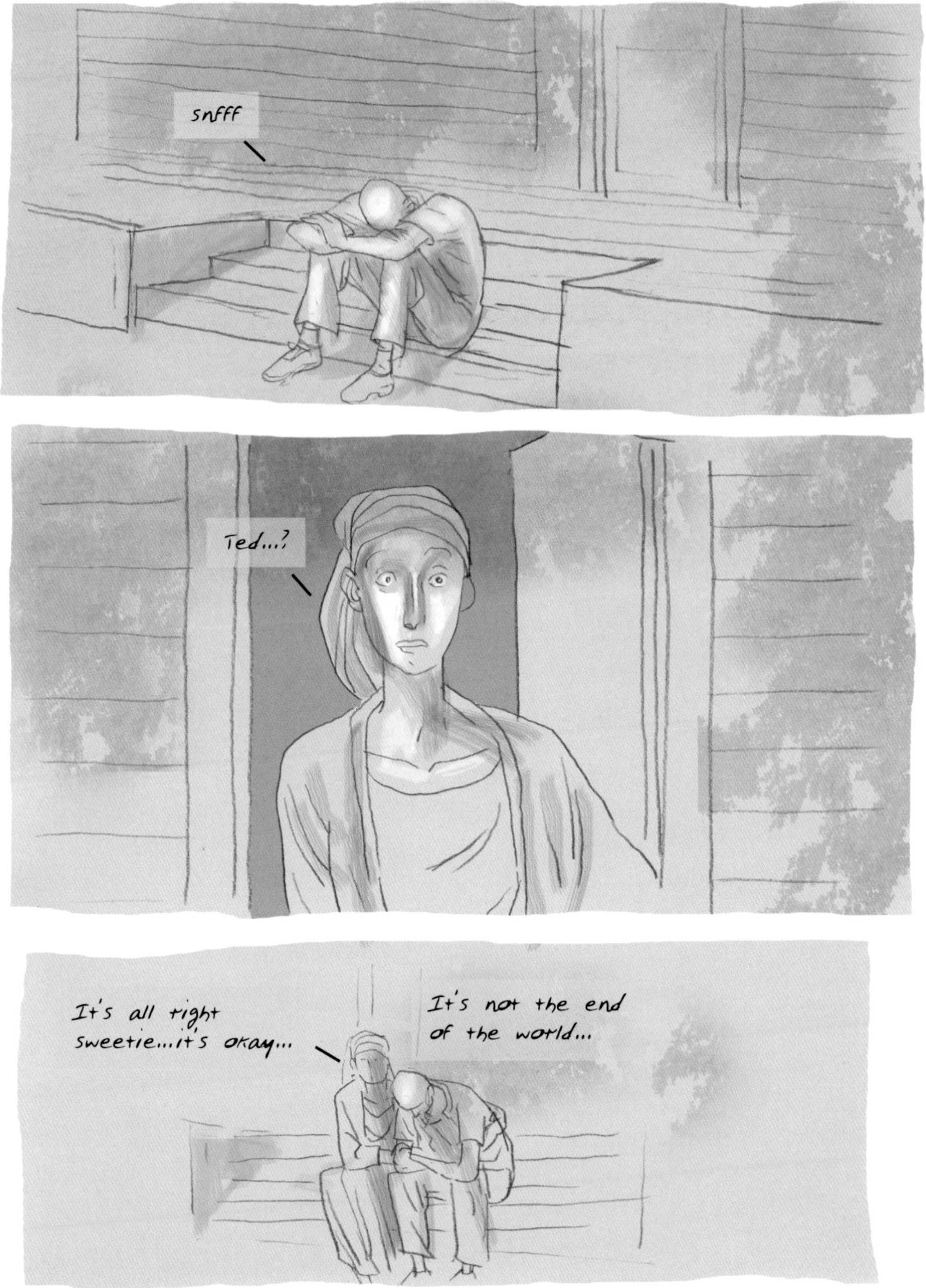
snfff
Ted...?
It's all right sweetie...it's okay...
It's not the end of the world...

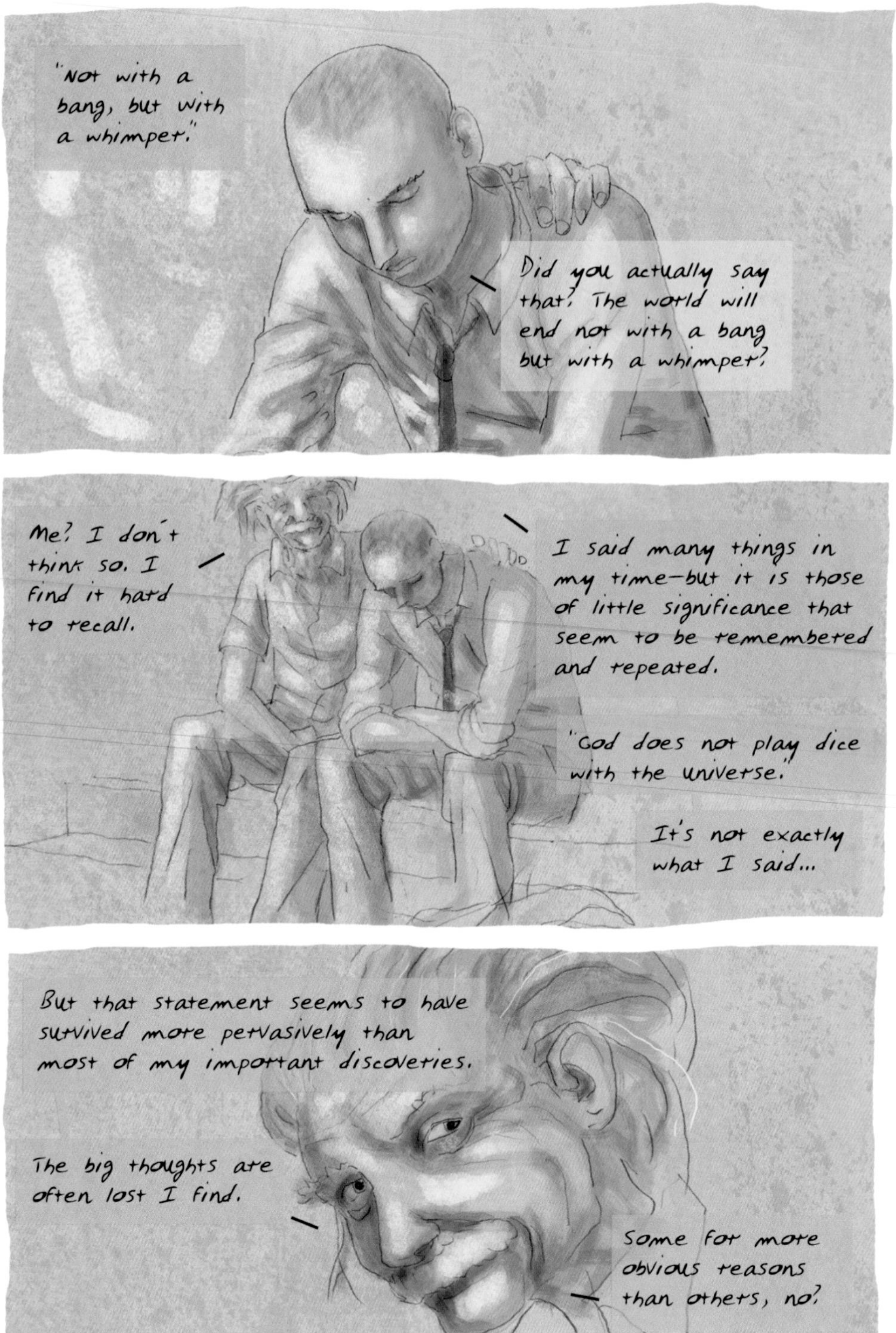
"Not with a bang, but with a whimper."
Did you actually say that? The world will end not with a bang but with a whimper?
Me? I don't think so. I find it hard to recall.
I said many things in my time—but it is those of little significance that seem to be remembered and repeated.
"God does not play dice with the universe."
It's not exactly what I said...
But that statement seems to have survived more pervasively than most of my important discoveries.
The big thoughts are often lost I find.
Some for more obvious reasons than others, no?

By the way, that was T.S. Eliot, the "whimper" thing.

Well, whoever it was, was a genius. My world has definitely whimpered.

Definitely?

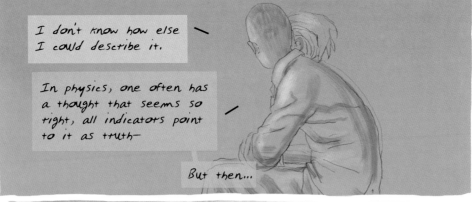

I don't know how else I could describe it.

In physics, one often has a thought that seems so tight, all indicators point to it as truth—

But then...

Boom!

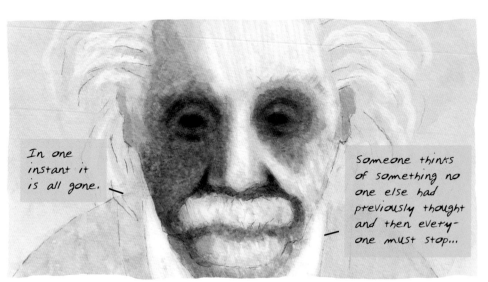

In one instant it is all gone.

Someone thinks of something no one else had previously thought and then everyone must stop...

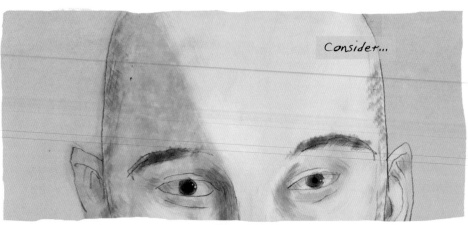

Consider...

...And start anew.

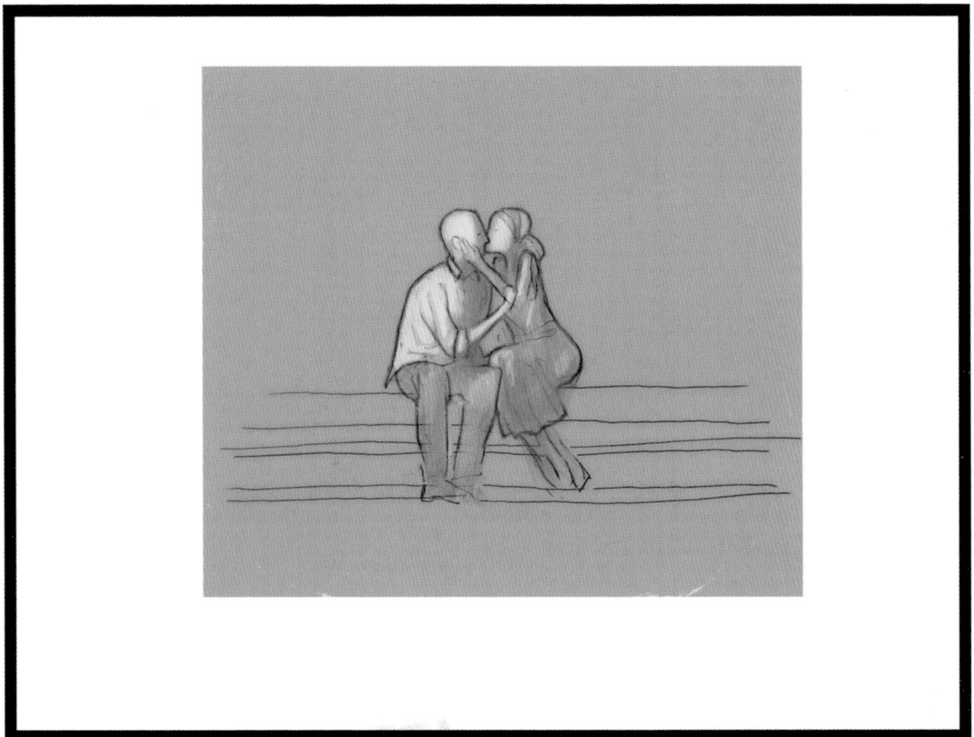

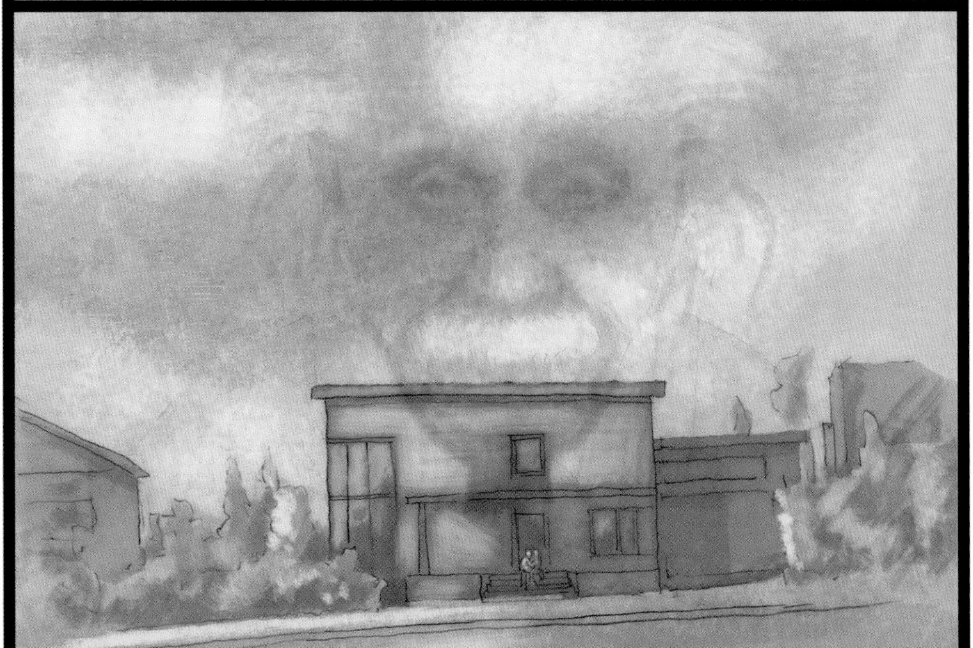

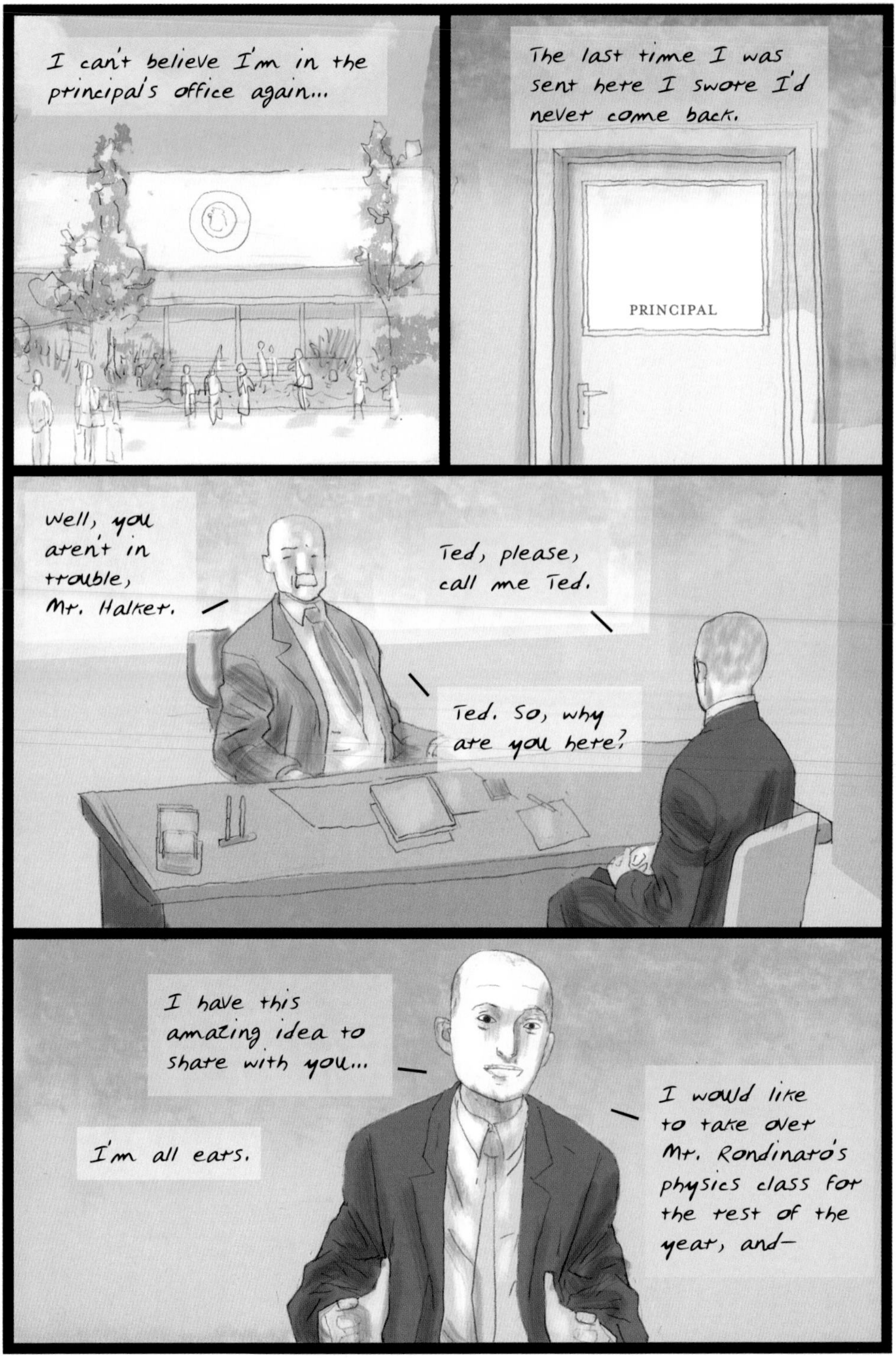
I can't believe I'm in the principal's office again...
The last time I was sent here I swore I'd never come back.
PRINCIPAL
Well, you aren't in trouble, Mr. Halker.
Ted, please, call me Ted.
Ted. So, why are you here?
I have this amazing idea to share with you...
I'm all ears.
I would like to take over Mr. Rondinaro's physics class for the rest of the year, and—

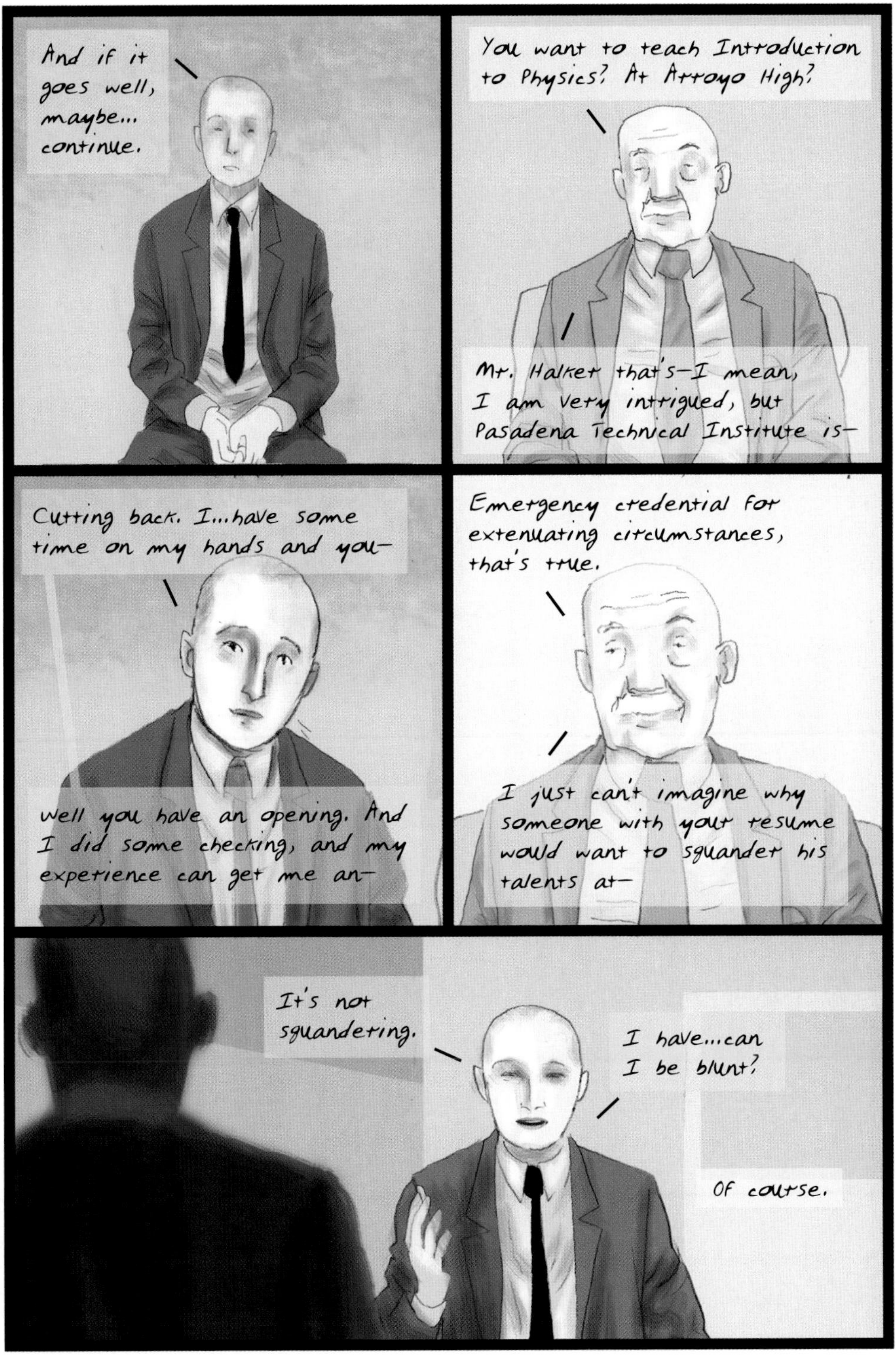
And if it goes well, maybe... continue.
You want to teach Introduction to Physics? At Arroyo High?
Mr. Halker that's—I mean, I am very intrigued, but Pasadena Technical Institute is—
Cutting back. I...have some time on my hands and you—
well you have an opening. And I did some checking, and my experience can get me an—
Emergency credential for extenuating circumstances, that's true.
I just can't imagine why someone with your resume would want to squander his talents at—
It's not squandering.
I have...can I be blunt?
Of course.

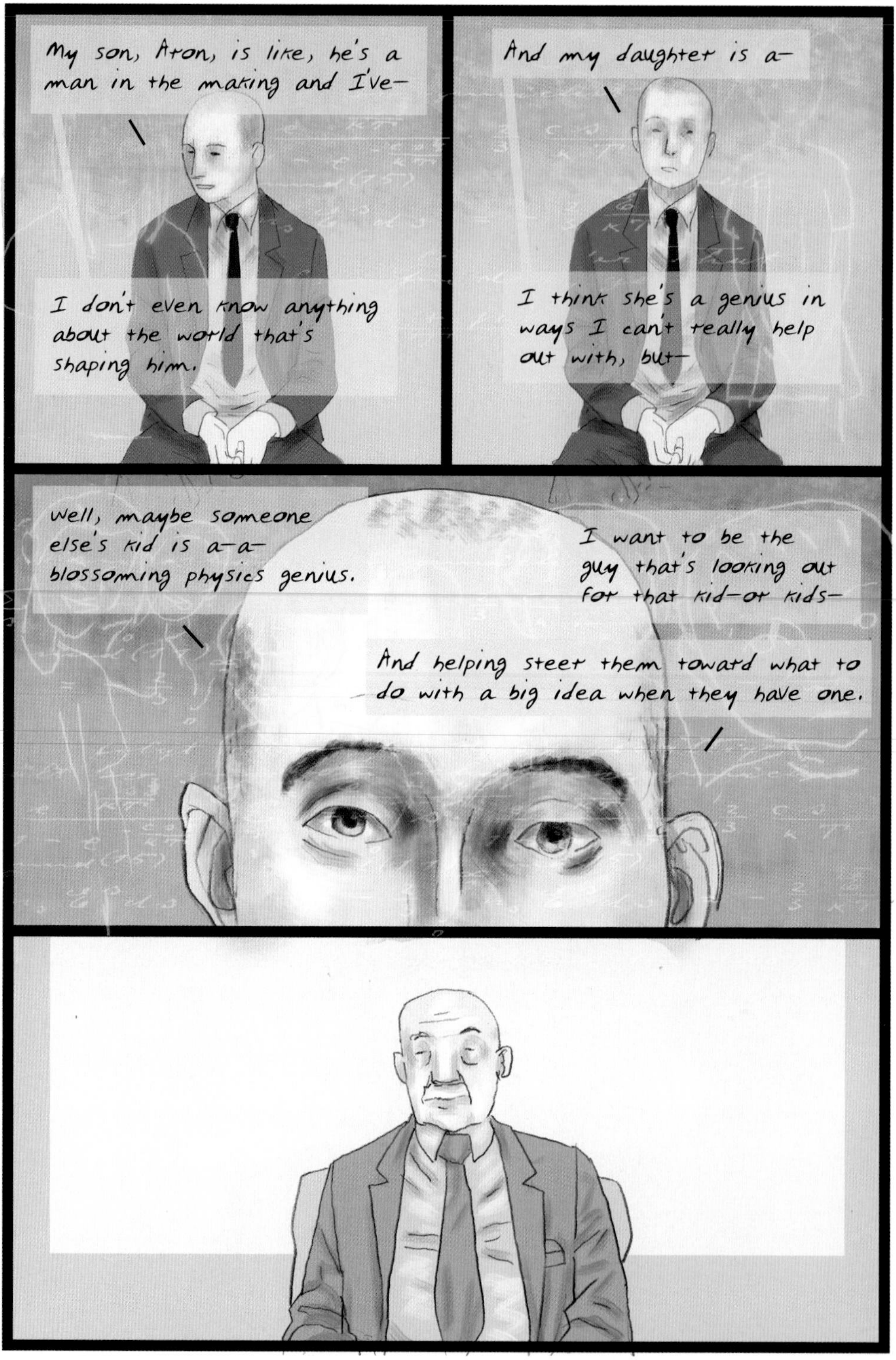
My son, Aron, is like, he's a man in the making and I've—
I don't even know anything about the world that's shaping him.
And my daughter is a—
I think she's a genius in ways I can't really help out with, but—
Well, maybe someone else's kid is a-a-blossoming physics genius.
I want to be the guy that's looking out for that kid—or kids—
And helping steer them toward what to do with a big idea when they have one.

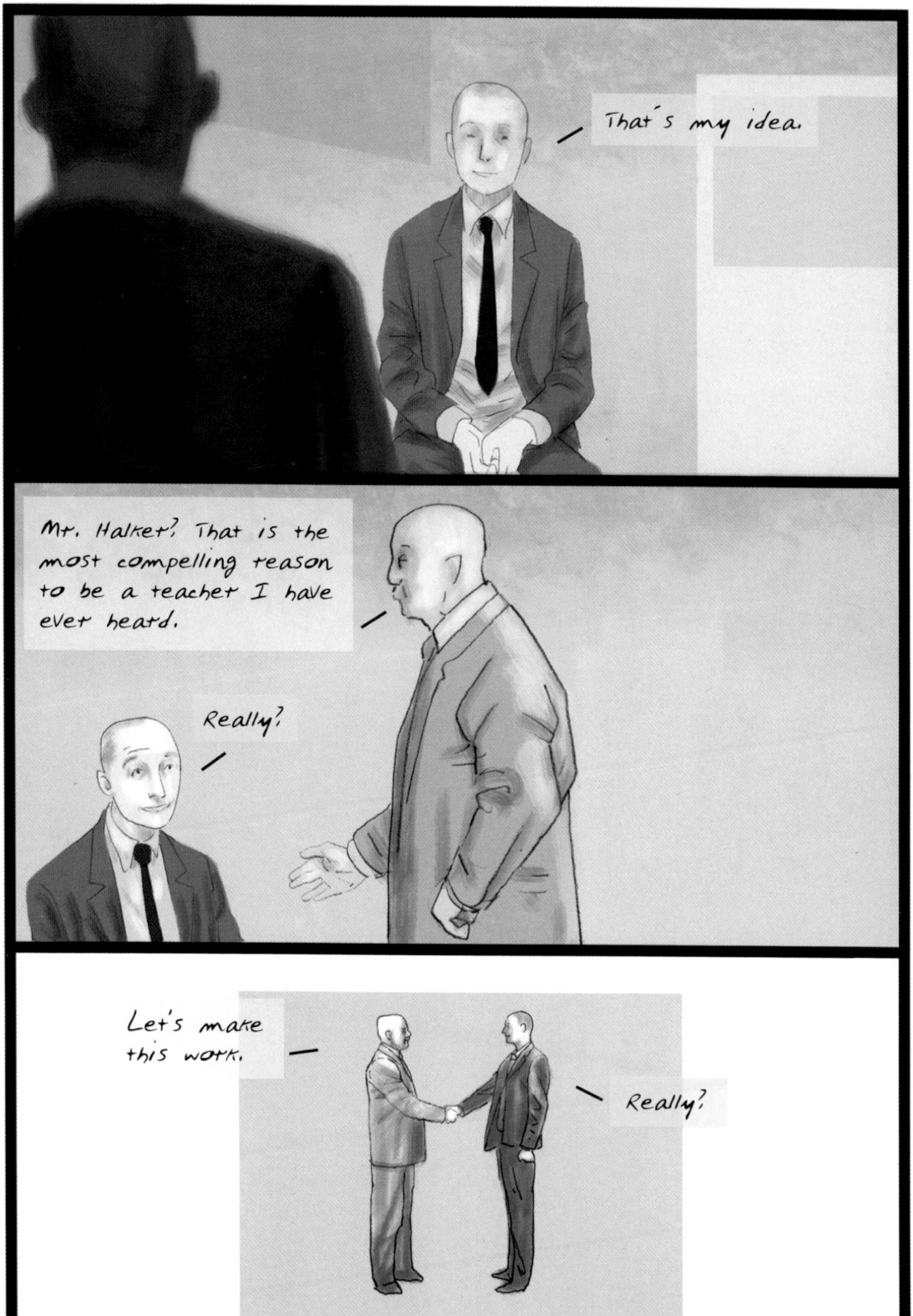
That's my idea.
Mr. Halker? That is the most compelling reason to be a teacher I have ever heard.
Really?
Let's make this work.
Really?

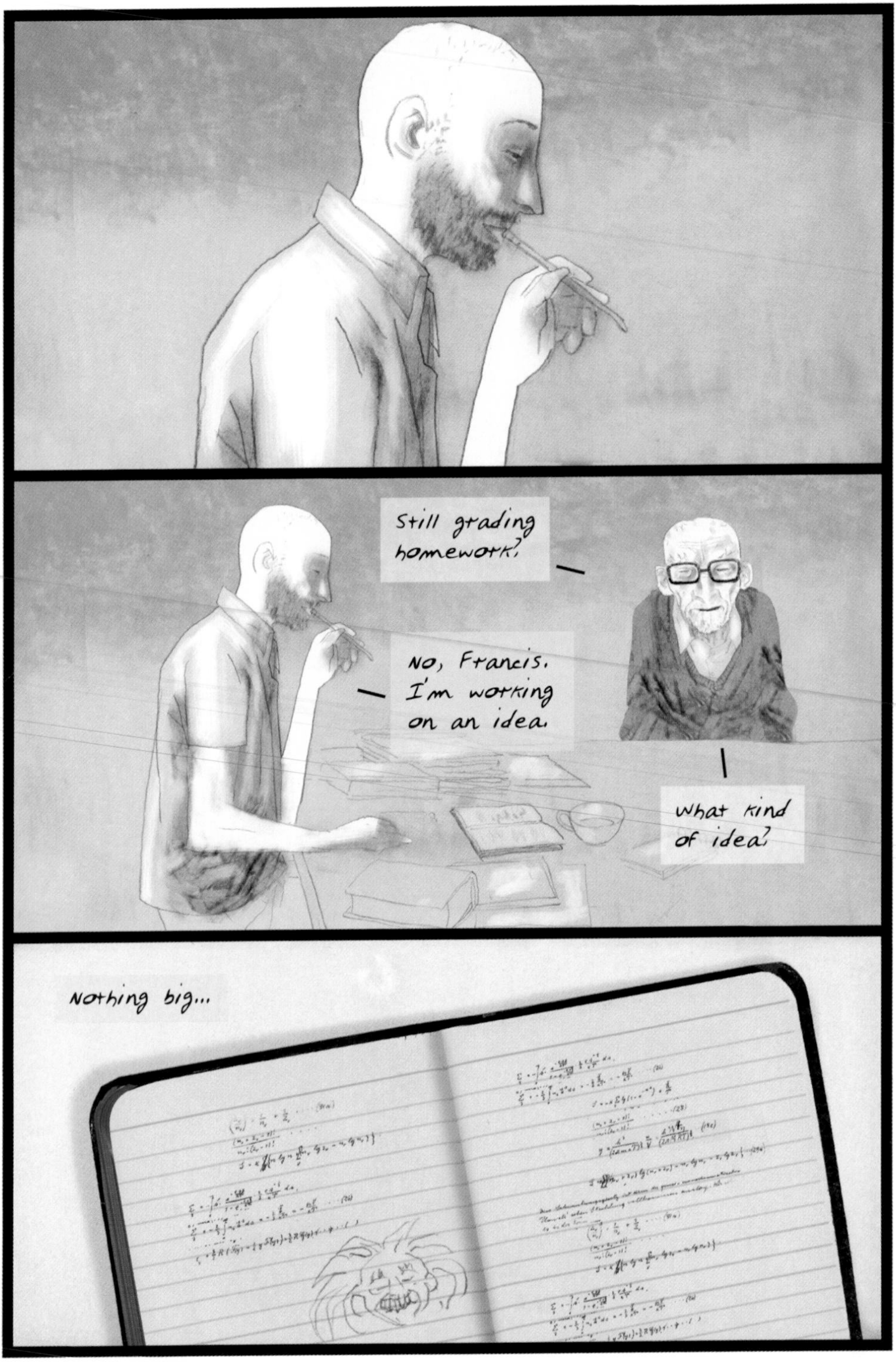
Still grading homework?
No, Francis. I'm working on an idea.
What kind of idea?
Nothing big...

Dedicated to Max Welch
Who took one of the greatest secrets ever known with him . . .

—S.S.

Dedicated to Hope for being there as a constant support,
and Michael for the old, old friendship.

Thanks to my three kids, Emily, Sophia, and Lulu, for a reminder
that the silly side of life should be for all!

And thanks to Steve and Mark for being very patient.

And never forget our old friend coffee.

—T.K.

First Second

Text copyright © 2013 by Steven T. Seagle
Illustrations copyright © 2013 by Teddy Kristiansen

Published by First Second
First Second is an imprint of Roaring Brook Press,
a division of Holtzbrinck Publishing Holdings Limited Partnership
175 Fifth Avenue, New York, New York 10010
All rights reserved

Cataloging-in-Publication Data is on file at the Library of Congress.
ISBN 978-1-59643-263-5

First Second books are available for special promotions and premiums.
For details, contact: Director of Special Markets, Holtzbrinck Publishers.

FIRST
EDITION

First edition 2013

Printed in China

10 9 8 7 6 5 4 3 2 1

BY ART
WE LIVE